# The Legacy of
# BARRY GREEN

**BOLEYN BOOKS**

Published November 2003 by
Boleyn Books
Tel: (01708) 379877

Printed by Cox & Wyman Ltd, Reading, Berkshire

Distributed by Vine House Distribution Ltd,
Waldenbury, North Common, Challey, East Sussex,
BN8 4DR, England.
Tel: (01825) 723398
Email: sales@vinehouseuk.co.uk

Set in Helvetica Roman

ISBN 0 9529641 2 0

Cover photographs by Action Images

For Shauna

For Gregory

# ACKNOWLEDGEMENTS

Many thanks to the following, without whom this book would not have been possible:

Bob and Mary Banks, Sylvia Prior and Lynn Cooper for their undying love and support, and for never questioning any of the decisions I have made over the last few years. I could not ask for a better family.

Peter Ross for the loan of the laptop computer.

All at Boleyn Books for their constant help and encouragement.

All my colleagues in Nottingham, Leeds and Manchester for helping me feel at home.

Big thank you to Perry Fenwick for doing the foreword.

Finally, thanks to Shauna for love and patience, helpful suggestions and constructive criticism. I couldn't have done it without you

*The publishers would also like to thank:*
M. Press (Sales) Ltd for pre-press production, Kate Bouchard, Peter Stewart, Richard Squibb and all at Vine Distribution Ltd.

# FOREWORD
## By PERRY FENWICK

In 1969, my father was the perpetrator of a very silly but quite deliberate act. An act that was to have serious and far-reaching consequences for the rest of my life. He took me to my first West Ham game.

In fairness to him, he was only repeating something my grandfather had done when dad was a boy some years earlier. It's tradition, you see? That night we lost and, over the last 34 years, some would say that's been a kind of tradition too.

"Get 'em young!" is the phrase and so at seven-years-old I had been given my first West Ham 'fix'. For 34 years I have been a hopeless addict. Of course, the taste and after-effects of my West Ham debut, just like your first beer or ciggie, were not pleasant. As I remember, we lost 1-0 to Arsenal. But like any determined junkie, it wasn't long before I acquired the flavour.

The intervening years have not been very kind. Of course there have been some highs to sustain my addiction. FA Cup victories in 1975 and 1980, Brooking and Devonshire at their peak, McAvennie and Cottee and the glorious Boys of '86 and, of course, the regular beating of Manchester United would send me high as the proverbial kite.

But the lows, it has to be said, have been low. By the

mid-90s, and by now a hopeless case, things were looking very bleak and after yet another embarrassing cup defeat (remember Iain Dowie at Stockport?) I contemplated ending it all and taking up bowls.

It was around this time I first met the eminent West Ham psychologist, Professor Robert Banks. I was attending one of my regular meetings at the Upton Park Priory (The Boleyn pub) for some post-match analysis and vocal exorcising with some fellow Hammers junkies when we were introduced. Immediately I realised there was a kindred spirit. He, too, had been a sufferer but through the medium of writing he had found a way to put things in perspective. He was straight-talking, honest and didn't promise a cure. He simply said: "Read my books, son." And so I did.

His previous two books and now this one, have taught me that being a West Ham fan is not an affliction, a bad habit or a cross to bear. In fact, I now realise that I'm a lucky boy.

Following the Hammers, like Robert and many others over the years, has taught me a lot. I know how to lose gracefully, how to be an optimist and never stop dreaming. How life can be wonderful yet at other times so cruel. And most importantly, that I am not alone. These are lessons for life that, I believe, every parent should instil in their children. In a round about way, that's what my old man set out to do all those years ago.

At times, I must admit, I had to question his judgement and motives but thanks to Robert and his West Ham 'Bibles', I now know his intentions were honourable, wholesome and true. And one day I shall take my son to Upton Park and know that, given time, the poor little sod will forgive me. Robert helped me – let him help you to help yourself.

I urge you to buy this book. Not just because it's a damn good read about being a football fan, nor just because Robert Banks sounds like he should have played in goal for someone, but also because Rob is still doing up his house and the extra few quid will come in handy!

Enjoy!

My name is Perry Fenwick and I am a West Ham United supporter.

*Walford*
*November 2003*

# CONTENTS

27. Down 4 U–WHU 1 Birmingham City 2  5.10.02
28. It's All Gravy–WHU 3 Leeds Utd 4   10.11.02
29. Lose Yourself–WHU 0 Southampton 1  2.12.02
30. Land Of The Living–WHU 2 Blackburn Rovers 1  29.1.03
31. Familiar Feeling–WHU 0 Liverpool 3  2.2.03
32. Move Your Feet–Everton 0 WHU 0  15.3.03
33. Out Of Time–Bolton Wanderers 1 WHU 0  19.4.03
34. All Over–Birmingham City 2 WHU 2  11.5.03
35. Misfit–AFC Bournemouth 0 WHU 4  15.7.03
36. Finest Dreams–Preston North End 1 WHU 2  9.8.03
37. Can't Hold Us Down–WHU 1 Reading 0  13.9.03

# INTRODUCTION

In a way, I feel quite sorry for kids today.

That might make me sound like I'm 103-years-old. Believe me, some days I feel like I am. It may even sound a little patronising but it's the way I feel.

Not only do today's kids have all the pressures of puberty, inexperience in the minefield of personal relationships, the cesspool of career opportunities to navigate and property prices rising faster than a patriot missile, but they also have to put up with truly awful football.

They say English football is the best in the world. There was a time when I would have agreed. Certainly, English clubs are among the most instantly recognisable, no matter where you are on the globe. Wear a West Ham shirt and someone will tap you on the shoulder grinning inanely.

And yet, these days, it all seems a bit . . . crap. When I put on my most expensive pair of Gucci rose-tinted spectacles and look back at the time when I started going regularly to watch West Ham in the early 80s, I feel that deep swelling of nostalgia that makes me believe that nothing will ever touch that period for memories, characters and downright good fun.

I'm wrong, of course. I missed out on watching such geniuses as Stan Bowles, Frank Worthington, Alan Hudson and Jimmy Greaves. Those who witnessed their skills first hand will no doubt tell me that I am wrong, that their era was the best. Those kids, for whom I feel such sympathy, will no doubt shrug their shoulders and wonder who and what I am going on about, before returning to *Match* magazine to fawn over "da wicked" pictures of David Beckham, Wayne Rooney and Michael Owen. Innit?

I can still recall the first night I went to Upton Park with my mates. That West Ham team had won their opening three games and were top of the old first division. Phil Parkes, Ray Stewart, Steve Walford, Billy Bonds, Alvin Martin, Alan Devonshire, Steve Whitton, Tony Cottee, Dave Swindlehurst, Trevor Brooking and Geoff Pike started the match against Leicester City, for whom Gary Lineker opened the scoring. Walford, Cottee and Swindlehurst replied in a 3-1 win that consolidated our lead at the top of the league. There was only one substitute allowed. The game kicked off at 7.30pm. The team contained no one born outside the British Isles. The new Adidas replica shirt cost £10.95. There was no sponsor's name on it. You could buy a pint of beer and drink it as you watched the match. From terracing. You didn't need a ticket, you just turned up. It cost £2.50 to stand and if you had enough front you could try getting through the under 16s turnstile for 50p. You could stand behind either goal or along the side in the 'Chicken Run,' what is now the lower tier of the East Stand.

None of these things, individually, made it better than it is today. Today, stadia are a lot more comfortable, some teams include international superstars and you can go to a game reasonably sure you won't end up in hospital.

But the fare that is served once you take your seat, or stand in front of it, is insincere rubbish. I want it back the way it was. My favourite game is dying.

Essentially, the thing that ruins almost everything in this world – money – has infected the game and it now waits along with other terminal cases – honesty, selflessness, integrity and decency – to die a long and very painful death.

Money and associated greed have ruined everything that was ever half-decent, from manufacturing industry to local government. The need to "cut costs," "show a profit," and "give the shareholders a dividend" has effectively spoilt the show for everyone. Hence those building societies that used to give you a tidy return and exceptional customer services became Public Limited Company banks and stuck up a metaphorical two fingers at everyone who values consumer choice and value for money.

Those banks that used to sit happily in the High Street became "Rat and Parrots" and "Orange Kippers" so that you couldn't so much as pay a cheque in without dialling 08457 and speaking to a recorded message in Dundee.

If anything breaks down, goes wrong or fails to happen when it was promised, you used to be able to speak to a human being and complain. Now you get a different 08457 number and speak to a recorded message in Bombay. They take your money efficiently enough but service? Oh, we didn't realise you wanted that, too!

And those football clubs that used to welcome you with open arms – yes, even you, Mr Working Class Man, who they understood couldn't afford to pay a fortune to watch the team they loved – became PLCs and hiked ticket prices up so high that only those with a salary approaching six figures could seriously afford to consider taking the family along on a regular basis. The shareholders grin. The foreign superstars laugh all the way to the 08457 number and those of us who loved the game as it was, cry: "We want our ball back!"

And the clubs reply: "F**k you!"

Wait until it all goes wrong. It will, trust me. What will happen then? What would happen, for example, if West

3

Ham were ever stupid enough to get themselves relegated? What would happen if it happened a second time? Imagine that. West Ham as a second division team.

I've been a football fan long enough to be more than a little bit cynical. There have always been men in our game, players, managers and members of various boards, who put their pockets before the good of the club and the good of the game. How many times have we heard the expressions: "It's a short career, I have to make the most of it while I can." Or: "Well, football is a business these days, isn't it?"

Rubbish. Football is not, never has been and never will be a viable business. It's a sport. A game. Nothing more, nothing less.

Those who choose to try and turn it into a business should take a note of the number of clubs currently making a profit in the Premiership. Not very many. You cannot make a viable business out of something when there are so many external influences on the outcome of the plan. A linesman (or referee's assistant, as they now like to be called) disallows a perfectly good goal. Champions League place missed on goal difference. The £5million you were banking on doesn't materialise. Sell best player. Get relegated next season. Sell the squad if you're lucky enough to have some still on a contract. Top business plan. But it's us mugs who pay for the mistakes and shore up "The Business" with our hard-earned cash. That's not business, it's charity.

Sure, individuals stand to make vast amounts of money through football (players mainly) as chairman after chairman throws good money after bad, bank after bank extends overdrafts into eight figures and fans extend themselves financially (over-extending in many cases) to watch the team they love. And who ends up footing the bill?

4

What is more galling is the fact that those who do make at least £30,000 a week – the top players – have no reason to feel anything for the club or the fans other than gratitude. Gratitude that they have been blessed with a talent that allows them to earn such a preposterous figure.

Some (yes, Mr Breen, I mean you) don't even have talent. Gratitude that idiots like you and me are prepared to pump cash at them and Uncle Rupert's Sky Sports empire until we are on our knees. Then they can turn around and complain about being mis-treated when they get subbed after half an hour.

No one begrudges someone with real talent the right to earn a lot of money. It doesn't make me angry to see successful, highly paid geniuses. I get angry at successful, highly paid mediocrities – and at people who can't tell the difference. There are too many people falling into both categories for anything ever to change.

That's what's wrong with the country as a whole. We have learned to accept that second best is acceptable. It doesn't matter if you only get 60%, because we'll lower the grades to make sure you get an "A" and that cushy university number your parents dreamed of. It doesn't matter if your accent is so strong only your close family can understand a word you are saying, you can still get a job reading the news on national TV. And it certainly doesn't matter if you don't give a sh*t about paying customers and the welfare of a football club steeped in tradition, you can still get a job as a Premiership chairman.

That's what's been wrong with West Ham as a club since the day they were formed. Mediocrity has ruled and we've been brainwashed into accepting it. Whatever it is that has opened my eyes, I can see everything so much clearer from afar. And what I can see makes me feel sorry for those who aren't old enough to remember happier times. Times when it didn't matter so much.

What follows is a summary of the events of the last three years at West Ham United seen through my totally unbiased – yeah, right! – eyes. There's a lot to get through. Read it and weep.

**Robert Banks,  November 2003**

# 1. Times Like These

## Manchester United 6 West Ham United 0  26.1.03

I had just seen West Ham humiliated 6-0 by Manchester United at Old Trafford. I was sitting on a Trans-Pennine train between Todmorden and Hebden Bridge with my future brother-in-law Andrew. He'd watched the match with me. Sympathetic to the end, he tried to lift the gloom by making conversation:

"So what's the worst defeat you ever witnessed?"

"Apart from today? 6-0 at Everton and I watched us lose 7-1 at Blackburn last year. Oh, and I saw us lose 7-1 at Old Trafford on the big screen at Upton Park."

"And what's the best result you've ever seen?"

"I once saw us lose only 1-0."

Not true, of course, but it's an interesting reaction and one which most West Ham fans would have given. It's the defining condition, the pathos and self-deprecating attitude. It sets West Ham fans apart from any others in the country. If someone asks that question, rather than recall the 10-0 win over Bury, the 8-1 win over Newcastle United, a 7-1 triumph over mighty Hull City or the 6-0 demolition of Barnsley, we implode and have a bigger pop at the club ourselves. Try it with an Arsenal or Manchester United fan and see what reaction you get. Call it a social science experiment.

It's quite bizarre and something you wouldn't do to any other loved one, any other member of your family. (Well, maybe.) Yet the love is so strong, so unconditional, you can poke fun at West Ham without fear of reproach. The team will always be the same. They'll always be largely incompetent but occasionally take your breath away with a moment of skill, a run of 10 decent games and, very occasionally, a whole season.

They never build on it, which makes them even more frustrating and even more lovable and even more tempting a target for sarcasm and irony. Even from their own adoring fans. Especially from their own adoring fans. Particularly from this, adoring, loyal, completely devoted yet now strangely detached fan.

## 2. Last One Standing

### England 2 Romania 3  20.06.00

Everyone is entitled to a watershed in their lives. Some have more than one. Some underprivileged folk never get one but you are, at least, entitled to one. Write to your local DSS if you've hit 35 and it hasn't arrived yet. It might have got lost in the post or chewed up by the dog. Mine turned up quite unexpectedly in June 2000.

I was feeling quite distant from West Ham United. I'd been without a season ticket for the first time in a number of years and it hadn't proved as painful as I had feared it might. I could pick and choose my games and, as a result, enjoyed them a lot more. It's a situation I would recommend.

But in June 2000 I was not a happy man. My girlfriend, Billie, Chloe or Suzanne, or whatever her f**king name was, dumped me in March. I had met her through an internet chat-room and made the fatal mistake of falling for her before I knew enough about her. I was totally besotted with her but only after I had fallen did I discover she was married and had a child. I didn't begrudge her that. Everyone is entitled to look for happiness but her insistence on secrecy verged on the point of obsession. She wasn't prepared to divulge basic information such as surname, mobile telephone number or even the area where she lived. Billie had been the name I had given her in *West Ham 'Till I Die*. Chloe had been the name she had given herself on the internet. Suzanne was the name her mother gave her. I think.

She would meet me at my house most weekday afternoons, when we'd make love, drink coffee and smoke cigarettes and then she'd go. As I didn't have any way of contacting her other than email (and she changed her address more often than most people change their underwear), each time she left I couldn't be certain I'd ever see her again, I had to rely on her to make contact. It was not an easy way to run a relationship and it took its toll on me both mentally and physically.

When we split, she cited misdemeanours occurring before we had got together but to her that was mere detail. She'd decided the time was right to move on and she would have blamed anyone but herself by then. I took the whole thing badly enough for my doctor to prescribe tranquillisers and counselling. I'd already been very ill over Christmas and the millennium celebrations – my doctor wanted me to take time off work but I couldn't see the point of sitting at home and brooding.

Work was also getting on top of me. I was a sales representative for the Co-operative Insurance Society, the CIS at the time, and, not being the most natural salesman in the world, was finding the going somewhat tough. Like Colonel Cathcart in *Catch-22*, the bosses kept increasing the targets we had to hit, while the boring but cumbersome and time-consuming administration side of the job did not diminish. Like Yossarian himself, I often found myself running around in ever-decreasing circles and, more often than not, crying myself to sleep, wondering how I would ever escape.

Money was also getting too tight to mention. Poorly motivated salesmen don't often earn mega-bucks and I was no exception. My obsession for West Ham United, my refusal since our arrival in the Premiership to let a week go by without seeing at least one game, meant my credit rating was now worse than zero. My cards piled up and the minimum payment got harder and harder to meet.

Like a highly paid striker facing a season in the first division, I decided I needed a change of scenery. The CIS were advertising jobs in Nottingham working on a new venture, processing sales and checking them for complicity with the Society's stringent guidelines. I applied, thinking this may be the escape route I needed. I heard nothing.

West Ham meanwhile prepared for the 2000-01 season in confident mood. After finishing in ninth place in May it was quite reasonable to expect that with experienced players of the calibre of Parlow Di Canio (I call him "Parlow" because it's what Harry Redknapp and Glenn Roeder used to call him. If it was good enough for them, it's good enough for me) and Stuart Pearce, emerging young talents like Joe Cole and Michael Carrick, the now established stars like Frank Lampard and Rio Ferdinand and recent acquisitions Frederic Kanouté and Davor Suker, they would lead West Ham forward well into the new century and cement us as a team challenging for Europe on a regular basis.

The feel good factor at Upton Park was not reflected at home, where my landlord, Mark, had decided to sell up, rather forcing my hand in the moving home stakes. I watched the letterbox intently each morning for news of the Nottingham job but none arrived and I began to fear the worst.

Then, out of nowhere, a watershed turned up. Just like that. Out of thin air. A trip to Sheffield to visit my good friends, Lucy and Richard, reminded me of the fact that life in the north was not actually as grim as people in the south would have you believe, so I bought a

11

couple of local papers to see what sort of work I could get and how much it would cost to rent a house. Everyone thinks when you travel north of Watford you can pick up a house for 50 pence but that's not quite the case any more. While rents were expensive, they were still a damn sight cheaper than London. I planned to get a job doing anything – even shelf-stacking or order picking – just to get me by until I could establish myself. Then I saw the advert from the CIS in the *Sheffield Star.*

I was disappointed. I thought they had gone through all the internal applications, found them to be unsatisfactory and advertised externally. But I rang anyway to see what the score was. I was advised that I had been selected to attend an assessment day in, of all places, Sheffield and there was a letter in the post. Sure enough, I arrived home in time to find the letter on the doormat. It felt like I only had time to get washed and dressed before walking back out the door and driving up to Sheffield.

The assessment went well and I was invited back for an interview in a couple of weeks' time. At last there was some light at the end of the tunnel – and this time it wasn't some bastard, shining a torch and bringing me more bad news.

Meanwhile Kevin Keegan was becoming the latest England manager to learn you don't win any prizes by leaving West Ham players out of the squad for a major championship. Euro 2000 was held jointly between The Netherlands and Belgium and I watched the opening game between Belgium and Sweden in the comfortable surroundings of Stuart the QPR fan's house in Lincolnshire, secure in the knowledge that I was nowhere near home and all the depressing thoughts surrounding it. Stuart the QPR fan had been a good friend to me for many years. His devotion to QPR is as deep rooted and loyal as mine is to West Ham. If West

Ham had a blank Saturday, I would go with him to Loftus Road and watch QPR around the time when they regularly finished in the top half of the table. It's been a real shame to see the way they have fallen away. I hope they'll be back soon. Stuart the QPR fan has always been there for me in my times of need. I was honoured to be his best man when he married Jill and an 'oh my Godfather' to his son, Callum.

On my return to Bexley, England opened their account by going 2-0 up against Portugal through Scholes and McManaman, only to lose 3-2. With Germany coming up next, things did not look good for England but in Charleroi we discovered the Germans actually had a worse team than us and we beat them 1-0 with a Shearer header. It meant avoiding defeat against Romania would be enough to see us through to the quarter-finals and a probable meeting with Italy.

As I watched Phil Neville concede a last minute penalty to hand the Romanians a 3-2 win and kick England out of the competition, a thought struck me. For all that we moan about England managers failing to pick West Ham players, what if Rio Ferdinand had lunged in and messed up everything for the whole nation? What if it had been Frank Lampard who had turned in a completely lack-lustre display in midfield and allowed the Romanians to dominate. What if it had been Joe Cole who'd missed a sitter from six yards? How would we cope with that? For the time being, I swept away the disappointment of failing to progress in Euro 2000, thanked the Lord that the nation hadn't been let down by any West Ham players and went to stick a few more pins in my Phil Neville doll.

With a fresh start within grabbing distance and the prospect of a successful league campaign for West Ham a few weeks away, I started feeling a little better about life. Not only that, I had a new book ready to come out.

Having worked like a Trojan on the manuscript over the summer, *West Ham 'Till I Die* was nearing completion. Roll on 2000-01, football once again proving a more than adequate retreat from real life.

# 3. Doesn't Really Matter

## Chelsea 4 West Ham United 2  19.8.00

By the time the new season started I had the job offer
in the bag. The opening game was against Chelsea at
Stamford Bridge and it was a glorious August afternoon
as Kev and I walked down Fulham Broadway full of beer
and optimism. Kev had been my best mate in football
since we had met through writing for West Ham's top
fanzine, *Over Land and Sea*. We had been to many
games together both as part of the *OLAS* crew and now,
more often than not, independently. Kev loves West
Ham as much as I do. He might deny it sometimes, say
he doesn't care, but I know what West Ham means to
him. And I know when he's lying.

The great thing about the opening day of the season
is that, for a few moments at least, you are joint top with
Manchester United. You are the equal of everyone, a
dream you hang on to until the first goal rattles in
somewhere around the country.

And rattle in it did. Jimmy Floyd Hasselbaink is one of
those players you find intensely irritating when he's
lining up against you because you know his ability alone
should be enough but he can't resist mixing it up with a
large slice of gamesmanship. After 20 minutes Shaka
Hislop went for the ball at Hasslebaink's feet and over he
went like a sack of Dutch tulip bulbs. Penalty! On
reflection, Shaka was lucky to stay on the pitch but he
might as well have been watching from the stands as the

penalty kick whistled past his head before he'd even had the chance to settle himself. One down and with Chelsea in the ascendancy, we consoled ourselves that, for at least another five minutes, we'd be level with Coventry City.

It was a warm day, warm enough for those with more confidence than me in the appearance of their bodies to remove their shirts and by half-time the lower tier of the old East Stand resembled the pleasure beach at Blackpool. The donkeys, however, were strictly confined to the pitch. Parlow levelled to bring hope but it was against the general run of play and, in the end, a 4-2 defeat was the result we deserved. The combination of warm weather, beer and a crushing opening day defeat sent my spirits plunging and my body to the tube station, where I got on a train home and slept it all off.

I wasn't concerned. Chelsea away . . . well, we didn't expect to win there and Leicester City at home to come . . . a match we NEVER lose. Then Manchester United at home, a match we rarely lose. No problem.

Work had almost been completed on *West Ham 'Till I Die*. The final chapters included the tortuous story of Billie/Chloe/Suzanne, or whatever the f\*\*k her name was, which I am not going to repeat here but the story was spelt out in graphic detail. Although she'd dumped on me from a great height, her opinion still meant a lot to me, so I ran the final 50 pages or so of the manuscript past her before going to press.

Her reaction was quite distressing. Considering she had practically ignored me for six weeks, I got a very emotional telephone call from her begging me to remove all the personal details. It could spell the end of her marriage. Urm, hello? Like I should care? She wasn't going to let this go. At first I brushed it off as a pathetic attempt to protect herself from a mild bit of embarrassment but after the fifth or sixth tearful telephone call, I felt I should give her a chance to explain.

This was a woman who had taken everything I had to offer emotionally, yet hadn't thought it necessary for me to know her real name. This was a woman who had berated me publicly for sleeping with another woman BEFORE our relationship had got off the ground, yet jumped into bed with a wine merchant called Tom while I was still licking the wounds inflicted by our abrupt split. I shouldn't have given her a nano-second of my time. But I'm a soft dipsh*t.

The way things were going at West Ham was starting to concern me. I had gone a full year without a season ticket but wanted to be in on the first home game of the season to see us beat Leicester City to a watery pulp in the traditional manner. As Leicester's record at Upton Park was marginally worse than ours at Anfield, it was not an unreasonable expectation.

I rang up the ticket office to be told the only seats available were £32 with an obstructed view. Since the definition of "obstructed view" has never been fully defined, I decided to pass. The words that sprang to mind were "You're having a f**king laugh, surely?" I rang Gary Firmager, editor of *Over Land and Sea*, knowing that where there was a will there was always a way. There was a seat in the press box going spare if I could see my way clear to selling *OLAS* for a couple of hours before the game. As this would constitute vintage nostalgia and incorporate a free ticket, I had no hesitation in accepting the deal.

Standing outside the main gates on Green Street, with a wad of fanzines in my hand and yelling at the top of my voice, took me back almost exactly six years to the night we met Newcastle United at Upton Park at the start of the 1994-95 season. Gary had only just sown the idea for my first book, *An Irrational Hatred of Luton*, in my mind and, as I was unemployed for a couple of months, spent all my time doing all things West Ham and gathering material for my first volume. I remembered how good it felt to be doing something so close to the club, yet totally unofficial. I was in there, mixing it but still retained some street cred.

I took my seat in the press box about five minutes into the match and watched a breathtaking 40 minutes in which West Ham did exactly as I had predicted and pulverised Leicester City. They did everything the coaching manual teaches about creative, attacking play – except the bit tucked away in Appendix One about putting the ball in the net. When the team re-emerged, I re-emerged too, with a belly full of sarnies purloined from the Ron Greenwood lounge. The players suddenly looked as though they'd been gorging themselves on fast food at half-time as well. Igor Stimac was sent off for a second bookable offence and the whole game plan went to the wall.

When Eadie scored, the prospect of Leicester City winning the game seemed inconceivable. There were many reasons for this. Firstly, Leicester City had not won a match at Upton Park since 1965. Secondly, this talented West Ham side could not possibly end the first two games of the season with nothing on the board. Thirdly, and perhaps most importantly in my view, the winning goal couldn't be scored by someone with a girl's name.

The referee, booed off the pitch, laughed and joked with his assistants, or "partners in crime", as we prefer to call them. In the press conference, the contrast between the two managers was stark. Peter Taylor gloated – he couldn't help himself. Harry Redknapp was dejected and although no one felt relegation was on the cards, we all knew nil points from six was not the kind of return we wanted if we were to make a serious challenge for Europe. Particularly when Manchester United were the visitors on Saturday.

When United arrived and took a two-goal lead into the last 15 minutes of the game it looked even worse. Nothing from nine points would be cause for serious concern. Beckham curled in the first from a free-kick about 35 yards out that left everyone asking why he could do it so often for United but consistently failed to do so for his country. Andy Cole added a second on the hour and the game looked as good as over.

But we'd shown enough in the first three games to suggest we were better than that and when Joe Cole won us a penalty by persuading Henning Berg to chop him down on the edge of the penalty area with 10 minutes to go that raised hope more than expectation. Parlow dispatched the spot-kick with customary aplomb and suddenly West Ham felt they could get something. In the dying seconds, a goalmouth scramble saw Mr Punch, Davor Suker, chin the ball over the line for an equaliser that was a sight for sore eyes.

With the first point in the bag, I realised that I'd actually committed myself to starting a new job in October in Nottingham but didn't have anywhere up there to stay. I hadn't even handed in my notice at my current job, nor had I got my head around the situation in any way, shape or form. Tranquilisers have that effect on you. The problem doesn't go away, you just don't give a sh*t any more.

Another phone call from Billie/Chloe/Suzanne, or whatever her f**king name was, prompted me to invite her round so she could show me exactly what parts of the manuscript were causing her concern. I had, after all, changed her name. We had very few mutual friends and we were no longer together, so I couldn't see the problem. She was panicking because I had found out her surname and address (spotty shop assistants can be very helpful when suitably bribed), so she needed me onside.

She came round armed with the manuscript covered in lots of little red lines, which amounted to virtually every reference to her. She was also armed with a lot of charm and a tape she had made of songs that meant a lot to us. She put the tape on and started to cry. This is something I will never understand about women as long as I live. She didn't want me for a lover but we couldn't possibly be just friends. And she didn't want me to move away or sleep with anyone else. Oh, and for good measure, I wasn't allowed to write the truth about it either. Seemed fair enough. She kissed me and told me she still loved me – it had been a mistake with Tom and she'd end it that very night if I'd have her back. I fell for it.

That night she got a train into town to see Tom and end it all. I met her at Greenwich station and drove her back to my house, where we talked, made love, drank wine, smoked and listened to music as we had done in the days when we had only a thousand problems, not the million that existed now. I believed every word she said, especially the bit when she looked into my eyes and told me she loved me.

To Billie/Chloe/Suzanne, or whatever the f**k her name was, sex was a way of getting what she wanted. She knew men in general, and me in particular, could not resist her. To her it was a game and she played it very well. She also knew that on October 21st I would be moving, lock stock and barrel, to Nottingham. She knew if she played it just right she could get rid of me and the offending paragraphs in the book that threatened the marriage she had told me was dead when I first met her. You have to hand it to her, it was a very clever move. I learned a very important lesson. Brains are located in the head, not the groin.

Had I seen through it from the start I would have published anyway and had the last laugh. The international woman of mystery was clearly so worried about the situation, she even gave me her phone number. This was a woman I'd been seeing for over a year and only now did she let me have a phone number. The surname and address probably still wouldn't have followed had I not got them through my own efforts but what did I care? All I needed to know was she was back in my bed smoking cigarettes, listening to music and drinking coffee on a Tuesday afternoon, when all my friends were hurtling up the A1 towards Sunderland. "Mugs"... I thought to myself, as she slipped open her silk robe and invited me inside. Funnily enough, they were thinking exactly the same thing about me.

# 4. Out of Your Mind

**Coventry City 0 West Ham United 3   23.9.00**

The game at Sunderland saw West Ham double their points tally for the season with a 1-1 draw, Suker again hooking in an equaliser. Two points was not a great haul from four games but the Stadium of Light was not an easy place to go in those days and we'd also nicked a point from United, so it was entirely reasonable to remain confident that all would be well.

The perfect place to pick up our first win of the season would have been White Hart Lane in a Monday night game sponsored by Uncle Rupert. It would have been the perfect place, had it happened. We played well for an hour and didn't deserve to go behind to a Sol Campbell header but you don't always get what you deserve in life. If you fail to take your chances, you can't sit and moan about the opposition taking theirs.

The Premiership had become a dog-eat-dog world. The old first division had always been competitive but now there had become three clearly defined sectors to the table and each sector had its own little battle for supremacy that made every game significant for one reason or another. Add to that the ridiculous decision by UEFA to extend qualification for the Champions League to third place, and every game took on the importance of a cup final. With the potential riches afforded by qualification, it actually became more important than a cup final. Winning the FA Cup or the League Cup merely means a place in the UEFA Cup – not a big deal to the Manchester Uniteds, Arsenals and Liverpools of this world.

The top section includes six clubs, Manchester United, Arsenal, Liverpool, Chelsea, Leeds United and Newcastle United, who are expected to finish in the top section. Then there is the bottom section, which would always include the likes of Bradford City, Coventry City, Southampton, whoever had been promoted the previous season and so on.

The middle section, teams which were unlikely to get relegated but were equally unlikely to qualify for Europe, included West Ham, Sunderland, Spurs, Aston Villa and Leicester City. Occasionally one team would appear in the wrong sector and make life interesting. For the time being, we stayed rooted in the bottom three, Sunderland defied gravity in the top three and Liverpool wallowed in mid-table anonymity.

So when we met at Upton Park on Sunday, September 17, 2000, Liverpool needed the three points as badly as we did to get us to our own respective "rightful places." What we had thought would be a temporary blip turned out to be lasting a bit too long for our liking. Liverpool took the lead through Gerrard and it took a spectacularly clumsy foul by Henchoz on Fredi Kanouté to earn us an equalising penalty. We looked tired, listless and unlikely to put things right overnight but we were, at least, working hard.

Once again I had a ticket for Walsall away in the Worthington Cup but chose instead to spend the afternoon in bed with Billie/Chloe/Suzanne, or whatever her f**king name was. It was bizarre. For some reason I thought that spending more time with her before I left would make the leaving of London easier to bear and make her want to see me more often when I came back. Once the relevant cuts had been made to the manuscript, I could see the cracks in the plan gaping wide open in front of my eyes. "How could it possibly work from such a distance?" she would say through crocodile tears. "The way we have it now works because we can see each other at a moment's notice." I couldn't tell if she was genuinely sorry or trying to wriggle out now the job was done.

Either way, Jermain Defoe announced his arrival on the scene with the winning goal at Walsall. I'd heard great things about Defoe, good enough to persuade me to go along to an FA Youth Cup tie at Upton Park where the young striker scored a quite superb hat-trick in a 5-0 win over Manchester United. His eagerly anticipated senior bow came in the salubrious surroundings of the Bescot Stadium and, in keeping with the proud tradition of great West Ham forwards, he scored on his debut, knocking in the rebound after Rio Ferdinand's second half effort had struck the crossbar. A vital strike, for not only did it show that here we had a striker of truly great potential (so fantastic in fact that Harry immediately sent him off on loan to Bournemouth), but it also provided us with our first win of the season. When it comes, you don't care who the opposition are, you grab it with both hands.

Highfield Road has always been a relatively happy hunting ground. The following sun-drenched Saturday we won there 3-0 with goals from Parlow, Cole and Lampard, all of whom converted crosses from Kanouté. The embarrassingly easy nature of the victory made us feel that maybe the early struggle had been completely out of character. What it actually signalled, however, was that Coventry City were a very poor side, destined for relegation. It was to be one of those days when everything went right. Having now obtained the telephone number of Billie/Chloe/Suzanne, or whatever the f**k her name was, we'd arranged that I would pick her up from work on my way home from Coventry. Then we'd go back to my place and she'd get a cab to pick up her car in the morning. A brilliant day, followed by a brilliant evening, one of the few days during the whole of 2000 that I can honestly say I didn't mind being me.

September was rapidly running out of days and a start date in Nottingham of October 23rd meant I had to pull my finger out sharpish if I was going to have a place to lay my head. In the end I pulled my finger out so quick you could hear the 'pop' in Newcastle. After an initial search of some very crummy flats and houses to rent for extortionate amounts of cash, I settled on a large shared house 15 minutes walk from the city centre. It was a bit of a rushed decision but one of those that just felt right. It proved to be an inspired choice. I paid the deposit and dashed back to London feeling like a ten-ton weight had been lifted from my shoulders. The adventure was going to happen, with or without the support or blessing of Billie/Chloe/Suzanne or whatever her f**king name was.

The second leg of the Worthington Cup tie against Walsall ended in a 1-1 draw, Steve Lomas heading us in front from another Kanouté cross in the first minute. The second division leaders grabbed a merited equaliser and, in the end, we were hanging on for a third round place against Blackburn Rovers.

The final Saturday of the month was spent in Nottingham checking out the local amenities and making sure I had made the correct choice. While in the general area I drove up to Sheffield to visit Lucy and Richard, listening intently as Joey Cole put us 1-0 up from yet another Kanouté cross at home to Bradford City, only for Dan Petrescu to outwit Trevor Sinclair and head an equaliser from a bizarre free-kick move. I urged the score to change for the better. Unlike the previous season's encounter, which ended 5-4, the game finished in a damp squib of a 1-1 draw. It was a match West Ham should have been looking to win if they were to have realistic European ambitions. But the longer the season went on without a win at Upton Park and drawing games that should have been won, Europe seemed a distant dream indeed.

# 5. The Lonely One

### West Ham United 1 Arsenal 2    21.10.00

The point from the match against Bradford City clawed us out of the bottom three and as we went into the October of a season that had promised much more, we expected much more. For me, though, the campaign did still promise much. The days when West Ham regularly struggled against the drop seemed so many years behind us. Yet it had only been three-and-a-half years since John Hartson and Paul Kitson arrived on the scene to drag us out of serious doo-doo and steer the ship on an upward course. We'd forgotten what it felt like, in such a short space of time, to stare relegation in the face. But here we were, getting on first name terms with the dreaded R-word before October had even started. The fact we hadn't had to face it for so long meant we were, in fact, a little blasé about the whole thing, not believing it could possibly happen to such a talented squad. I was as guilty as anyone, shrugging off our lowly position and not being at all concerned about the prospect of wearing my West Ham shirt to the pub to watch England's World Cup qualifier against Germany. The final England international at Wembley before the bulldozers moved in to rebuild the old place.

Despite being so detached from the whole thing, watching the match in a pub in Bexley, it was still an emotional occasion watching England in their red shirts taking on Germany in white. It was hard not to be moved by the sense of occasion. Strange, because England's finest hour at Wembley had come two years before I was born. Why it should send a shiver down my spine when I think of it, I'm not too sure. It's yet another unexplainable anomaly of the football fan's predicament. The 1-0 defeat in the pouring rain and Keegan's subsequent resignation did not make for a pleasant afternoon – but the day would have its compensations.

Billie/Chloe/Suzanne, or whatever the f**k her name was, phoned early evening. She left her car at Eltham and I went to pick her up. She'd gone to town on her appearance. We stopped off for a drink and something to eat before going back to my place with a bottle of wine. I didn't know it then but it was to be the last time. She knew it of course. She'd known weeks before but, as usual, I was the last to find out.

The following Saturday, West Ham managed another 1-1 draw, this time a creditable one at Portman Road, where high-flying Ipswich Town, another of the teams marauding in the wrong sector of the table, took the lead through Marcus Stewart in the first half. Stewart had been one of those players Harry had been linked with years before, when Marcus was knocking goals in for Bristol Rovers. Gary Firmager and I interviewed him at the time for the fanzine and both formed the opinion that he was a nice chap but not Premiership calibre. Maybe we had been wrong to dismiss him. Following a productive spell at Huddersfield Town, Stewart had signed for the Tractor Boys and was now banging them in from all angles. Parlow volleyed in an equaliser in the second half, proving that form is temporary, class is permanent.

That evening, Billie/Chloe/Suzanne, or whatever the f**k her name was, decided to go out drinking in town rather than spend what could possibly have been our last Saturday night together. I knew our relationship would not continue after I left for Nottingham, it wasn't practical. It hadn't been good for my health when I had lived around the corner, so it certainly wouldn't help being 150 miles away. I had hoped, however, that she'd want to cherish every moment we had left together. But no, she'd achieved the main objective and I'd been left in no doubt about the way she felt. It seemed cruel but not completely out of character. I realised now was the crunch time – within the next seven days I would change job, move house by 150 miles and lose a girlfriend. If you're going to change, change big.

One thing, I knew, would always stay the same. West Ham would always flatter to deceive. With results starting to pick up we could have expected better than the 1-2 defeat at home to Arsenal. Pires put the Gunners in front, then a sloppy own goal from Rio meant Stuart Pearce's cleverly disguised free-kick was nothing other than damage limitation. I was unloading my stuff in Nottingham as this was unfolding before me. The first item out of the car had been the stereo, so the football could be monitored during other, more mundane tasks. Having unpacked, put all my books on the shelves, underwear in the drawers, made the bed, put posters on the walls and got the computer up and running, I sat back and looked at my student style bed-sitter that was costing me the princely sum of £45 per week. I was 31-years-old. What on earth was I doing here?

I thought it over as I drove to a garage that evening to buy the sandwich and bottle of Coke that would form my dinner for the evening. Moving is a costly business and with payday eons away (Thursday), it was sandwiches or nothing all week. There was no phone line in my room, so I couldn't even go online. The rest of the house was pretty much empty, most of the other occupants choosing to return home to parental nests, so I was left with my portable telly and collection of West Ham videos to pass the time. I felt excited yet lonely, tired yet restless. But the presence of the Hammers videos on the screen helped me forget I was in a strange town a long way from home, where I knew only two people in the immediate area.

On my first Sunday alone in Nottingham, I seriously doubted the wisdom of my move. It rained hard from an ink-black sky as I walked to the nearest phone box, dodging the requests of the resident beggars and prostitutes, demanding anything from the price of a cup of tea, and not afraid to open the door of the phone booth to ask for it.

After beating off the third or fourth request from the local scrotes, I got through to mum and dad and pretended everything was fine and dandy. I tried not to let on that I feared I'd made my greatest ever mistake.

The following day I walked the short distance to the Jarvis Hotel, where I had been instructed to report for training. This was an unusual situation. Normally when you start a new job, there are people around you who have been doing the job for years and are able to show you the ropes, help you to get acclimatised. This, however, was a new venture and for all 17 of us it was our first day.

There were enough of us from similar backgrounds for me to make friends immediately. Andy and Yvonne had left exactly the same job as me in Ripley for exactly the same reason. Craig had done the same from Macclesfield office. Mick and Keith, our "Rolling Stones", came via the Coventry office, Big John from Retford, Dave and Cath from Lincoln. A gaping wide net had been spread but the mesh had been fine enough to trawl far and wide and, as it turned out, capture the salt of the earth. Our manager, a guy called Chris Broughton, joined us a week or so later having been the District Manager at Sheldon in Birmingham. He was returning to his native Nottingham, a land I was soon to learn he loved deeply – and I was soon to find out why.

In addition to ex-CIS sales staff, a sprinkling of new blood from outside the Society added a different perspective and a certain degree of spice to our training in the early weeks. Tony had been with Abbey Life, Ian and Rebecca with HSBC and Nick, who had come from Lloyds TSB, all had a different slant on things. It made agreement on anything virtually impossible but added a lot more fun to what could otherwise have been a very dull training programme.

We were training in the hotel because the office we were due to occupy had not yet been completed. We had been due to "go live" in December but that date rapidly became January, April, May, etc, until we were finally let loose on an unsuspecting sales force in June 2001.

Meanwhile there was lots of training to be done and this began in earnest. In the breaks, football was the main topic of conversation. Having worked in the London area all my life, I had been used to colleagues supporting London clubs and, of course, the inevitable Manchester United and Liverpool sycophants. Here, however, I had colleagues who supported a myriad of different clubs, from Glasgow Celtic through the obvious Nottingham Forest and Notts County to Aston Villa, Birmingham City and Coventry City. With five of those six clubs outside the Premiership at that time, it gave me a whole new perspective on football.

Although I had moved away from London, I hadn't left West Ham. Having been away for only a week, the lure of a home game against Newcastle United was too much and I was back in the East End easily in time for kick-off on the following Saturday. I may have only been moved for a week but things had definitely changed. Green Street didn't look the same. The people milling around me looked different. I couldn't quite put my finger on it but I knew the move I had made was permanent. There was no going back now. It scared me a little bit.

I took comfort in the familiar surroundings of the Bobby Moore stand and watched as West Ham battled for their first home win of the season. Newcastle at home is never an easy match but in recent years they have proved fairer game than they did in our first few seasons in the Premiership. A pulsating game ended in a 1-0 win for the Hammers, Fredi Kanouté scored the winner in the second half, capping a build-up in pressure that almost lifted the roofs off all four stands at Upton Park. Convinced that having got the first home win out of the way we would be all right, I got back to the car and drove the 150 miles back to Nottingham in what seemed like no time at all. My first week at work had been a success, topped by a fine display and three points for West Ham. What more could I ask for?

I suppose a friendly, nearby pub with Sky TV serving cheap grub and good beer would have been too much to ask but the Newcastle Arms was there on my doorstep and did just that. On a Sunday I could pop in and get sausage and chips for £2 and a pint for £1.50. Sorted. Being in the middle of student land helped, of course – the local pubs were tripping over themselves for the students' business and apart from having to dodge pools of sick and exploded kebabs on the walk in to work every morning, there was no definable downside. I had a word with the landlord and checked that he would be showing the Worthington Cup tie against Blackburn Rovers on the Wednesday. He confirmed they would be, I took my place at 7.30pm in an almost deserted pub, sitting comfortably in front of a massive screen, pint and sausage sarnie in hand. Maybe that Uncle Rupert wasn't such a bad bloke after all?

Something I didn't take long to notice about Nottingham was the friendliness of the people. I watched the Blackburn game in the company of a complete stranger and talked long after it had finished about the state of the modern game, our own recollections and hopes for the future. I know it could have happened in any pub in any part of the country. But I know for a fact, if someone had come up and started talking to me like that in a pub in London, I would have considered them a weirdo. In Nottingham I considered it friendly. It was possibly a symptom of the fact I was alone in a strange place that magnified the smallest show of friendship. Either way, it was thoroughly appreciated and the Newcastle Arms quickly became my local for that very reason.

Christina, my pen-pal from Nottingham, who I started writing to in 1985 following an advert she placed in 'The Hammer' matchday programme, was always on hand to make sure I was settling. She was busy working on her wedding plans – she was due to fly out to Sri Lanka the following Christmas to marry Chris but they both always made time for me. If they were going to a show or a concert in the immediate vicinity, they would always invite me along. I never felt like I was playing gooseberry but I didn't want it to get to that stage, so I didn't always accept their invitations. On my first full weekend in Nottingham they took me along to the Royal Concert Hall to see Phil Jupitus and have an Italian meal afterwards. They helped me find my feet in Nottingham and, for that, I will always be grateful.

# 6. Walking Away

**Leeds United 0 West Ham United 1  18.11.00**

Work had been completed on my second book, *West Ham 'Till I Die* and I raced home from work at lunchtime to find the first copy sitting in a padded envelope on the table in the kitchen. Living in a shared house, it was a matter of trust that your post would be there in the evening – but to be fair there was never a problem with mail going missing.

I'm sure many people dream of having a book published. I always did and I remember the elation I felt when I first laid my hands on a copy of *Irrational* but it was magnified a thousand times when I first saw a copy of *West Ham 'Till I Die*. I'd not had a great deal of input in the design and layout of the jacket. I'd largely left that up to other people, so I had very little idea what it would look like, what it would feel like. It was my second book, my second major achievement. I floated back to work and showed off.

That evening was the first time I realised how handy it could be to live in Nottingham when it came to away games. Courtesy of our old friend Uncle Rupert, we had to play Derby County at Pride Park on a wet Monday night in November. While most West Ham fans had booked a half day off work and struggled with the conditions on the M1, I strolled home from work, had a shower and a bite to eat, jumped in the car and drove the 15 miles to Derby and still had 45 minutes to spare before kick-off.

One thing I hadn't counted on, however, were the weather conditions. Normally, a trip to Pride Park is simple enough – park in the hospital grounds, then cut across the fields down by the canal, about a 15-minute walk to the away end. Tonight, however, the rain was torrential. Our path across the fields was blocked by ankle-deep puddles, an over-flowing canal and a security guard the size of Mount Kilimanjaro. We were instructed to get on a bus that would take us the convenient, 200-mile route around to the away end, via a traffic jam reminiscent of a South American capital city, not an East Midlands industrial town.

I missed the first 10 minutes of the game but, as it turned out, I wished I had missed all of it. One of the dreariest 0-0 draws of all-time ensued but I was trapped in my seat as I wasn't going anywhere until the coaches picked us up and took us back to the car park.

Only when I returned to work the following morning did I understand the hatred that exists between Nottingham Forest and Derby County. Let me re-phrase that. I understood the hatred Nottingham Forest fans have for Derby County. I've never had the opportunity to hear the opposite view but I'm sure the complete lack of respect works both ways. "I see you couldn't beat the sheep-shaggers, then?" was a phrase used more than once that Tuesday morning. I couldn't quite understand the vitriol. Derby was 15 miles away in a different county. But, of course, these things are more deeper-rooted than most outsiders could ever understand. After all, of all the London clubs, who, other than West Ham fans themselves, would put Millwall down as the chief focus of our fear and loathing?

The Nottingham/Derby rivalry went back years and was about more than just location. Derby were successful at a time when Forest were not and vice-versa. Both clubs had been managed by Brian Clough, still a god in Nottingham. These intricacies of Midlands football were all lessons I had to learn but I lapped it up.

I was, however, incredulous that they were surprised we hadn't beaten Derby. I was always grateful to come away from anywhere with a point, so even though the game was appalling I was grateful for what we had.

I've never been one of those people who says they'd rather see us play well and lose than battle out a dull 0-0 draw. At home, yes, maybe I have some sympathy with that argument and it always fills me with pride when I hear supporters of other clubs saying: "Ah, West Ham, they always play good football." Their idea of a good footballing side is one that rolls over and gives them three points. It's not the same as mine. My ideal would be a team that plays classy, composed football at home but is able to dig in and get a result away when required – even if it means not beating a bunch of sheep-shaggers.

With my book hot off the press, I was keen to gauge reaction so made the trip down to London the following Saturday to buy up copies of the matchday programme and *Over Land and Sea*, both of which contained favourable reviews. I wasn't doing as much promotional work as I had been for Irrational, partly through choice but partly because of the practicalities involved. I hadn't been intending to take in the home game against Manchester City but as I was in the vicinity and a spare ticket ended up in my pocket, I thought, what the hell?

It seemed that the hard work done in the summer had finally started to pay off. Something, somewhere, seemed to click after about 50 minutes of the match, when after falling 0-1 down to a first half strike from Prior (I say strike, it kind of bounced in off his head), everything suddenly fell into place. Kanouté cut in from the right and squared for Lomas to equalise against his old club. Sinclair also attacked the space down the right and squeezed one in to give us the lead. Another Kanouté cross landed on Ian Pearce's head and he finished with a flourish. Then, in the dying minutes, referee Winter appeared to be the only person in the stadium (the only one that mattered, anyway) to notice Dunne tugging at Fredi's shirt in the penalty area and a spot kick was duly awarded.

Parlow has received a fair amount of criticism in the past for the quality of his penalty taking. His miss against Aston Villa the previous year in the Worthington Cup quarter-final 'replay' was a case in point and led to Lampard having a stand-up argument with him the next time we were awarded a penalty in the famous 5-4 win over Bradford. On this occasion, though, 3-1 up and with seconds on the watch, chipping City keeper Weaver from 12 yards seemed an entirely sensible approach. The effect was devastating, the morale lifted higher than any words of encouragement could ever do. The captain led by example and what an example. It was Wednesday before the smile started to loosen from my lips.

The prospect of playing Leeds United at Elland Road should have made that smile fade much sooner than it did. However, I knew from early on in the season that it was a game I would have to miss, as my good friend Katherine was getting married.

Elland Road is one of those trips I make every year, because one day – one day – we'd win there. I've seen us win at Highbury, White Hart Lane, Old Trafford, Maine Road, Goodison Park and St James' Park but a Hammers away victory in Leeds hadn't happened since 1981 and, well as we were playing, I couldn't see it happening in 2000 either. While I sat dutifully through the Catholic ceremony in a dull and dreary Bexleyheath, text messages were received at regular intervals, telling me that a Nigel Winterburn goal had given us a half-time lead. Hard though it was to believe, I scurried away after the service to drive on to the reception and pick up news of the final score. West Ham had won 1-0. Nigel's goal had been enough for the three points and they had done it without me. Bastards! I was prepared to forgive them this once but heaven help them if they ever do that when I'm not present at Anfield.

Billie/Chloe/Suzanne, or whatever the f\*\*k her name was, had so far managed to be pretty elusive since I'd left for Nottingham. She figured it was over so didn't see the point in prolonging the agony (that was my version of events anyway, she was actually too busy latching on the next unwitting victim to care very much about me). I sent her a text message, as I knew she was working on the Sunday, and asked her to meet me for lunch so I could give her a birthday present and a copy of my new book. She grudgingly agreed but wouldn't shift out of reception. She took my gifts and the conversation fell flat. I wanted her to say how much she missed me. She didn't. Same old story.

I couldn't help wondering where it had all gone wrong as I drove back up the M1. In reality I knew it would never work, with her still being married and having a child she doted on. I can't criticise her for that and I know I could have handled it better but all the time I could hear myself saying "If only".

"If only I could meet someone else," I thought, as I pulled in at the BP station on the A610 outside Nottingham that evening. A thought that was running through my head just at the very moment the pretty blonde girl in front of me dropped her purse and all her change went rolling around on the floor. I helped her scramble around picking up the coins and when I looked at her, she said: "Thank you" and smiled at me. A very important part of my insides melted. She paid for her petrol and went back to her car, just when I saw the edge of a pound coin sticking out from underneath the counter. I picked it up and dashed out after her, catching her just in time. "You missed one," I told her breathlessly.

"Thank you," she giggled and smiled a sweet smile. I did something I have never done before or since. Without thinking, I blurted out: "I think you're really nice – can I give you my phone number?" My look of shock was mirrored by hers. I couldn't work out why she'd be shocked, she probably got offers all the time, but I stiffened myself and raised my chin a little ready to take the knockout blow.

"I can do better than that," she said, reaching across and tearing the lid from an empty packet of Embassy Number 1s. "Here's my mobile number – call me some time!" and with that her little Fiat Uno was away and I was standing there gobsmacked. The only noise I could hear came from the forecourt attendant over the tannoy. "You paying for that petrol or what, midduck?"

Maybe the whole thing – victory at Leeds, the standoffishness of Billie/Chloe/Suzanne, or whatever her f**king name was, Sarah (the name the girl at the garage scribbled on the cigarette packet) giving me her phone number – was some sort of sick joke. Joke or not, having plucked up the courage to ask a complete stranger for a date, I now had no bottle whatsoever when it came to making the call. "I'll do it tonight," I'd promise myself, then realise there were a hundred more important things that needed doing, mainly involving cleaning, cooking or sleeping. It was worse than the procrastination that sets in when exams are on the horizon. I got crap 'O' level results but my bedroom was spotless.

More importantly, I had to come to terms with the sale of one of our favourite sons, Rio Ferdinand. £18million is a lot of money by anyone's standards and I can imagine there were a few disbelieving faces at the West Ham board meeting when Leeds United's offer was put forward. If I'd been there I would have found it hard to suppress a snigger. But it was true and Rio had gone. Of course, it hadn't happened overnight, these things rarely do, but playing Leeds at the weekend (and beating them, more to the point) seemed to have accelerated things. With a new stand well under way and a bank overdraft bigger than the national debt of a small African country, the world record fee for a defender was an offer no club in our position could refuse. Rio was sacrificed on the altar of all that is good about the West Ham youth policy. He conducted himself with great dignity. The board duly released funds for Harry to buy new players but when other clubs see us with pots of cash, I always know what to expect. It would have been naive to expect anything else. After 25 years as a football fan, if nothing else I've learned that it's always the fans who get screwed.

Deep down – well, not that deep down – that's what I hoped would also be the case with Sarah. "I'll ring her if we win at Southampton on Saturday," I promised myself, a pledge that would add a little extra spice to my Saturday afternoon spent, for the first time since moving, in Nottingham.

I had also hoped that I wouldn't get too much grief at work about the sale of Rio. There were no Leeds fans to give me a hard time, so I thought I stood a good chance. "Nah then, Rob," said Big John as I walked in the next morning. "I'm sorry to have to tell you that I'm leaving. The Prudential have put in an £18million bid and it's too good an opportunity to miss. I need to move on to a bigger company."

"Piss off," I said.

Promising myself to call Sarah if we won at The Dell was only slightly less risky than if I'd promised to do it if

Steve Potts scored a hat-trick of headers from the half-way line. It wasn't likely to happen.

That's the fantastic thing about West Ham – when you thought you had them sussed they go and do it again. Prove you wrong.

All seemed to be going to plan when Oakley belted in a low drive to make it 1-0 to Southampton. But a Kanouté glancing header and a left foot thunderbolt from Stuart Pearce gave West Ham a 2-1 lead at half-time and had my hand hovering over the telephone. Beattie equalised and it looked like a night in with a take-away after all. Trevor Sinclair had other ideas, however, and with a great run and shot gave West Ham their first victory at The Dell for nearly six years. Not much of a statistic, I know, but you'd think a team like West Ham would be able to muster more than one win during that time at a place like Southampton.

With victory assured, I had to pay-up on my promise, otherwise I'd never trust myself again. It was very strange how my courage had disappeared so quickly after the confidence of the garage forecourt. I reasoned with myself. Would she have given me the number if she didn't want me to call? I guessed not and dialled the number.

A voice answered. "Sarah?"

"No, It's Millie."

"Oh, right. Is Sarah there?" Maybe she'd given me a fake number?

"She's just popped aht duck, she won't be long."

I thought the whole point of mobile phones was that you could take them out with you.

"She asked me to call," I started, then realised she didn't know my name. In fact our only point of reference was our meeting at the garage. I got all embarrassed again.

"We met at the BP garage. It's Rob. Can you ask her

to ring me back, please?" She asked no questions, which was a relief.

"Okay duck, she won't be long, baht 10 minutes or so."

I thanked her and went to lay down on my bed. My bedroom in Nottingham was also my lounge and dining room. It was about 12 feet square and had it not been so nicely decorated and furnished with so many of my own possessions, it could easily have been called a cell. Cell or not, I chose to spend a lot of time in there. It was comfortable, I had a phone line in now, so could talk to friends, go on the internet, or simply lay back, listen to music and wait for Sarah to call. She didn't. I resisted the temptation to phone back. Maybe it had all been an elaborate wind-up?

After back-to-back wins away at Elland Road and The Dell, the average West Ham fan would have been justified in expecting a relatively easy win over Sheffield Wednesday at Upton Park in the fourth round of the Worthington Cup. Again I promised myself that if we won I would try Sarah again but, this time, West Ham let me off the hook by losing 2-1 to a side struggling to come to terms with relegation from the Premiership the previous May. Despite going close through Frank Lampard in the first minute, Hammers found themselves 0-2 down just after half-time and left with a mountain to climb. No heroics to win 4-3 like the year before – lightning, it seemed, did not strike in the same place twice.

## 7. Can We Fix It?

**Everton 1 West Ham United 1  16.12.00**

Mark, my former landlord and housemate, came up to visit the following Saturday. In his newly acquired Maserati, he made the trip in a little over two hours and we went for a stroll and a beer in town. My trips away at weekends had been taking their toll on my pocket and I had to resign myself to watching the scores roll in at the pub. West Ham had beaten Middlesbrough 1-0 at Upton Park with a goal from Parlow. I got back to my room in time to watch the goal on *Match of the Day* – a classic strike by Parlow, drifting in from the left and unleashing an unstoppable right-foot shot into the bottom corner. This man had so much talent, it was so frustrating that he could not bring himself to use it every week.

It was getting on for midnight but, fuelled by a little Dutch courage and a general feeling of well being that comes with a home victory, I thought I'd try Sarah again. This time she answered. "Hello you!" she said and I froze, momentarily. That was the greeting Billie/Chloe/Suzanne, or whatever the f**k her name was, used all the time. When I got my voice back, I found that she remembered me and wanted to go out for a drink. I suggested the salubrious surroundings of the Newcastle Arms at 7pm on Sunday evening. She didn't want picking up, she knew it, so she'd meet me there. She sounded pleased to hear from me. I was pleased she'd remembered me. I clean forgot to ask why she hadn't phoned back last Saturday. I didn't care and grinned myself to sleep.

After a longer than average lie-in, I spent most of Sunday getting myself ready for my date. I was installed at my usual table at the Newcastle Arms by the appointed hour. I had a drink. Then another. Then another. Eight o'clock came and went. I rang her mobile. Answerphone. Message left. Ten o'clock came and went. I rang again. Answerphone. By closing time I'd had about eight pints and was not in the best of moods as I staggered back up the hill to my room. Half expecting to see a note of apology scribbled by the communal phone, or a message on my own answer phone, I was to be disappointed again. Not meant to happen, forget it.

I scraped together the money for another trip to Upton Park the following Saturday, for the game against Aston Villa. Michael Carrick scored a brilliant goal with a left foot shot from way out that pinged against the left-hand post, then crashed against the right before going in, leaving their keeper rooted to the spot. West Ham were well on top at that point and should have gone on to win easily but, instead, they allowed Hendrie to equalise within a few minutes and somehow never regained the momentum required to overhaul them.

On the way home, my mobile rang. It was Sarah. I watched the screen flash for a couple of seconds while I decided what tone to adopt. Angry? Hurt? *Laissez Faire?* I decided on the latter. Something had come up, she was sorry. She'd been out without her mobile (that, at least, figured). If I was still interested, I could go round and pick her up tonight at 8pm. If I was honest with myself, I was still interested but decided not to make too much of an effort. I jotted down her address and as soon as I got home, showered, changed and had my usual 'in a rush' meal of two slices of marmalade on toast and a Mars bar.

I arrived at the given address and knocked. Millie answered. "You must be Rod?"

"Rob," I corrected.

"You must be Millie?"

My conversation was unusually scintillating that night.

"She's just popped ahht but she won't be a minute."

I rolled my eyes, experiencing a little bit of *déjà vu*.

"Have a seat, like a cuppa?" In for a penny, I thought. I sat down and Millie trundled off to the kitchen. I looked at the sofa opposite. Declining the shouted offer of sugar, I lifted the cushion under my arm to find a spoon and some silver paper underneath. My heart sank. I got up, walked out and drove off without looking back. I never called her, she never called me. It ended before it had begun, thank God.

It might have been that Sarah wasn't doing drugs but it explained a few things if she was. I could have stuck with her and tried to help her – and every now and then I experience pangs of guilt that I didn't. But drug addicts, be they smokers, drinkers or smack-heads, have to want to be helped. I could have been banging my head against a brick wall. I'm sure I did the right thing by walking away. Besides, she was probably off her face when she gave me her number – I'll never know.

That Wednesday I got my first taste of Nottingham football. Forest were at home to Huddersfield Town, now managed by ex-Hammers boss Lou Macari. As Forest had very generously (and somewhat desperately) lowered their ticket prices to a fiver for the night, I decided to go along with Big John. Forest lost 3-1 and I thought it best to keep quiet about the fact that I had never seen Nottingham Forest win a game at the City Ground.

That Friday was to be the last day we spent training at the hotel. Our offices in the centre of Nottingham had been re-fitted and were ready for occupation the

45

following Monday. We celebrated with a combined Christmas bash and wetting of the new office's head. I woke up with a very sore head and someone called Gail. We both looked as surprised as each other. Neither of us had any idea what had happened after about 10pm the previous evening and we both preferred it that way. I had a thumping headache but had to get up and get on my way to the game at Everton, so I made Gail some breakfast and then took her home still blissfully ignorant of what had occurred the night before. It was Christmas, I reasoned, I should allow myself the present of believing that she hadn't been able to resist my charms and had begged me to take her home to bed.

The journey to Goodison Park took longer than it should have from Nottingham, mainly because I was still finding my way around and didn't realise you were allowed to cut across country rather than stick rigidly to the motorways. I opted for the M1 to Leeds, then the M62 to Liverpool, which, when I looked at the map later, was an incredibly tortuous route that could have been done in half the time if I'd cut across to Stoke and gone up the M6. We live and learn.

The season of goodwill had not extended to Merseyside. Everton fans are whiney little sods at the best of times but when they failed to score after 45 minutes against us, they started getting bored and laying into us verbally. Normally, Everton would be two or three up by half-time against West Ham, so their frustration was understandable. But the acidity of their vitriolic comments had to be heard to be believed. I was sitting in the last seat before the gangway, separated only by a couple of stewards from the snarling hoards. I'm the first one to have a pop at football but when all is said and done, it's a laugh. These guys meant it.

Their mood didn't improve when Watson gave Everton the lead in the second half and it only darkened after Fredi Kanouté's turn and shot from just inside the area levelled the scores at 1-1. Something quite bizarre happened a few minutes from the end of the game. A football memory that ranks alongside seeing Tony Cottee score four and West Ham 10 against Bury, it's up there with a win at Old Trafford and Kevin Keen starting in a number 12 shirt by mistake, it was that unusual.

Parlow, the target for much of the abuse levelled by the Everton fans during the second half, produced a sequence of play the like of which I had never seen before and, in this day and age, doubt if I will ever see again. With Everton keeper Gerrard down and injured making a clearance, a cross came in for Parlow to nod the ball into an empty net. But, seeing Gerrard lying on the floor, he caught the ball in mid-air to effectively stop play and allow the stricken goalkeeper to receive some medical attention.

The warmth of the applause and the standing ovation afforded to Parlow made the hairs on the back of my neck stand up. Possibly this was because of the marked difference in opinion the Everton fans suddenly showed, or maybe it was pride that one of our players had done something perceived to be so worthy.

There was a difference of opinion, of course. He's professional footballer, he should have taken the chance to score a winning goal. But Parlow is smarter than that. It wasn't a 100% clear-cut goal scoring opportunity. Had he gone for it and missed, he would have got stick from both camps. Had he scored, Everton fans would never have forgiven him and, given his history in the sportsmanship department, may have earned himself a tag that he would never be able to shake off. It is doubtful whether it was running through his mind at the time – these decisions have to be made in a split second – but he certainly chose the right option.

By plucking the ball out of the air, the Everton fans

commended him on his sportsmanship. The West Ham fans puffed out their chests with pride and said: "See, we told you he was just misunderstood." And the press had a field day, finding anyone who had stood to win large sums of money on a 2-1 West Ham victory, as they were about the only people who had a bad word to say about him. Perhaps the only real losers that day were West Ham. The extra two points would have done very nicely, thanks. But it's just not the West Ham way. What's the point in winning if you know, in your heart of hearts, you didn't quite play the game?

We had hoped that Harry would invest the money he was allowed to spend from the Rio Ferdinand transfer wisely. We had reason to be optimistic, given his track record, but there was always the spectre of Boogers, Raducioiu, Dumitrescu and Harkes peering over the fence and reminding us that just because he signed Bilic, Berkovic, Hartson, Kitson and Parlow, it didn't make Harry invincible. He'd signed enough donkeys to keep Blackpool pleasure beach in business for a century.

The first two signings he did make caused me a little discomfort. Rigobert Song had played a blinder for Liverpool when I saw him at Anfield in the 2-2 draw a couple of years before but there had to be a reason why Liverpool were so keen to get rid of him. The same could be said of Titi Camara, the man sporting the most ridiculous name of any footballer ever to play for West Ham and who looked like a cross between Uncle Fester and Frank Bruno. Although Camara had finished top scorer for Liverpool and had scored the winner against us at Anfield the previous year, that, to me, was no proof of pedigree. I'd fancy my granny to score against West Ham at Anfield.

Song had a steady enough debut at Goodison Park, making waist-high headers and generally playing like a complete nutter. Had he kept that up, we might have been able to accept him but, instead, he turned into a nightmare.

Camara proved to us at Leicester City that he didn't need to make that transformation. Fredi gave us the lead but Izzet equalised before half-time. In the second half, Ian Pearce found the season of goodwill had come early in the West Ham penalty box and gifted an easy goal to the ever dis-likeable Savage. Harry gave Pearcey a bit of a slating in the post-match interview, which I thought was a bit unfair. With planks like Camara playing up front, slicing volleys so high they came back down with snow on them, it was hardly surprising we lost the game. But then, Harry had invested a lot of money in Camara – he was hardly likely to hold his hands up and admit to, arguably, the biggest mistake of his career, was he?

After the game I trudged back to the car and drove south along a foggy M1 to London to spend Christmas with the family. Although at work we had moved into our plush new offices, we were still training and there was little work of consequence to be done, so I had no qualms whatsoever about taking the time off.

On Boxing Day we met newly-promoted Charlton Athletic at Upton Park and I took in the game on my way back to Nottingham. Something of a bogey team for a few years, they beat us on their last visit on their way down and, in 1992, on our way towards promotion to the Premiership. I was not expecting an easy game. However, it proved as easy as it gets at this level, West Ham winning the game 5-0 with some fantastic strikes. Parlow's first goal appeared to be a brilliant back-of-the-heel flick but further analysis showed that it was, actually, an own goal by Richard Rufus. Like we cared? Fredi added a second and Frank Lampard a third before Trevor Sinclair notched the goal of the season with a stunning volley from about 25 yards out. Fredi completed the rout with a well taken one-on-one, sending me home happy.

I wasn't so happy to get back, though, when I found that an inch of snow had fallen in Nottingham and the power had gone off in the house. With no one else around, I endured a cold and sleepless night, reminiscent of the bad old days in my horrible little flat in Beckenham. Fortunately, Bridie, our chirpy Irish cleaning lady, knew where the fuse box was and it was all fixed the next morning. I prepared for a trip to see Stuart the QPR fan in Peterborough to celebrate his son Callum's first birthday with victory at home to Chelsea but, in true West Ham style, the game was called off just two hours before the game was due to start.

I spent New Year's Eve at a party at the Newcastle Arms. I met a gorgeous, slim, blue-eyed blonde girl called Shauna, who lived in Bradford but was there with a group of friends celebrating New Year as they had heard Nottingham was a party town. We chatted for ages and, optimistically, I gave her my phone number. She had a boyfriend. I was seeing someone on-and-off. She didn't tear it up and throw it away, which was a start. She said she'd ring if things changed. I didn't hold my breath.

As midnight approached, Shauna had moved on without so much as a kiss under the mistletoe. I felt the time had come to take stock. The move to Nottingham had, overall, been a success. I was enjoying life a lot more. Money hadn't improved, in fact things were getting steadily worse. West Ham were still, well, West Ham and women continued to run rings around me but there was time to sort all that out. One thing at a time.

# 8. Things I've Seen

## Manchester United 0 West Ham United 1  28.1.01

New Year is all about tradition and 2001 was no exception as we conformed with our traditional spineless capitulation at Old Trafford. The only mystery surrounding this one was how we didn't concede seven like the year before, as, first Rigobert Song, and then Stuart Pearce made defensive errors that would make a schoolboy blush. Two-nil down at half-time was a positive situation for us, given the pummelling we'd taken. When Yorke made it three, it looked like collapse might be on the cards but, due more to a lack of exertion by United rather than any heroics on our part, Kanouté nodded a consolation goal near the end of a 3-1 defeat.

FA Cup third round day is a very special one and when you were working, as I was, in an office full of such diverse football tastes and persuasions, it made life doubly interesting. Nottingham Forest were due to play Wolves in the third round on the Sunday. Big John persuaded me to go even though I had now confessed to him that, up to that point, I'd been something of a Jonah where Forest were concerned. Come to think of it, I've never seen Nottingham Forest win at the City Ground against any opposition, a run which must now extend into double figures. One day, when I'm extremely bored, I'll work it out exactly.

First there was the small matter of the Saturday afternoon and yet another trip to Walsall. I wasn't filled with glee at the prospect of playing Walsall for the second time in the same season at Bescott Stadium but they didn't represent a massive threat to our progress into the fourth round. I was surprised, though, when I bought a copy of the Walsall fanzine to read the editorial saying they were a bit pissed off to be playing West Ham again! Not because they thought they'd lose, but because it would have been nice to get a bigger club. Ungrateful sods. It reminded me of 1994 and the expression on the then non-league Kidderminster Harriers players' faces when they drew us in the fifth round. They looked like they'd all just been laid off. Personally, If I was a non-league, or lower league player, I'd be delighted to play West Ham. At least we'll give you a fighting chance.

Again I was able to experience the benefits of living in Nottingham when it came to travelling to away games. Being slap-bang in the middle of the country, I could travel to the West Midlands in under an hour. As it turned out, my body clock was still on London time and I arrived in Walsall early enough to get a parking space right by the away fans' entrance, buy a McDonald's and read the aforementioned offending fanzine.

In a way I could understand the fanzine's point of view. I stood in front of my seat awaiting kick-off with no particular appetite for the game and the atmosphere, for an FA Cup third round tie on a Saturday afternoon, was a bit flat to say the least. Lampard put us 1-0 up after a clever back-heel from Kanouté sent him racing through against the keeper. But Song was obviously not a huge fan of the FA Cup and wanted to see us knocked out immediately. His lethal hesitation in the area allowed Wrack to nip in and score an equaliser just before half-time to reinforce the point that just because these guys were second division, it didn't mean they couldn't snap up a chance when it was presented to them. Especially when it was presented to them with a f**king gold ribbon on it.

Class told in the second half and a Cole cross was firmly headed in by Kanouté. Camara did something very unusual by making a pass that found a colleague and stayed on his feet. He squared for Kanouté to fire home a shot of such ferocity and unstoppable venom, it put me in mind, briefly, of a goal I saw Michel Platini score for France in the 1984 European Championships. The ball travelled just over the top of the grass, not rolling, not in mid-air, seemingly floating like a hovercraft but travelling like a train.

Of course, West Ham being West Ham, couldn't see out the last five minutes of a cup-tie with a two-goal winning margin in their pockets and Brett Angell, a former assassin from his Stockport County days, made it 3-2 just before the end.

Having parked so close to my seat, it took forever to get away but why should I care? Once on the road I'd be home in 45 minutes. Well, I would have been if the cam-belt hadn't snapped like an elastic band at 70 mph on the M42. Bit inconvenient, that. The RAC took my car to my usual trusted garage in Eltham and took me home to Nottingham, via the Newcastle Arms. The next day, Dennis, my trusted mechanic, gave me the bad news – £1,100 worth of damage. Ouch. On the up side, I'd just received a cheque for £1,800 as an interim payment for the sale of my book of customers when I worked as a sales rep. But I could think of better ways of spending it.

On the Sunday I put it all behind me and met Big John in The Magpies, his usual haunt before a Forest home game, and had a pint or six with him. It was a blisteringly cold day and I knew that it was daft to drink so much before going to sit outside in the bollock-freezing cold but you do these stupid things, don't you? Trying to keep up with Big John, however, was folly indeed. He's not called Big John for nothing and a pint glass in his hand looks like a thimble. A pint disappears down his neck before you've had a chance to sit down. To add insult to injury, he doesn't even start slurring his words after three, like I do.

Big John was there with his wife, Chris (I was beginning to wonder if every other person in Nottingham was called Chris) and 12-year-old daughter 'Are Amy'. I thought 'Are Amy' was a funny name for a child but he always referred to her as 'Are Amy', so it must have been a Nottingham thing. I thought it rude to ask.

I walked carefully over Lady Bay Bridge to avoid spilling anything and took my seat in the Brian Clough stand waiting to be entertained by a cup-tie between two of the better teams in the first division. I was to be disappointed. Not as disappointed, admittedly, as Big John and Are Amy, as Forest went down 1-0 to a Proudlock strike mid-way through the second half. Are Amy's training had clearly been working as she stood on her seat shortly after the goal was scored, pointing at the Wolves fans and yelling: "Sit dahn shurrrooop!" It was music to my ears and by far the most entertaining incident of the afternoon.

I was fortunate enough to be able to walk home from the game and followed a very optimistic man who had brought a transistor radio with him to listen to the fourth round draw. The only one that mattered came out towards the end. Manchester United v West Ham United. Oh bollocks. Well, that was that for another year.

As was usual after a day out with Big John, I went back to my room, fell sound asleep and didn't wake up until Monday morning.

I had to make arrangements to get back down to London to collect my car the following Saturday, which Dennis assured me would be good as new by then. As luck would have it West Ham were at home to Sunderland that very afternoon and I was able to kill two birds with one stone. I still had the problem of getting to

London, though. I solved this by taking a National Express coach for the bargain fare of £12 one way, much cheaper than the train and a lot less than I would have spent in petrol. It was painful to part with such a lot of cash just to have my car put back the way it was. But I suppose it did have a new engine in it, which had to count for something and, Dennis assured me, he'd "given it a tickle 'round with the hoover, too." Ah, well, that's a grand well spent then. To be fair, the car handled like a dream, as it always did when Dennis had run his magic hands over it. The man is not a mechanic, he's an artist.

The Sunderland match was one to forget in a hurry and I did. I don't remember us having very much of the game at all against a very organised Peter Reid side. When Reidy had them firing on all cylinders, his sides were always hard to beat. A Varga header and a quickly taken free-kick from Don Hutchison gave the Black Cats a deserved 2-0 victory and any hopes I had been nurturing about an FA Cup victory at Old Trafford quickly disappeared.

Although Christmas was still fresh in the memory, I'd been doing a lot of travelling and felt I needed a break, so I booked a couple of days' holiday so I could take in the game at Charlton and enjoy it properly. Uncle Rupert's band had decided to cover the game so it was moved to the hugely inconvenient Monday night slot. I wasn't particularly bothered. When you've done Newcastle away on a Monday night and been up for work the next morning, there's not a lot in terms of travelling to a domestic football match that fazes me but I felt I needed to take time out and enjoy this one.

Some more new faces had arrived on the scene. Sebastien Schemmel had played in the FC Metz side that West Ham had beaten in the Intertwobob Cup the season before. Harry had been impressed by the right-back and had taken him on loan for the rest of the season. His manager at Metz reportedly called him: "The most mentally unstable player I have ever worked with". Nice one, Harry, we thought, he should fit in perfectly. Christian Dailly also arrived, from Blackburn Rovers, a signing I was equally underwhelmed by. I thought he was possibly the most physically unstable player I had ever seen at the club, with the probable exception of David Kelly. Or Paul Hilton. Need I go on? I'd seen Dailly outclassed playing for Dundee United, Derby County, Blackburn Rovers and Scotland and I saw no reason why he would add anything to the solidity or balance of the team. Hannu Tihinen also arrived on loan, A Finnish international I had never heard of but Brita, my Finnish-Welsh friend, said good things about him and I was prepared to give Harry the benefit of the doubt on that one.

I went down to London on the Saturday morning and saw a lot of family and friends and generally did a bit of catching up. I even got a reply to a text message I sent to Billie/Chloe/Suzanne, or whatever the f***king hell her name was, and we met for a lunchtime coffee in one of our old haunts in Bexleyheath. She seemed sad but bitterness coursed though my veins and I found it hard to muster any sympathy. I realised at that point it probably never was love. Obsession, infatuation, lust, call it what you will, it was never love. Had it been love I would have been more tolerant, as would she. To this day I don't know what true love is – but I know what it isn't.

True love does mean always forgiving and no matter how much sh*t they threw at me, I always came back for more from West Ham. The three new signings all played at The Valley and when Bartlett nipped in to put Charlton 1-0 up, it looked like same old story and a bit of revenge for the 5-0 drubbing we handed out to them on Boxing

Day. It certainly seemed like a lot more than a month ago that we were playing flowing, controlled football and sweeping all before us. Now we were scrappy, disorganised and leaky at the back but the three new boys showed promise and when you have someone like Parlow in the side there is always the chance of something spectacular happening. So it proved that Monday night. With 10 minutes to go, he fired a terrific shot into the top corner that would have hit me square in the mush had it not been for the net. A 1-1 draw was a decent result to take from a place like Charlton and the optimism I had been starting to feel about a result at Old Trafford began to grow.

It was illogical, totally illogical. Our last 10 – count them – visits to Old Trafford had ended in comprehensive defeat. Why should this one be any different just because we had a few more fans up there and the game was being shown live on ITV. What difference would that make?

And yet, the longer the week wore on, the more confident we would get a result I became. The fans of other clubs at work all said we stood a chance. What possible basis did they have for such an assertion, given recent form and the results of our last 10 visits? If the assumption was based on the idea that 'luck had to change at some point', then it was fair enough but it's hardly a theory Stephen Hawking might have come up with. Scientific or not, the old 'feeling in my bones' was beginning to grow and for the first time in many years I found myself counting down the time in days and hours to when I'd be watching us kick off. Not adult behaviour and probably symptomatic of the fact I had nothing better to do with my time than to dream wistfully of victory over United on Sunday.

To help pass the time on the Saturday, I went to watch Notts County's FA Cup third round replay against

Wimbledon. It was a bizarre experience – pay a tenner and sit where you like. The attitude of the County fans amused me. Their average crowd almost doubled for the visit of recent Premiership regulars Wimbledon, yet the supporters who went week in, week out were complaining about the presence of the 'fair-weather fans.' I had a degree of sympathy. I remember going to games at early stages of the 1985-86 season among crowds of 19,000. Then, when it looked like we might even win the championship, come April, I struggled to get in the ground at all. But I wouldn't have changed it – it showed we'd been successful. Those County fans who dream of progress should remember it won't happen on the back of home gates of 6,000 and shouldn't moan if they can't get their regular seat because some part-timer, who doesn't even support the Magpies, has got his fat arse in it. Anyway, County lost 1-0 in the last minute of extra time, so they could relax in the knowledge they would be back to a more comfy 5,893 again the following week.

I consulted the AA website and obtained the most direct route to Old Trafford. I found out it was not necessarily the quickest way but it was very pretty, consisting mainly of winding roads and stunning views of the Derbyshire Peak District. I arrived in plenty of time and parked at a school near Old Trafford Cricket Ground, meeting Liam and Sean, two Wakefield-based Hammers, and Brita in a hastily improvised bar at the local leisure centre. My confidence was dented when I overheard the conversations of the gathered United fans. Their main point of discussion was not whether they would win but by how many. Don't get me wrong, I am the first one to knock our own chances if I think we are going to get beat. But when I hear other people suggest it, it makes my blood boil.

I had to leave and take up my seat in the dizzy heights

of the old Scoreboard End, taking in all around me. It's a phenomenon of the all-seater stadium that with half an hour to go to kick off there are usually very few people in their seats, as there is no atmosphere as such to soak up. After all, if your seat is guaranteed, you might as well stay in the pub. Today was different. There was a buzz of anticipation around. If positive mental energy has anything to do with results, if it was possible that 9,000 travelling fans just wanted it more than the 57,000 home crowd, then I'm prepared to believe it. Certainly our mood was infectious and as the public address system belted out *The Ballad of John & Yoko*, one of my favourite Beatles songs, I felt a renewed confidence that this was to be our day.

And it was. What a fantastic day. It's easy, with the benefit of hindsight, to say I knew we would win but I did and many others around me all said the same. Kanouté was full of tricks. Cole was full of hard running and determination. Michael Carrick's watershed had turned up in the post and he was maturing into a West Ham mainstay – his drive in midfield was just amazing. The three new boys played out of their skins. Not one of the 11 on the park had an off day, which was the way it had to be if we were going to get a result.

What pleased me more than anything was the fact that United *really* wanted to win. They fielded a full strength side and ended the game with four strikers on the park – Solskjaer, Yorke, Sheringham and Cole. They also had Butt, Keane and Beckham in midfield. But, close as they came, they couldn't break us down.

The longer it stayed at 0-0, the more confident we grew of getting a result. The more possession we obtained, the easier it became to break up United's attacks. The breakthrough, when it came, was worthy of the magnitude of the victory. Cole slipped a neat pass through to Parlow, who we could all see was clearly onside. Although Lampard, in the middle of the park, may have been a tad off-side, he was not interfering with play. Instinctively, I looked at the linesman. No flag. "Go on, Parlow, you're onside!" I, and 8,999 others, yelled. Fabien Barthez, United's French keeper, seemed confused by the fact that just because he had his arm up at Old Trafford, the linesman didn't automatically follow suit. While Barthez was giving the 'lino' a hard stare of which Paddington Bear in his prime would have been proud, Parlow slipped the ball into the far corner of the net. We went loopy and so did the players.

Understandably so. Despite United throwing everything but the dressing room bath at us in the last 10 minutes, we held firm (well, we were a bit wobbly at times but we didn't let one in and that's the main thing) and, at the final whistle, we went potty. Parlow came over to the camera in the corner of the stadium, pointing at his chest and delivering a monologue no doubt proclaiming his own brilliance. He needn't have bothered, we were doing a pretty good job of that ourselves. The man was already a massive hero at Upton Park, the day's events rocketed him to legend status. I was proud to have been there to witness it.

But there was more to follow. As we shuffled out down the stairs, 'Bubbles' was being sung at a considerable volume until we reached street level, when everything seemed to go quiet. You could have heard a pin drop as 67,000 left the stadium without saying a word. For a group of fans normally so gobby, it was bliss to hear the United faithful drowned in the sound of silence for once. Then, from the corner of my eye, I spotted a man in claret and blue halfway up a lamppost. At the top of his voice he yelled: "Unlucky, you northern c**ts!"

I couldn't help it. I burst out laughing, as did most of the people around me, many of whom, to be fair, were

United fans. Whether the guy got home in one piece or not, I don't know.

A 90-minute wait to edge the car anywhere near the road was a small price to pay for such a joyous day. I arrived back in Nottingham deflated by just one fact – the fifth round draw had paired us with Sunderland at the Stadium of Light. Having just won at Old Trafford, I felt anything was possible. But if this was going to be our year to win the cup, we were going to have to do it the hard way.

The following Wednesday gave West Ham fans the opportunity to welcome home the conquering heroes with victory over Spurs at Upton Park. But Spurs had got incredibly dull since George Graham, the bloke in the raincoat, took over, so it ended 0-0.

# 9. Stutter

### Liverpool 3 West Ham United 0  3.2.01

I haven't said very much about what West Ham meant to me at this period of my life. It would be true to say I had undergone one of the most fundamental changes in my life in the few months leading up to Christmas 2000. I had moved not just my job but my home, not just to another part of town but to another city in another part of the country. Add to that the break-up of a highly emotional relationship and you might begin to understand this was the time when it all started to sink in. If anything, West Ham played its most important role in my life, keeping a thread of continuity running through my existence. Had that part changed as well, I don't think I would have been able to cope.

If it hadn't been for the wonderful unpredictability of West Ham in particular and the warmth and friendship generated through being a football fanatic in general, I'm sure I would have gone nuts. A promotion at work helped me to settle and realise this was what I wanted to do. We had still yet to 'go live' but were busying ourselves travelling around the country offering assistance at various District Offices. I travelled to Edinburgh, Middlesbrough, Grimsby and Basingstoke in various capacities, staying over in plush hotels and generally having the time of my life. It wasn't easy work but it was fulfilling, had a definite purpose and made me feel like I actually made a difference, which is important to me.

My manager, Chris Broughton, had written a book about Nottingham Forest called *Forest Ever Forest*. Aware that I'd had a couple of books published, he asked me to proof-read it for him. This was a task I thoroughly enjoyed and launched myself into 100%, offering opinions and discussing various options. I was delighted, and a little surprised, when he asked me to write the foreword. Chris had been at school with Garry Birtles and had got him to write an introduction. It's a great book and I'm not just saying that because I had a role in its production. It charts the rise and fall of Nottingham Forest from second division obscurity to double European Cup winners and back again. Something I doubt any club will ever experience again in such a short period of time.

The first Saturday in February gave West Ham the opportunity to prove to the world that the win at Old Trafford had not been a fluke, a chance to show we could pull off amazing results more than just once a season and that we had some permanent backbone, spirit, fight and determination. The fixture was Liverpool away.

On the first Friday of February, however, I was feeling extremely poorly and only dragged myself into work because it always looked bad if you took a Friday or a Monday off. I wanted everyone to see how ill I was before making my excuses and disappearing off home around 11.00am.

I went home via Boots, where I stocked up on painkillers and menthol products and went straight to bed. Once Bridie had finished her cleaning, the house was always blissfully quiet during a weekday and I slept soundly until being awakened by the sound of a telephone ringing. Still half asleep, I picked it up.

"Ughhh?" I grunted into the mouthpiece. I made it sound a bit worse than it actually was, just in case it was someone from work.

"Yeah 'ello, is that Robert Banks?" an accusatory voice enquired. I grunted again. "It's Stuart Pearce, West Ham United."

Bloody hell. Here was one of the most influential and important English footballers of recent times, a hero, neigh a god in Nottingham, ringing me at home and I'm talking to him stark bollock naked. Not only that, I was talking to him like it was completely inconvenient. For a moment I had forgotten why he was even ringing.

I'd got Pearce's book, *Psycho*, for Christmas and had enjoyed it so much I thought I would write to him and ask him if I could interview him for *Over Land and Sea*. I never dreamed for one moment he would actually ring me back but here he was, making that effort and catching me unprepared. I explained I was off work ill and not in the best frame of mind for doing an interview. Besides, I hadn't expected him to agree to it so had done very little in the way of preparation or note-making. On top of all that, I had no way of recording the interview and my shorthand was on the non-existent side of poor. Bearing all of the above in mind, I asked him if he would ring me back on Sunday evening. He was good as gold.

"Yeah, all right. About seven?" I have to admit I was a little bit star-stuck.

"Seven it is – good luck at Anfield tomorrow." I cringed to myself. That was a crawly thing to say but what the hell, the man was a legend, I dare say he was used to crawling amateur hacks.

Pearce's call did me the power of good and I slept soundly for hours feeling genuinely refreshed but still full of cold. I realised that as I would be spending most of tomorrow at football, I needed to get some preparation work done for the interview. I decided not to dwell too much on his past but concentrate on his West Ham career to date, tactfully avoiding the subject of penalty kicks and Germans.

On Saturday I stopped off in Stoke on my way to Liverpool and bought a telephone with a speaker so I could tape my telephone interview with Stuart. As I completed my journey I began to fantasise about West Ham winning at Anfield and Pearce grabbing a controversial winner, with me gaining the first exclusive interview after the momentous event. It didn't happen, of course. In one of our more mundane Anfield performances, we got blown away, 3-0, with Smicer getting a swerving opener and Fowler adding a brace either side of half-time.

Pearce had one of his worst games for West Ham. I felt a bit guilty – he'd probably been a bit nervous about the interview.

As 7.00pm approached on Sunday, I began to feel slightly nervous myself. Psycho was noted for his directness and his intolerance of stupid questions. From his book, I knew he had been let down by the newspapers failing to print exactly what he had told them, or giving a story a subtle twist to make it more interesting but, sadly, a lot less than the truth. I half expected him not to call, especially after the shambles of the display at Anfield, but dead on seven he rang and we chatted for almost an hour.

Pearce was open and honest and gave full replies to every question I posed him. However, when it came to typing it up, when I cut out all the "You know what I means," "To be honest with yous," and "It's as simple as that reallys," there was only five minutes of usable material. But it was my five minutes and I was proud of it.

One of the things Pearce had mentioned was that while the FA Cup win at Old Trafford had been very nice, we actually needed to put some Premiership points on the board if we weren't going to end up in serious bother. It was something I had been conscious of for a little while, as, apart from the cup victories, it was now mid-February and we'd only gathered one league point since Boxing Day.

A home game against Coventry City would normally provide the perfect opportunity for three points, especially as they floundered in the bottom three and were destined to be relegated at the end of the season. They had looked very ordinary when we won at their place back in September and as I settled back with a pint in the Newcastle Arms that Monday night, I expected nothing less than a comprehensive victory. I was to be disappointed. Despite Parlow hitting the bar early on, Coventry were having their 'we might be relegated but we're going down fighting' phase. John Hartson had joined them from Wimbledon and was determined to show us a thing or two. He had a first half goal disallowed and always posed a threat whenever he got into our box.

It was West Ham who drew first blood and it looked likely to be enough when Joe Cole slotted home an angled drive, taking both the ball and hapless defender Gary Breen into the net. I always think you should get extra points if an opposing defender ends up in the net with the ball, and extra points still if they end up on their arse looking stupid and pretending to be injured. Victory looked assured but this was West Ham and in the last minute a harmless looking corner bounced off the top of Christian Dailly's head and looped over Shaka Hislop for the equaliser. It was too late to do anything about it and the morale-boost of a first home goal of 2001 evaporated as quickly as it had arrived. Still, I thought as I wandered home, it could be worse. We could sign Gary Breen.

The following Saturday, Uncle Rupert pulled out all the stops in his own personal quest to make life as totally f**king awkward for as many people as possible, when he decided we should play Sunderland away on a Saturday at 12 noon. It's all right for him in his personal jet but the average West Ham fan had to be up at 4.00am to make the trip north to Sunderland in time for kick-off.

For me, of course, 150 miles north of most West Ham fans, it was a little easier. But I still had to be up fairly early to drive 70 miles up the M1 to meet Liam and Sean, the Wakefield Hammers, who were giving me a lift from the service station at Woolley Edge.

The atmosphere at the Stadium of Light was somewhat subdued. Most Hammers fans were tired and tetchy after the early start and the long journey, not to mention, for the most part, a complete lack of beer. It was a bright, sunny day and while the atmosphere was nowhere near comparable to Old Trafford in the previous round, after 20 minutes of the game it was clear to me there would only be one winner. All Fredi Kanouté had to do was to beat the offside trap for once in his life and we'd be home and dry.

Sunderland, for all their good organisation, posed no threat whatsoever and I knew all we had to do was break through once. Kanouté slipped the offside trap after a clever through ball from Frank Lampard found his feet. The keeper, Sorensen, raced out to meet him but Fredi slipped the ball under his advancing body as he reached the edge of the 18-yard box and that was that.

We went home happy, of course, but the euphoria was not as great as the previous round. What didn't dawn on me until I got back to the car and settled down was that we were now in the sixth round, the quarter-final, and had as good a chance as anyone of making it to the final at Cardiff in May.

When it gets to the sixth round, the adrenaline starts to flow. A home draw and you know you are within touching distance. Of the other remaining teams, only

Arsenal and Liverpool represented a major threat but if we met them in the semi-final or later, we were in with a real shout. The draw paired us at home to Tottenham. I made sure my diary for May 12 was reasonably clear.

Meanwhile, Stuart Pearce's assertion that we needed league points to steer us clear of trouble still nagged away at me. I drove to the game at Bradford City with a lad called Tom, who lived in Derby and had got in touch via Northern Hammers. I was happy to help out with a lift and as it was my first visit to Bradford since a hastily ferried-in-ferried-out affair in 1989, I was keen to try a lunchtime curry in one of the numerous local hostelries before the game. It proved harder than I thought, though, as Tom and I searched high and low for a curry house that was open, before settling for a rather insipid restaurant located within a dreary hotel. It was highly disappointing.

It was only a short walk to the away end at Valley Parade, where the second major disappointment of the day ensued. Our end of the ground was jam-packed. The stand was tight, offering very little room for manoeuvre and had less than inadequate toilet facilities. After a 20-minute queue for a waz and frozen through to the bone, I sat with my knees tucked under my chin and watched West Ham gain a much needed victory against a doomed Bradford City.

Lampard scored twice in a 2-1 win that was still very hard work, Bradford equalising in the second half and proving to be a tough nut to crack. It was clear though, despite being awkward to play against, City did not have the quality needed to survive in the Premiership.

I dropped Tom off in Derby and continued my journey home in the thickening snow. I rushed because I had a date but I was stood up again. I have a sign on the front of my car – invisible to me but visible in huge letters to anyone else – saying: "I am a mug, please pull out in front of me, I love it." I'm sure I have something similar tattooed on my forehead that only women can see. This one pulled the old trick of arranging for a mate to ring her mobile five minutes after we'd been due to meet, to give her an escape route. "I've got to go, my little lad has fallen down the stairs." I wouldn't have been so upset if she'd had kids. Or didn't live in a bungalow.

# 10. Shut Up And Forget About It

**West Ham United 2 Tottenham Hotspur 3 11.3.01**

With 35 points on the board going into March, it was not going to be enough to avoid relegation and everyone, with the exception perhaps of Harry and the squad, knew it. After playing some superb, scintillating football in November and December and recording a couple of famous cup wins, the incentive to go on and win mundane league matches just didn't seem to be there.

To me, this was very frustrating and highly annoying, for while I didn't have to travel such distances to the majority of away games, I still made the effort to go to as many home games and away matches in London as I could manage. That, coupled with the spiralling cost of attending Premier League fixtures, meant I would have liked to have seen a bit of effort occasionally. A bit of huff and puff when things weren't running as smoothly as they should. Not a lot to ask.

I travelled to Highbury more in hope than expectation and met up with Kev for an early morning beer before jumping on a tube to try and scrounge a ticket. Kev sent me any tickets he didn't want for the long away trips. His arthritic neck was causing him a lot of discomfort and he couldn't face the long hauls, so he sent them on to me. For the away games he did want to go to, I had to make my own arrangements. On this occasion, it meant getting to Arsenal's ground early and getting out my begging bowl.

I was reasonably used to this. Since the introduction of all-seater stadia, turning up without a ticket has become an occupational hazard but I am proud to say I have never missed a game because I couldn't get one. Where there is a will, there is always a way and it doesn't have to include lining the pockets of a shifty ticket tout. It seems hard to believe now but years ago, for a big game like Arsenal v West Ham, only the select few would hold a ticket – the rest of you just had to make sure you got there early.

I arrived at Highbury to find the usual *OLAS* crew, most of whom were ticketless. Simon Smith (and his amazing dancing bear) was at the head of the queue if one turned up but there were at least half a dozen between him and me. I felt my chances of a ticket in the West Ham end were pretty slim. An American bloke called Louis, who was of Colombian extraction and loved the whole Premier League scene, joined me in my quest. He had jumped on a plane on Friday night, arrived with his bag on his back and the clothes he stood in. He decided Arsenal v West Ham was the game to watch. Poor man. He claimed no allegiance to any particular team, so I made it my mission to turn the poor unsuspecting stray into a die-hard Hammer. Just to prove it could be done.

Half an hour later, a large silver BMW pulled up and a head popped out asking if anyone wanted tickets in the West Stand. We all looked at each other. Not really. I didn't want to have to watch the game surrounded by Arsenal fans but I had travelled a long way and Louis had ventured even further. I suggested to Louis if we got ticketed up now, we could head off for a beer before the game started. He nodded with the enthusiasm of the innocent and we paid less than face value for the tickets, leaving the others to sort out their own dilemmas. Teamwork, that's what it's all about. In the end, I believe

Simon Smith (and his amazing dancing bear) found a bent turnstile operator who turned a blind eye for £20 and a fiver for the bear. It's a great comfort to me in these days of big money transfers and strict government regulations that there are still enough crooks in the game to make it interesting.

Louis was eager to learn all about British football, so I thought I'd start right at the bottom of the footballing food chain and take him to The Gunners pub. Here we could sample the most basic Neanderthal, pond-life behaviour at first hand, without fear of any harm coming to us, as long as I kept my jacket done up to my neck. Of course, it was an opportunity not often afforded to a travelling supporter – we only got in there because we held tickets for the Arsenal end. Once inside, though, I couldn't wait to get out. They were singing all sorts of mean and nasty things about West Ham, something Louis found highly amusing but which I found far too difficult to deal with and considered dumping my ticket there and then and going straight home. If I found it hard to cope with now, in a pub before the game, with the score at 0-0, how would I cope when Arsenal knocked in their third or fourth of the afternoon and started showboating?

Louis persuaded me not to jack it in just then. He was enjoying the whole experience and had no axe to grind either way, so didn't quite understand the hurt I was feeling. Eventually we compromised. I agreed to stay another 10 minutes if we could then go and get a beer at the stadium.

We took our seats, possibly the most uncomfortable and with the worst view in the whole of Highbury. Believe me, that is some achievement. By half-time, Silvain Wiltord had scored a hat-trick, we were 3-0 down, didn't even look like scoring and most of the people around me had sussed I was a West Ham fan. I couldn't wait to get out of there but Louis was lapping it up. It was possibly the worst game I'd seen all season but he was hooked.

He had nowhere to go. His flight back to the States didn't leave until Sunday lunchtime, so he had quite a few hours to kill. I took him back to Kev's on the tube and we had a few more drinks before I made my apologies and left the two of them to it. Ever hospitable, Kev gave Louis a night out on Turnpike Lane. I don't think Louis has ever been quite the same since. Now a confirmed West Ham fan, he turned down the opportunity to go clubbing in the West End to sit in Kev's front room and listen to Bob Dylan CDs until 4.00am. He would certainly have a tale to tell his colleagues back home when they asked him what he got up to at the weekend.

As for me, I was due in Manchester on the Monday morning for a fortnight's work, helping to iron out problems with the computer programs for the new Stakeholder Pension. It was interesting work but I missed my little corner of the office in Nottingham and we were working long hours, arriving back at the hotel with just enough time to grab a beer and a bite to eat before going through it all over again. Preparation for the FA Cup quarter-final against Tottenham was not going well. Chelsea hadn't won away for over a year but they turned us over at Upton Park, 2-0, on the Wednesday night. It left us still poised precariously on 35 points and needing a huge improvement in both form and luck if we were going to get past Spurs in the sixth round.

It was a very different atmosphere to our previous quarter-final. Against Arsenal in 1998, it had been an evening kick-off for the replay at Upton Park and the game was a titanic struggle between two teams on top form, one of which had lost only once at home all season, the other poised to go on to win the Double. I'll leave you to work out which team was which, although it was hardly credible that West Ham could fit either bill!

This time it was a Sunday afternoon kick-off, thanks again to Uncle Rupert. The 4.30pm start was highly inconvenient as it meant a late night getting back for me and I had to set off for Manchester again on Monday morning. But this was a cup quarter-final against Spurs and I wasn't going to miss it for the world.

Normally, I would have fancied us to win. Maybe not comfortably, but to win all the same. This time, though, it seemed the FA had decided our unwelcome presence in the latter stages of the competition had to come to an end. They made the draw just before our match kicked off and decided the winners of our game would face Arsenal in the semi-final.

On the Upton Park PA system, Jeremy Nicholas turned down the sound as he played *Bubbles* and let us sing *á capello*, which brought a lump to my throat. The home crowd roared louder than I'd heard them for many a game but Spurs had the smell of the Arse in the semi-final in their nostrils and they raced out of the blocks. For the majority of the first half, they were much the better side and Rebrov put them 1-0 up. It was raining hard and control of the game shifted from one team to the other. Just before half-time we were awarded a free kick on the edge of the box. Stuart Pearce hammered home with a characteristic snarl. One apiece at half-time and everything to play for. We had to win – we had won at Old Trafford and the Stadium of Light to get this far. Not only that but we had slain another major demon in the third round and managed to beat a side two divisions below us. This had to be our year. Surely Spurs at home, after that lot, was a piece of piss?

Evidently not. Another goal from Rebrov and a Gary Docherty header put Spurs 3-1 up and the game was effectively over. Bulgarian striker Svetoslav Todorov pulled one back for Hammers towards the end but it was too little, too late. Once again, with a glittering prize beckoning, we as a club had fallen flat on our faces. While sitting on our laurels and congratulating ourselves on our achievements so far, some clever little sod had nipped in and tied our bootlaces together. Not only that, they'd tied them together with such a difficult knot it would take ages to get us back on our feet.

Okay, so maybe Arsenal would have wiped the floor with us in the semi-final at Old Trafford. It would have been nice to have had the chance to find out. While the atmosphere before the game may have been very different to the sixth round replay against Arsenal in 1998, the atmosphere afterwards was virtually identical.

No-one spoke, other than to yell: "You f**kin' muppets, West Ham!" I bumped into my old mate Buzz. Normally, no matter what the circumstances, he'd have a smile on his face and a joke to tell. He scowled back at me with a look of mutual disappointment. I knew I didn't have to talk to him to know how he was feeling. We all felt sick.

Life had to go on, though, and I drove back to Nottingham painfully aware I'd have to iron five shirts before going away to Manchester again the next day. Some days, it never rains.

West Ham started the month with 35 points from 27 league matches. They ended it with 35 from 31 matches. First Ipswich Town came and nicked a 1-0 win, then Everton repeated the dose with a 2-0 win in a match that also saw Stuart Pearce sent off. I received news of the latter defeat while watching Nottingham Forest v QPR with Stuart the QPR fan. A pretty unsatisfactory day for everyone, QPR were about to be relegated from the first division, Nottingham Forest's drive for a play-off place seemed to be running out of steam and West Ham seemed to be hurtling for the trap door in the basement of the Premiership. The kick up the arse the defeat by Spurs should have provided did nothing but deepen the gloom. The players had talent and had shown before they could play. They would just have to buckle down and show us again.

## 11. Butterfly

**Manchester City 1 West Ham United 0  28.4.01**

April began with another trip away through work, this
time to Basingstoke. I crammed a lot in while I was down
there, zooming off on one evening to visit my parents in
Hastings and joining my colleagues, Big John, Andy and
Dave, on a trip to Vicarage Road to see Watford beat
Nottingham Forest 3-0.

The first Saturday in April saw West Ham travel to Villa
Park in an attempt to halt the disastrous slide which had
seen them edge ever nearer to the Premiership
basement. With three minutes to go it seemed another
defeat would ensue as we trailed 1-2 and didn't look
particularly inspired, I decided to start shuffling towards
the exit in the hope of having the same effect as a
couple of years previously. By leaving early on that
occasion, I managed to persuade Trevor Sinclair to
score the equaliser in a 2-2 draw. This time, it was Frank
Lampard but the effect was the same. I knew I would
pay for my disloyalty. Walking back to the car, I was
showered by a passing motorist who, it seemed,
deliberately drove through a muddy puddle, but I
reasoned with myself that I'd had to leave early, as I had
to be back in Nottingham for a night out.

Mark, my former landlord, came up for the evening
and we went out to Rock City, a premier music venue,
where we saw the band 'Less than Jake', who Mark had
been wanting to see for ages. I just went along for the

ride but, I have to say, I thoroughly enjoyed the show. It occurred to me, though, as we stood at the back of the room watching people dive around over one another in the pit, it was all a bit dangerous. Here were a lot of young people, all with high levels of alcohol and God knows what other drugs in their blood streams, diving around with a driving beat behind them and adrenaline coursing through their veins. It would only take a small spark to ignite a disaster, yet no-one is made to sit rigidly watching a rock concert from a numbered seat, made to get to their seat half-an-hour before the show starts, or prohibited from swearing or behaving in an anti-social manner. I suppose it's all about being a family show but it makes you wonder. I sincerely hope we don't have to have the equivalent of a Hillsborough disaster before things are changed. I must be getting old. I'm turning into a right spoilsport.

Thirty-six points still wasn't going to be enough to avoid relegation, so we needed something from home matches against Derby County, Leeds United and Southampton to ensure Premiership status was preserved for the 2001-02 campaign. We played Derby on Easter Saturday and, being my sister's birthday, I drove down to London and took in the game first, watching a classy first half display blow Derby away. A Cole shot bounced off Kanouté's knee for 1-0, then Lampard got the second and Cole got a third without any assistance from Fredi's gangly legs. A 3-0 half-time lead often means a less frantic second half and that's how it proved, the match ending 3-1 but leaving everyone a bit happier on 39 points.

Something was rumbling away in the bowels of Upton Park. Discontent among the fans seemed to spread throughout the whole club. This clearly wasn't anything on the scale of the Bond Scheme of 1991-92, or the Red Card protests against the board's refusal to speak to millionaire racehorse owner Michael Tabor in January, 1997. A lot of people around the club were just deeply unhappy. The main reason for it was the sale of Rio Ferdinand. Not so much the sale but the age-old question: "Where's the money gone?" Not even that. We knew the vast majority of the money we got for Rio went into the building of the new Dr Martens Stand, which was, by now, taking shape like a massive overcoat around the existing West Stand. What was bothering people was the fact that players no-one rated – even from day one – seemed to be arriving for vast sums. It seemed money burned a hole in Harry's pocket and managers of other clubs knew this. When Gerard Houllier heard West Ham had sold Ferdinand for £18m, I'll bet he could not believe his luck and seized his opportunity to unload useless lummoxes like Titi Camara and Rigobert Song for ridiculous amounts of cash.

There were, of course, other players arriving who were a bit tasty but they tended to come on loan. We could never afford to keep them, because they had proved to be so good their value suddenly tripled and we had no cash left because we'd wasted it on useless lumps of Anfield sh*te. Tihinen and Schemmel were cases in point. They had both proved to be good players but after the impetuous purchases of Camara, Song and Dailly, it seemed unlikely we'd be able to keep them on.

For all the rumblings and rumours, we were still acutely aware 39 points was unlikely to be enough to stay up and things didn't improve at Newcastle on Easter Monday. I'd arranged to be given a lift up by Chris, an *OLAS* regular who ran in the London marathon with Gary Firmager the year before. We had once watched a 0-0 draw at Villa Park together and that sort of experience can bond people. When he offered me a lift I jumped at the chance and, together with Chris' son,

Kim, we drove up to Newcastle early and sat down for an all-you-can-eat buffet at a Chinese restaurant just yards from the stadium. I have always enjoyed my trips to Newcastle, there's always so much to do and you never have to go far from the stadium. For a few years in a row we'd go to Big Luke's, another all-you-can-eat emporium, and eat and drink so much we usually slept through the majority of the game. Not always a bad thing away to The Toon.

Our tickets placed us in the new part of St James' Park, a mile above the pitch. It was so far up I started to suffer with vertigo and despite having a beautifully clear view of the field, the players just looked like ants as they trotted about. It was like watching a game of Subbuteo through the wrong end of a telescope. From Mars. To me, this was not how best to watch football and demonstrated the way things were going in the Premiership. It was a case of getting as many people, paying the highest possible prices, into the ground. It didn't matter that fans needed oxygen and a pair of Mission Impossible binoculars to see the game, just take their cash and get them in. It stinks.

It also made for a somewhat detached feel to the game. A four-year unbeaten run at St James' Park was just itching to be broken and we found ourselves 2-0 down early in the second half from goals by Cort and a spot-kick from Solano, before Frank Lampard scored a rare away penalty. Hopes of an escape from 2-0 down, like the previous year, were dashed as the whistle went and I carefully climbed down the stairs trying to avoid developing a severe case of the bends. I was quiet on the way home. I hate games on Bank Holiday Mondays at the best of times, let alone long trips ending in defeat, relegation trouble and decompression sickness.

Leeds United have never been a team to roll over and give us three easy points at Upton Park. Since our return to the top flight we had only managed one win over them and having lost to us at Elland Road back in November, and, meanwhile nicking our most promising young player, they were in no mood to get turned over again. Their 2-0 win left us in serious cack. Inevitably, Rio Ferdinand scored their second. To his enduring credit, he did not celebrate but walked calmly back to his own half to await the re-start. He knew which side his bread was buttered. With only away matches at Manchester City and Middlesbrough and a home game against Southampton left, I fancied us to get at least four points, which would be plenty. But when you are dealing with West Ham, you just never know. You wouldn't bank on them to get *anything* away from home and with the pressure on against a Southampton side they would be expected to beat, what would be the outcome?

I tried not to think too hard about it. Surely a team as talented as West Ham could manage three points from the last nine available? It was hardly a foregone conclusion, as in 2001 when we had only managed 10 from a possible 42. Hardly European form.

Louis had been in touch and asked me to get him a ticket for the game at Maine Road. He flew into London on the Friday morning and spent a boozy afternoon in Turnpike Lane, renewing his acquaintance with Kev and Bob Dylan. Then he got on a train and met me in Nottingham after I'd been to see Neil Finn in concert. (That's the ex-front man from Crowded House, not the 17-year old who played in goal for West Ham at City on New Year's Day, 1996 but then you knew that.)

As we walked through the streets of Nottingham, poor Louis had his tongue hanging out. Nottingham is a great night out and it was that time of evening when the pubs were chucking out and the girls were all queuing for clubs and wearing very little. On this warm April evening, Louis thought he'd died and gone to heaven. In fact he was merely standing outside McCluskey's muttering "Oh man!" under his breath every few seconds.

There wasn't a great deal of room in my bedsit but we managed to clear a space on the floor for Louis to sleep on and by pulling the bottom drawer out of the chest and rolling a blanket on top of it to make a makeshift pillow, he managed a reasonably comfortable night's sleep. The following morning, suitably showered and breakfasted, we headed for Manchester and I showed Louis, a native of New England, what the Old England looked like in its full spring glory. It was certainly a picturesque drive, pockets of sunshine between heavy showers over open countryside, then we got lost in the darkest depths of Manchester and I had to stop and ask directions. The last time I had driven to Maine Road had been in a minibus with 15 of us on board – everyone offered an opinion on the best route that day and we still got lost. It was a relief to have an American with me who would offer no opinion other than what a depressing sh*t-hole Moss Side was.

We took up our seats and were greeted by a sight to behold. It was Buzz's 30th birthday and to celebrate he had hired two limousines to make the trip up – and all 12 of his party were dressed as Elvis. There the laughter ended, though, as we endured another pathetic display against a City side fighting an ultimately losing battle for their Premiership lives. A mistake from Ian Pearce deflected in a shot from Goater, possibly the ugliest footballer I have ever seen and that, from a man who has twice seen Iain Dowie at his football club. It stayed until the end. Todorov had missed the sort of chance he would normally tap away in his sleep and Joe Royle's men celebrated like they had officially survived. But Louis, myself and a dozen Elvis impersonators left the ground painfully aware we still had 39 points and only two games left to reach the promised land of 42. City's win put them five points behind us with two games left to play. It was a long shot for them but they had shown enough courage and determination to suggest they could win their final two games. We'd not shown enough to suggest we could win the toss.

Louis stayed and treated me to a Mexican meal before I dropped him at Birmingham airport the following day. He was due to come over again in July and I promised him similar hospitality, maybe a friendly match and possibly a West Ham victory.

# 12. What Took You So Long?

**West Ham United 3 Southampton 0  5.5.01**

It was ironic that the last home game of 2000-01 season should precipitate so many changes by ultimately confirming the status quo. West Ham beat Southampton comfortably, 3-0, with second half goals from Cole, Parlow and Kanouté. But the winds of change were blowing strong though the corridors of Upton Park. This would be the last time we would have the opportunity to watch a match from the old West Stand. Good thing too, many people said. It was old, decrepit, uncomfortable and gave an abysmal view. Even so, it was like trading in a rickety old first car. I'd had some good times in that stand. I'd watched Paul Ince grow from sheepish youth team player to arrogant toe-rag in the 4-1 demolition of Liverpool. I'd seen Colin Foster pirouette like a ballerina and smash a volley into the top corner of the goal at the South Bank end against Everton, gaining us an FA Cup semi-final place in the process. And I'd seen us win promotion from a seat in the lower tier. It held many happy memories. I didn't want to be sat up in the stratosphere and shell out £42 to watch a series of claret and blue dots moving around on the pitch.

But progress, they say is unstoppable. At least the new kit, made by Fila, was the dog's bollocks. Traditional and stylish, the ever-popular claret body and blue sleeves, straight forward, no messing about with piping or flashes. Very classy. A shirt fit for a team moving on to better things. I was prepared to believe we were heading that way. Despite the atrocious end to the season, I got the impression all the team needed was a smart kick up the backside and we'd be back challenging for a place in Europe, maybe even a bit of silverware.

The biggest change, though, was yet to come. As I filed out of Upton Park that afternoon, I had no idea about the maelstrom about to be unleashed, or the turmoil that was to follow. On May 11, Harry Redknapp was sacked as West Ham manager.

I'll never forget it. I was buying a bacon sandwich from the bakery opposite my office when my mobile rang. It was Simon Smith (minus his amazing dancing bear) offering me not only the news but a complete breakdown of how, why, where, who, what and when. I thanked him, hardly able to take in the news, went back to my desk, sat down and ate my sandwich before mentioning it to anyone else.

To a man, everyone at work was shocked. I was shocked and I was a West Ham fan. I hadn't seen it coming. The club had a tradition of not sacking its managers. With only nine in its entire history and five since the war, the West Ham manager's position has been dubbed 'The safest job in football.' Ron Greenwood held the post for 13 years. John Lyall, his successor, for 15. Billy Bonds could have been West Ham manager for the rest of his working life had he chosen to. Harry had been in the position almost seven years, or a lifetime in modern football terms.

There can be no doubt Harry Redknapp almost single-handedly made West Ham a success in the Premiership through his astute dealings in the transfer market. His great signings of players like John Hartson, Paul Kitson, Slaven Bilic, Marc Rieper, Eyal Berkovic,

Steve Lomas, Parlow, Trevor Sinclair, Fredi Kanouté et al were nothing short of genius. But the totals in the debit column had proved costly. Marco Boogers had signed in 1995 for a million quid and after a few substitute appearances (in one of which he famously sliced Gary Neville in half) reportedly ended up sulking in a caravan somewhere in Holland. Add to that the names of Gary Charles, Mark Bowen, Iain Dowie, John Harkes, Florin Raducioiu, Ilie Dumitrescu, Rigobert Song, Titi Camara, Robbie Slater, Don Hutchison (the first time) Christian Dailly (at any time) *et al*.

Maybe the truth of the matter is that if you throw enough mud against the wall, some of it is bound to stick. Harry had also brought home favourites Tony Cottee and Julian Dicks but, at the same time, he also re-signed the likes of Steve Jones – a lovely lad but Premiership class he was not.

I wrestled with it for a few days. Was it possible that just because he had wasted a few million quid, he had been sacked? Or did he know something we didn't and decided to walk? Had he resigned in protest at not being given more of the Rio Ferdinand money? To be fair, what he'd already had he might as well have put on a three-legged horse. Think of the money he made for the club with deals on players like Eyal Berkovic, Stan Lazaridis and Slaven Bilic, then think of the money he just plain wasted. On balance, I felt he was a better manager than he was given credit for anywhere. While he had a fantastic ability to grab the occasional bargain, he had a tendency to give shelter to waifs and strays resident at the last chance saloon and a very nasty tendency to sign a complete waster. Maybe it was time for a change, I thought. Whatever had happened, he wasn't coming back, so I channelled my powers of speculation towards who should replace him.

My first choice would have been Alan Curbishley. I

had met Alan on a tour of Barcelona a few years previously and admired his straight-talking style. Born in Forest Gate and a former West Ham player, he had proved his managerial ability at Charlton Athletic, twice getting them promoted. The only doubt I had about 'Curbs' was that whenever I mentioned West Ham to him, he would pull his face into a such a shape you'd think he'd just come second in a lemon-sucking competition. He had bad memories of the way we had let him go and I think he felt little affection for the club.

I'd met other managers and potential managers on that trip. Keith Peacock had managed Charlton Veterans through an unbeaten run of three years. Steve Gritt had saved Brighton from the drop into the Conference and Alan Pardew made no secret of his managerial ambitions, quizzing Bobby Robson when we met him at the Nou Camp. Pardew didn't strike me as the type to make it as a manager. But then, what did I know?

At work, Michael, the only Arsenal fan in the building, teased me that George Graham was currently unemployed and was looking to add West Ham to the collection of London clubs he had f\*\*ked up. I found it very hard not to rise to the bait, particularly the almost daily email I would get saying it had just been announced on Radio Five Live that Graham was taking over at the weekend and was already having the walls of the office painted red and white.

My second choice would have been Stuart Pearce. A success when he took over at Nottingham Forest, his position there had been somewhat undermined by the Pierre Van Hooijdonk situation and the board bringing in Dave Bassett above his head. He was a man who had the utmost respect of players and fans alike and would certainly not have accepted second best. Which is possibly why he buggered off to Manchester City at the earliest opportunity.

Parlow was another possibility. As a player-manager he would, for once, be justified in opening his gob and demanding more effort. But if he couldn't handle it when Frank Lampard tried to stop him taking a penalty, how would he cope with a run of four successive defeats?

There weren't a great many options available. First team coach Glenn Roeder took charge of the team for the final game of the season, a long, hard, unnecessary and predictably fruitless trip to Middlesbrough. I'd had a sneak preview at his CV and had a suspicion that if money had been the cause of Harry's departure, the inexperienced but willing Roeder might be the board's preferred option. My preferred option was to bury my head in my hands and moan quite a lot about the situation.

I'd met Gary, a fellow West Ham fan, in Nottingham and we'd watched Liverpool win the UEFA Cup in a local pub, then met up again in Middlesbrough and tried to decide who was going to be our new manager. We both agreed it would probably be Roeder but, no disrespect to Glenn, we hoped for a bigger name with a bigger reputation. I watched the papers, the websites and Teletext every day for a scrap of news but none came. Simon Smith (and his amazing dancing bear) emailed me confidently predicting his inside 'source' had told him Curbishley would be our manager by the end of the week. On hearing the news I confidently decorated my workstation of the picture I'd had taken with him in a Barcelona seafood restaurant.

I was disappointed when, after Curbishley and Steve McClaren both turned West Ham down, Roeder was finally appointed. I didn't have any photos of him at all....

I was still out on the road a lot through work, which meant weeks at a time away from home. Now the football season was over and there was no major international tournament to get engrossed in, I concentrated on going out and having a good time at weekends. I met a girl called Alison, who didn't do drugs (unless you count dishing them out as part of her job as a nurse). She had her own house in a part of Nottingham called Arnold. A typical Friday night would consist of a pizza and video, depending on her shift, and a typical Saturday evening would generally be the same. It was what I had been looking for. It was all I ever wanted – quiet evenings in, the occasional night out, good company, good conversation. Just not with Alison.

After a few weeks, I realised I'd made a mistake. On my birthday we went out for a meal and when we got back to my room she was expecting some hot action – but I fell asleep. I woke up to find her gone and a scribbled note indicating she wouldn't be back. It might sound harsh but, in a way, I was relieved. It saved me the trouble of that awkward "This isn't working" speech. She was perceptive enough to realise it. She was an Arsenal fan anyway, it would never have worked, so the search for mutual compatibility continued.

At work, we finally went 'live' on June 25th and we got the chance to buckle down and get involved in the tasks we had been trained to do. We had brand new computers with massive screens, state of the art software to run on them and were made to feel like the most important part of the company plan. I was happier in my work than I had ever been at any time.

Part of the reason for that was the quality of my colleagues – they were all stars. But it was also partly due to the perceived importance of our role and the fact we held absolute power over any stroppy members of the sales force who may care to challenge our opinion. "If you don't like it, I'll put you through to my manager but he'll only say the same thing as me," was my favourite phrase. I got my own way every time.

I was starting to get my own way quite a lot. I lived a

pretty much carefree existence in Nottingham. I could come and go as I pleased, return to London for the weekend, attend any football match I fancied, go out with colleagues on a Friday night and try to mask my painful shyness in trying to talk to girls. It wasn't difficult in Nottingham, the city is crammed wall-to-wall with women.

So why was I so unhappy? Probably because the one thing I craved more than an FA Cup win for West Ham, was to feel I belonged. To feel loved. To feel I had a reason for existing, not just getting from day to day and having a reasonable time, using a football club to fill in the dull bits. I needed a purpose. The reason I had moved to Nottingham in the first place was not to find any missing pieces of an existing jigsaw, rather to throw the existing jigsaw away and go for a completely new one. I had the edge pieces in place and the easy bits with the boats on, now all I had to do was the sea and the sky. It was just that there were 800 pieces left.

## 13. Heaven is a Halfpipe

**Nottingham Forest 1 India 1   15.7.01**

Glenn Roeder also set about doing a jigsaw, only it seemed he didn't have a picture on the lid of the box. He brought in Paul Goddard as his number two. Of course, we knew 'Sarge' from his days as a player at Upton Park in the early 80s. It's a sign of the times that the £800,000 we paid for him in 1980 built a new stand for QPR. Now, 21 years on, we had sold a player for £18million and still had to find more cash to get a stand completed. Admittedly, the new Dr Martens Stand was a slightly bigger project than the School End at Loftus Road but you take my point.

Roeder also made a major signing in July, paying Aston Villa £3.5million for goalkeeper David James. I was puzzled by this move. We had some perfectly good goalkeepers at the club. There was nothing wrong with Shaka that a crash course in coming-off-his-line wouldn't put right. In Stephen Bywater we had one of the most promising, young English goalkeepers in the country. And Craig Forrest was, in my view, better than Shaka. So why go out and buy a man of no fixed ability or hairstyle? True, he was one of the best shot-stoppers in the game and, on his day, was a match-winner. But on any other day, his flapping about could cost a goal.

Then there was his feud with Parlow, dating back to a Worthington Cup tie in December 2000. Parlow had reportedly called James a 'cretin'. Now they were playing in the same team, I prayed they would both bury the hatchet – preferably not in each other's backs.

Having said all of the above, I saw James play in a friendly at Peterborough and he made Shaka look distinctly ordinary, just by his presence. He's a tall, imposing figure, completely the opposite to Shaka in that you sometimes want to nail him to his line. His distribution and all-round play that night was second to none. West Ham won the game 2-0, Kanouté got the first, then Jermain Defoe scored a cracking second goal late on, a low drive from the edge of the box.

It seemed Defoe would feature heavily in Roeder's plans. No new strikers were being sought, so we assumed he was happy to settle for Parlow, Defoe and Kanouté as the main three. Other arrivals included Laurent Courtois, a nippy French winger from Toulouse, while fellow Frenchman Sebastien Schemmel signed on a permanent basis. At £465,000, he represented excellent value, mentally unstable or not. Hannu Tihinen and Kaba Diawara, who had also shown promise on loan, were released. Croatians Davor Suker and Igor Stimac moved on and were barely missed. Stuart Pearce's departure to Manchester City meant the only true pensioner left at the back was Nigel Winterburn.

The other major departure of the summer had seemingly been a done deal before Harry had left. Frank Lampard joined Chelsea for £11million. His departure so soon after that of his mate, Ferdinand, represented the break-up of the 1995-96 youth team that swept all before them. After a few barren years, we had now sold two home-grown players who had raised £29million between them. Joe Cole, Michael Carrick, Jermain Defoe and Stephen Bywater may all go the same way one day. Although Defoe and Bywater did cost fees, these were only a fraction of what they will be sold on for. And for a club the size of West Ham, that kind of production line is vital.

On the whole, the squad Roeder had at his disposal showed a good balance and depth, a fair blend of youth and experience and a determination to show the previous season's brush with danger had been a one-off. By the time the season got underway there would still be transfer money available. Despite the disquiet over the departure of Harry and the disappointment of losing Lampard Jnr, there was every reason to feel optimistic that despite his Premiership inexperience, Glenn Roeder would have every chance of making a success of the job.

I had promised to take Louis to a friendly but when it came it wasn't quite in the form I imagined. Nottingham Forest were playing against the Indian national team and as Louis was over for the weekend, I nipped down to London to collect him. West Ham had no game that day, so I showed Louis the delights of Forest's City Ground, after introducing him to a pint of mild at The Magpies. A combination of the flight, the drive, the pint of mild and a less than riveting game resulted in Louis being sound asleep as half-time approached. I shook him awake but he pleaded with me to let him sleep, he was so exhausted. I agreed but wasn't going to let him sleep through a football match. We left the second half and I took him back to the bed-sit so he could get a proper kip.

He was apologetic about making me miss the game and bought me another Mexican meal to thank me for my hospitality. He was flying on to Spain the next day to do a pilgrimage. I swapped him my old West Ham shirt for a pair of khaki Colombian walking shorts and bade him farewell. He sent me a picture of himself wearing my old West Ham shirt at the Bernabeu. It was a start, maybe an omen for European football?

# 14. Someone To Call My Lover

**Liverpool 2 West Ham United 1  18.8.01**

The first Friday of August, coincidentally, brought West Ham to Nottingham to play a friendly against County, or Caahnty, as they are more locally known. I went to the game with Phil, a colleague and County fan. Going direct from the office in town, we stopped off for a couple of pints in the infamous and totally politically incorrect Hooters bar. I'd never been in there before – it was an eye-opener, I can tell you.

The Test match was coming to the end of the day's play at Trent Bridge, so pedestrian traffic was heavy and we walked over to The Magpies for a bite to eat and met up with Nottingham Gary. County's Meadow Lane is just the other side of Trent Bridge to Forest's City Ground and we were positioned in our seats in time for kick off. West Ham lost a terrible game 2-1. Adam Newton, who had ironically been on loan at County up to then, scored our goal. Newton was unlucky. As part of the youth team including Cole and Carrick, he was possibly the player with the third biggest weight of expectation on his shoulders. Sadly, despite a successful loan period at County, it never quite happened for him. I know this was only a friendly but we were sh*t, not to put too fine a point on it. With the season due to start in two weeks' time, I feared the worst. No cohesion, unable to string more than two passes together, David James going walkabout, shambolic defending and non-existent strikers. I trudged out of Meadow Lane feeling thoroughly depressed. Phil, on the other hand, had a grin as broad as the River Trent and offered me a pint, which I gratefully accepted.

Maybe I was being hard on them. To my knowledge it had been our only friendly defeat but then judging by the quality of the opposition, that was nothing to crow about. The following weekend, while the Nationwide League season got underway, West Ham faced one final friendly against FC Utrecht of Holland, the match being played in Jersey. A trip to the Channel isle was out of the question, so I contented myself with another trip to The Magpies, another drinking session with Big John and another game at the City Ground that Forest failed to win. A 1-1 draw between Forest and Sheffield United was hardly enough to lift my spirits, spirits that were currently drowning in far too much beer for a Saturday afternoon. Maybe living within walking distance from a football ground wasn't such a great idea after all, I thought to myself, as, by 6.30pm, I was fast asleep in my room when most sensible people would have been just getting started.

I awoke around 11pm and went on the Internet to check my email. As often happened on these occasions, I would forget to switch off the alert telling all my internet friends I was on line and several long conversations followed. By 1am I was ready for bed. As I logged off, the telephone rang.

It was Shauna, the girl I had met at the New Year's Eve party. She had got rid of the old boyfriend, just bought a new flat and was questioning the wisdom of it, having spent the third night in a row staring at four blank walls and with 27 pence in her current account until payday. I was delighted to hear from her – I'd given her my number but didn't have hers, so had to wait for her to make contact. Shauna had a black and white cat called

Delia, who was a new arrival after buying the flat, and she had a job working for an internet security company. After my trials and tribulations with Billie/Chloe/Suzanne, or whatever her f\*\*king name was, I was cautious about getting too close to anyone for a while. But Shauna was different. There was honesty almost to the point of brutality about her conversation and within a few minutes I was hooked.

We talked long into the night before finally making our excuses and promising to speak again soon. I slept soundly and heavily but when I woke on Sunday morning, I felt compelled to ring her but promised myself to wait until she called me. I didn't have to wait too long. We spoke again for a long time and again that evening after exchanging mobile telephone numbers and texting each other most of the afternoon. I gave her my work email address and suggested she drop me a line the next day. She did just that. There was an honesty and openness in the way she spoke and wrote. It was like a breath of fresh air.

We found it so easy to talk. After about two hours on the telephone on Monday evening it seemed daft not to suggest meeting up again for a quick drink. "Okay," she said. "When?"

"How about tonight?" I said, thinking, this is ridiculous, it's 8.30pm now and by the time I get to Bradford it'll be time to turn around and come home. "Okay," she said, calling my bluff a bit. "Have you eaten? I can put something in the oven for when you get here."

With that I was in the car, stopping only at the off-licence to pick up a bottle of white wine. When I got to the address she'd given me, she made me wait outside until she was sure she was ready, then she came out to fetch me. I was stunned. She was even more gorgeous than I remembered! She was slim, blonde and attractive with piercing blue eyes. She was so shy and coy with it that I could already feel myself falling for her.

She led me up to the flat and I could immediately tell I was home. It might sound strange but as soon as I walked in, everything felt right. I'd found what I was looking for. All I had to do was convince Shauna that she had, too!

As it turned out, she didn't need a lot of convincing. After drinking a bottle of vino between us there was no way I could drive home but was told I was welcome to sleep on the sofa bed and grab a shower in the morning, before going back to work. I was invited to return the following evening and the evening after and the evening after that. I had a ticket for the opening game of the season at Liverpool and was told I was welcome to come straight round after the game.

I needed no second invitation and, before long, Shauna's flat had become my primary base. And since both of us felt we had found what we were looking for, we decided there was every reason to settle down and get married.

The whirlwind change in my personal life felt so right, it was hard to explain all the finer details to friends and family, who I felt sure wouldn't understand and would think I had flipped. To be fair, my immediate family didn't think I had flipped (at least, if they did, they didn't tell me!) and wished us both every happiness. Shauna's mum and brother, her only immediate family, were similarly understanding and accepted me into the fold as though I'd been there all along. The jigsaw was starting to take shape. It was obvious I couldn't drive the 84 miles from Bradford to Nottingham every morning and the 84 miles back every evening for much longer. I applied for a transfer to the Leeds office and also for a permanent job at Chief Office in Manchester. Had I been in the slightest bit religious, the phrase 'The Lord will provide' would have sprung to mind. I certainly didn't have a clue how I was going to make it all work but I was hopelessly in love and when you are hopelessly in love, you somehow manage.

Ah, yes, football. The opening day of the season arrived. A week before I had been sitting in a drunken haze watching Nottingham Forest v Sheffield United, then collapsing into bed to sleep it all off. Seven days later I had a new life. West Ham had a new manager, too, and I wondered if this was all a sign, a sign of better things to come, starting with a victory at Anfield.

Words I had written some seven years previously preyed on my mind as the teams warmed up on the Anfield turf prior to kick-off. In *An Irrational Hatred of Luton* I quite clearly remember stating when life was going badly, West Ham did well and helped me through. When life was going well, they always seemed to nose-dive. With life going so well, albeit on a somewhat rudderless and helter-skelter course, I hoped West Ham would not suffer as a result and it would not be all my fault for having such a good time.

Of course, defeat by Liverpool did not necessarily mean West Ham were in a downward spin. As we hadn't won there in the league since 1963, defeat at Anfield meant things were chugging along as per usual. It was raining hard, horrible warm rain that runs down the back of your neck and the first time you feel it is when your underpants get soaked. In the difficult conditions, a wet slippery, billiard-smooth pitch, West Ham acquitted themselves well, looking organised and disciplined but rarely threatening to score.

Liverpool went 1-0 up through Owen in the first half but, just as we had done in 1999 in the famous 2-2 draw (it comes to something when a 2-2 draw is regarded as famous), we were awarded a penalty in front of The Kop. I suppose it's not such a rare occurrence these days but in the 70s and early 80s no one ever got penalties at Anfield. Except Liverpool, of course, who seemed to average more than one a game. The secret of winning penalties at Anfield, I have found, through extensive and painstaking research, is to get into their penalty area. That helps a great deal.

Svetoslav Todorov got into the Liverpool penalty area, scaring the Liverpool defenders by abandoning his Alice-banded hairstyle and adopting the Bulgarian village idiot look. Whether that was a factor or not, he got scythed down in the penalty area by Henchoz and despite the fact it was West Ham playing at Anfield, the penalty was awarded. Parlow scored with a flourish, chipping Arphexad in the Liverpool goal the same way he had beaten Man City's Weaver the year before. It was cheeky, particularly in front of The Kop, but Parlow didn't owe anything to anyone. He was a law unto himself and one we were glad to have on our side. He trotted down the touchline and gave Roeder a high-five in such a way as to suggest it had been choreographed. I think Roeder was actually as surprised as anyone and maybe a little dismayed at Parlow for trying an audacious chip instead of belting it low and hard into the corner. It would be a steep learning curve for Glenn.

Owen grabbed his second in the second half to win the game for Liverpool. It was a quality strike, showing pace, quick feet and speed of thought. I walked away from Anfield in the rain scarcely believing Liverpool had won four trophies the previous season and thinking Owen had been the only real difference between the sides.

Shaka Hislop had started the season in goal because David James had been injured playing for England in a friendly against Holland at White Hart Lane. No disrespect to Shaka but it was disappointing our much heralded new signing had not been able to make the start of the season through a leg injury – an injury he hadn't even picked up while playing for West Ham. I remembered Richard Hall, another of Harry's great white elephants, and the injury he picked up in a pre-season friendly at Carshalton, after being tackled by a postman. Then I remembered Simon Webster breaking his leg in training and decided to stop thinking, it was too dangerous.

Goalkeeping injuries paled into insignificance, however, when, the following Tuesday, we learned of the death of Les Sealey at the tender age of 43. Les had been with West Ham on and off since 1995 and made two appearances in goal but had famously appeared as an outfield player in a 1-0 defeat at Highbury in September 1995. Les was an Eastender born and bred but his playing career had taken him to Coventry City and Luton Town before he played in a replay of the 1990 FA Cup final for Manchester United against Crystal Palace. After winning the game 1-0, he gave his winners' medal to Jim Leighton, the man he had replaced from the first game. I never met Les Sealey but I understand that gesture was typical of the man. A bouncy and highly motivated character both in training and in the dugout, he would be sorely missed by everyone at the club, not least by the fans, who enjoyed a special relationship with him. His Uncle, Alan Sealey, who had scored both goals in West Ham's European Cup Winners' Cup final triumph in 1965, also died young. It certainly put things in perspective.

With the new Doc Martens Stand still not completed, the midweek fixture against Chelsea was postponed, so now our first game at home would be against Leeds United the following Saturday. I had not been planning on making the trip anyway and certainly hadn't been planning on going out to buy an engagement ring, but that's how I spent my Saturday afternoon. Saturday night was spent being all loved up. I still had to switch on the TV the moment we got in to check the scores, of course. I was mightily relieved to see West Ham had chalked up their first point of the season, kept a clean sheet and, by all accounts, played measured, controlled football as they had done at Anfield. Joe Cole had been unlucky to have a goal disallowed. Maybe I had been too hard on Roeder. Maybe he would prove us all wrong to doubt him?

## 15. Help, I'm a Fish

**West Ham United 3 Newcastle United 0  23.9.01**

I wish I could remember more details about my first few weeks with Shauna. It was an important time in my life and in many ways I was so wrapped up in the whole thing I never stopped to take note, make mental photographs and remember things. I remember September 1st, though. Germany 1 England 5. If she's honest, Shauna will admit she only sat through the game to please me but if you're going to sit through a game, what better way to do so than with England thrashing the old enemy in their own back yard? While I wouldn't want Shauna to be so enthusiastic about football that she tags along to every game with me, it was good that a match like this sparked enough of an interest for her to be enthusiastic when England were on the telly. Particularly with a World Cup less than a year away.

She had some interesting views. She thought Glenn Roeder was German. This I can understand. The name does sound a bit German, like it should have an umlaut in there somewhere. When he stands in the technical area wearing that long, black leather coat, you have to admit he does look a bit like an extra from *'Allo 'Allo*. From then on, I always referred to Glenn as Herr Roeder.

Tomas Repka finally arrived from Fiorentina after a protracted on-off saga. Repka was a Czech Republic international and as the Czechs had a decent side, we were expecting great things. Not only that, the fact he had ummed and ahhed so long about coming, and we had shelled out £5million for him, justified our expectations. Also, of course, our only previous Czech international, Ludek Miklosko, was an Upton Park legend and had also returned to the club as a goalkeeping coach. He had been influential in persuading Repka to join West Ham. Any mate of Ludo's was a mate of mine.

Derby County away proved to be a longer drive than the previous year, as I made the trip from Bradford, stopping off at Meadowhall along the way down to buy a much-needed new pair of trainers. Shauna was knocking me into shape. I had been single for a long time and hadn't lived with anyone for nearly 12 years. While my dress sense wasn't terrible, I wasn't particularly bothered if my trainers were falling to bits. Shauna made me see the error of my ways and, shod in a brand new pair of Adidas Campus, I parked up in the usual spot at Pride Park on a beautiful, sunny September afternoon. While the weather and the drive may have been fine, the result was another dreary 0-0 draw.

I wasn't particularly worried. We had looked the better side, although, admittedly, that wasn't saying much and a clean sheet was always welcome away from home. Jermain Defoe missed a chance he would normally have expected to bury but on the whole I was happy to double our points tally and concentrate on enjoying my Saturday evening and Sunday.

Tuesday, September 11th, 2001 is, of course, a day that has already gone down in history as one of the blackest on record. It began routinely enough, as I drove to Nottingham to spend a half-day at work before popping back to the bedsit (which I had kept on while still working there) and then driving on down to Reading for the Worthington Cup tie in the early afternoon. I was tired when I got home from work at lunchtime, so got my head down for an hour before switching on my computer to read my email. A headline popped up on my home page – something about a plane crashing into the World Trade Centre. I ignored it. This sort of thing probably happened all the time, they were big buggers, after all, those Twin Towers at the World Trade Centre. But as I got into the car and switched on the radio, I realised it was a little more serious than some idiot in a Cessna flying into a tall building. You don't need me to give you the details. As I headed south on the M1 it was clear this was a terrorist attack the likes of which had never been seen before. I listened to the whole story unfold on the radio, feeling sick to the stomach. I was over half way to Reading by the time I realised the full horror of what had gone on. I was tempted to turn back. Surely the game would be called off? Sports bulletins were, understandably, few and far between. Traffic was starting to build up and I wondered if this was the start of the end of the world. I had found happiness just in time.

I arrived at the Madejski Stadium in Reading to find the game was going ahead, which I thought a little disrespectful, but, on the other hand, what good would calling off a football match do? Life had to go on, after all. I had been one of the first to show my annoyance at the postponement of the Sunday games following the death of Diana, Princess of Wales, but this seemed so huge. The loss of human life on a scale unimaginable. People phoning home to loved ones to tell them they loved them before facing their inevitable deaths. But it's okay – Reading are at home to West Ham tonight, that'll take your mind off it. I was finding it quite hard to reconcile my emotions as I sat down to watch a game that scarcely mattered.

As the action ebbed and flowed (mainly ebbing, it

must be said), I found it impossible to concentrate. The figures on the pitch floated around as if in a dream. Maybe I was still asleep and the whole World Trade Centre catastrophe had been a figment of my twisted imagination. A third successive 0-0 draw proved to me it wasn't a dream. Had it been a dream, one of my dreams, anyway, someone would have scored. Extra time proved no more fruitful and a penalty shoot-out ensued. I don't recall the finer detail. I think Scott Minto missed the sudden death kick but Defoe had already missed the chance to put us through, so it would have been unfair to blame Minto. It would have been unfair to blame anyone. The whole world seemed so unfair.

I got back to my car to find someone else also thought the world unfair and had taken it out on my car windscreen. With a hammer, by the looks of it. I called out Autoglass but I had no idea where I was parked and, struggling through football traffic, it took them an eternity to find me. By the time they had done their bit and relieved me of £50 in the process, it was 1.00am and I still had to drive back to Nottingham. I did so dangerously full of fatigue and got home at about 3.30am. I expected to find the house quiet, with most people in bed, but everyone was up and watching the TV. The images of the two planes flying into the New York skyline confronted me, then the scenes as the towers collapsed and people rushed about in utter bewilderment. It was one of those events you will always look back on and remember exactly what you were doing at the time. It was also one of those times, when losing a football match and having to fork out for a new windscreen seemed to be pretty pathetic things to moan about.

The lack of goal scoring was not such a problem as long as we didn't concede. Unfortunately the organisation that had been so evident at Liverpool and at home to Leeds United in the opening games of the season had started to slip away and we were rapidly reverting to headless chicken mode. At Middlesbrough, Repka and Song made the kind of defensive errors you normally only hear people talk about in pubs after several pints. They claim they happened to them at school but you never really believe them. To add insult to injury and a 2-0 defeat, Repka got himself sent off. He was starting to look like five million quid down the Upton Park plughole – a plughole that had seen a fair few quid pass through the u-bend in its time.

Newcastle United at home provided our first three points of the season and a first indication that maybe we'd be all right after all. Don Hutchison had re-joined the club and become our record signing for the second time in the process, a rare distinction indeed. He claimed he'd grown up a lot. But he said that when he joined us the first time on exactly the same day in 1994. Why should we believe him now? He went a long way towards convincing us by diving into the six-yard box to head the first goal. Parlow captained the side wearing an American stars and stripes flag as his armband in tribute to the thousands who had died in New York, Washington and on United Airlines Flight 93 in Johnstown, Pennsylvania 12 days before. To cap the tribute, he scored a stunning second, before Hutch sold a superb dummy to allow Fredi in to make it 3-0. It was an impressive result against an improving Newcastle side and sent me home with plenty to ponder.

Defensively, despite four clean sheets from the last five games, I still worried about our capabilities. Repka was, hmm, how can I put this without being rude? Combative. Yes, combative would be a suitable euphemism. Since Julian Dicks had retired, we'd not really had a defender who could not only kick people up in the air but could also play. Many had tried but none succeeded in filling the boots of Billy Bonds as a player. Repka seemed likely to join that ever-lengthening line. Christian Dailly worried me even more. Every time the ball went within a few yards of him, I could feel the draught from 25,000 people drawing a deep breath. A wake-up call was on the cards.

From an attacking point of view, we had three of the best strikers in the Premiership and one of the most creative and talented midfields in the country, so I had no doubt we would always score goals. It was the defence that bothered me.

The wake-up call I had predicted came at Everton. I drove to Merseyside for the second time in the space of a few weeks, figuring it was better to get them both out of the way early on. I met Brita in the Stanley Park for a pint and we discussed our chances. We both agreed, despite the battling draw last season and Parlow's display of sportsmanship, Everton were unlikely to show us anything other than a clean pair of heels.

And that was exactly how it turned out. The defence I had fretted about proved woefully inadequate against an Everton side who, it has to be said, were not the most imaginative in the world. In the end, 5-0 was kind. It could have been a lot more. I trudged home. Fortunately, I was about to experience my first proper Bradford curry, at the Ru Palais in Baildon. I went with Shauna and her brother, Andrew, his fiancée, Terri, and Shauna's mum, Norma. Andrew hadn't seen the results. He believed me when I told him we'd won 2-0. I left it at that.

## 16. Flawless

**West Ham United 2 Chelsea 1  24.10.01**

We both had some time off to celebrate Shauna's birthday, which, as it happened, was two days after my dad's. We took a trip down to London and Hastings, then came back to find my transfer to the Leeds office had come through and I was to start there on Monday. It was a bit of a shock and I was going to miss everyone I had made such good friends with in Nottingham but there was no way I could have kept on doing 170 miles a day. I'm not sure who would have cracked up first, the car or me.

The first thing I noticed while working in Leeds is that Leeds United fans have no sense of humour. That's probably why they are Leeds fans, I suppose. Liam and Sean, our Wakefield-based Hammers, had warned me of this fact but I hadn't quite been ready for the barefaced truth of it. You always think people exaggerate a bit about these things. Leeds fans find nothing funnier than taking the piss out of you but point out the smallest failing in their own team's make-up, poke a bit of fun back and they don't like it one little bit. Lighten up, guys.

You can imagine my predicament, therefore, when the Saturday before I started at Leeds, we lost 5-0 at Everton and then the Sunday after, we lost 7-1 at Blackburn. I knew we would lose at Blackburn – it was a foregone conclusion, as traditional as roast beef and

Yorkshire pudding. I wasn't prepared, however, for the manner of the defeat, or the severity of it. Three down in the twinkling of an eye, Carrick managed a great strike before half-time to seemingly lift spirits and brace us for the fight ahead in the second half.

Knowing full well what was likely to happen, I had spurned the chance of half-price tickets in the West Ham end, provided via the CIS's continuing sponsorship deal with Blackburn Rovers. Part of the reason for this was I had, at least, seen us win at Blackburn before, albeit in a penalty shoot-out in a famous 1998 FA Cup fifth round tie. Also, the game was on Pay Per View TV in my new adopted local, The Great Northern. To my delight, domestic bliss meant I had lots of things I'd rather be doing – I'm quite happy to admit it and it doesn't make me a bad person for wanting to put a shelf up rather than travelling all the way to Blackburn to see us get spanked.

And what a spanking. By the time the match ended, I dared not turn my back in case another one flew in. It was embarrassing. I felt for young Grant McCann, coming on as a substitute before slicing his clearance straight into his own net. You usually only get once chance at this level. That was his.

I couldn't wait to get out of the pub. Something had made me wait until the bitter end, as though I could somehow keep the score under double figures as long as I kept watching. I felt a little bit sick after the game. I'm not scared of relegation. I'm not scared of losing. I'm scared of humiliation. That's what was facing me and every other West Ham fan across the country. When players capitulate the way they did that day, they don't realise the profound effect it has on the people who swear their allegiance and have to put up with bucket loads of sh*t being thrown at them on a Monday morning. And bucket loads is what I got.

Fortunately I'd had my interview at Manchester and had been offered the job. I accepted gratefully, not only on the basis it would be a good career move but also there would be a wider diversity in the football chat on a Monday morning. It wouldn't all be focused on Leeds – a subject that had started to piss me off and bore me f\*\*king rigid after about 20 minutes.

I always think of myself as the tolerant sort and I probably am. But if they are ever looking for ways of extracting information from suspected terrorists, I would suggest they lock one in a cell with three Leeds United fans for half an hour. They'll be singing like a canary.

My former colleague at Nottingham, Nick, a Villa fan, had already taken a job at Manchester and reported the coast was clear, so I decided to risk it. It was another major move for me. It would mean a 42-mile drive each way every day across the Pennines, on the notorious M62, but I felt the chance to work at the head office of such a major UK firm was worth the risk.

The Saturday before I started in Manchester, West Ham faced an early relegation 'six-pointer' against a similarly struggling Southampton side at Upton Park. Having felt personally bruised by each of the 12 goals I had watched us concede in the last two games, I opted instead for a day-trip to Blackpool with Shauna.

Even though it was late October, the place was throbbing with people – very strange people at that. By the time I had managed to find a parking space, Kanouté had already put us 1-0 up, climbing high to nod in at the far post from a Winterburn cross. Then I switched off, or rather, tried to switch off. But knowing your team is 1-0 up with half an hour to go is almost as bad as knowing they were 1-0 down after five minutes. You desperately need to know what happened next. I didn't have the confidence to think we would hold on to win against Southampton. This is West Ham, it doesn't work like that.

We took a stroll along the pleasure beach, had a wonderfully romantic ride on the big wheel (I chickened out of the Pepsi Max) and ate fish and chips looking out over the sea in the darkness of the early evening. All around us there was hustle and bustle of youths, groups of young lads on stag weekends, groups of women on hen weekends being an embarrassment to themselves and anyone else unfortunate enough to see them. Complete meat-heads in the main, the kind of people who whip their shirt off at the merest hint of sunshine and who call their kids 'Chlamydia' because they think it's classy. It is an awful, scary place. I loved it. Hardly Falaraki but it wasn't far off. Eventually curiosity got the better of me and I suggested we return to the car and drive through the illuminations. Then I could have the radio on and find out the score.

Unbelievably, Radio Five rattled through every game except ours. Not unbelievable at all really. The media always appeared to ignore us and now I lived in the north of the country I should have expected nothing less. I had to wait until we'd got home before Teletext provided me with the missing information. We'd won 2-0, Kanouté adding a second when nodding in a rebound after Parlow had hit the bar. Relief – not only that I had found out the result, but that we had kept a clean sheet and taken a much-needed three points. The defeat was clearly too much for the Southampton board, who sacked manager Stuart Gray almost immediately. Clearly the stigma of losing to West Ham was too much to take.

The boost was much needed, because Chelsea were due as midweek visitors. This was a game I really didn't expect us to gain anything from. Chelsea were unbeaten and playing with a swagger and style that was always expected of them but only ever materialised in patches. This was another game I'd have to watch on Teletext. I'd only started working in Manchester on the Monday and taking time off to watch a football match would have been viewed dimly indeed.

I was late getting home and couldn't believe my eyes when the score-line read 2-0 to West Ham after 15 minutes. Carrick had belted home a superb right-footed drive after just six minutes and Kanouté added another from an almost identical position a few minutes later. Chelsea pulled one back through the irrepressible Hasselbaink, who also hit the post in the second half, but West Ham held on for one of their best ever victory-in-the-face-of-adversity results. It reminded me of the 4-1 Littlewoods Cup win over Liverpool in 1988, when, after getting mullered in the league every week and facing a team that was strolling away with everything, we cut loose and played.

My colleague Clare, a fellow southerner, backed me up on most things due to our geographical roots. As she is a Chelsea fan, though, I couldn't resist a dig and altered her screen saver to reflect the previous night's score. It doesn't happen very often but when it does, you have to make the most of it.

Maybe I'm hypersensitive but that's all football rivalry should be about – a little laugh and a joke here and there at the other's expense. Too many people take it far too seriously and can't see the funny side. I've had little choice but to see the funny side for 28 years. I should be used to it by now.

I'd been reluctant to go to Ipswich for the game the following Sunday but Shauna insisted I went. The game was on PPV again and after nursing painful memories of Blackburn away, which was shown in a similar cruel fashion, I feared a similar outcome. Ipswich Town had finished fifth in the Premiership the previous season, a position high enough to gain them a place in the UEFA Cup, but this season they were struggling severely to match the high standards they had set for themselves. Portman Road has been a reasonably happy hunting ground for us, so in the end I agreed it would be a good idea to go.

A beautiful sunny Sunday lunchtime greeted me in Ipswich as I sat outside the Drum and Monkey pub and considered the game ahead. With two good victories following two harrowing defeats, it seemed the season could already hinge on the outcome of this game. Victory would show the watching world (not that they cared) we were made of stronger stuff. Defeat would mean the effort put in against Southampton and Chelsea meant nothing, the players had learnt nothing and we'd been hoodwinked into believing we had a half-decent side.

But again, it's not about winning and losing as a West Ham fan. Had we lost at Ipswich and put in a good performance it wouldn't have mattered. It's about showing commitment, desire and passion. If you're unlucky to lose, that's okay. If you're lucky to win, that's still okay – I'll take the three points – but somehow it doesn't give me the same pleasure. Maybe I'm weird.

Ipswich is a long way from Bradford and I'd made the trip on my own, too, having only decided to go the day before. I saw Gary and we had a long chat about the state of things. He actually sounded quite upbeat. I was still unsure, thinking the season could still go either way. We had too much talent to go down but we were also clearly capable of losing to very poor sides and once the heads drop it's a hard rut to get out of.

Ipswich found out to their cost. The euphoria of a fifth place finish the season before had clearly addled their brains and now they were struggling to find any sort of consistent form. Midweek UEFA Cup ties against the likes of Inter Milan seemed to be sapping all of their strength and they were finding it hard to concentrate on the bread and butter of the league.

That was to our advantage. Parlow slipped through the defence to fire in an angled shot to put us 1-0 up at half-time but shortly after the restart, Shaka pawed a soft clearance into the path of Hreidarsson, who neatly volleyed it home. It was a shaky period of the game but somehow our nerve held and we emerged victorious. A probing run from Hutchison ended in Kanouté spinning and sweeping in a scuffed shot to make it 2-1, then Jermain Defoe, on as substitute for Parlow and, bizarrely, wearing his captain's armband, scored his first Premiership goal after being put through in a one-on-one situation. We were already in injury time when that happened but, West Ham being West Ham, still managed to let Ipswich pull one back. Former youth team player Matt Holland swerved in a great shot from about 40 yards out to make it 3-2 and give us a nervous final minute or so.

The month of October had ended with three successive victories and yet I still had very little confidence in the way we were playing. We looked the business in the new kit, when we turned it on. We played with a style and a swagger of which Moore, Hurst and Peters in their prime would have been proud. But when we were bad, we were shocking. I hoped Herr Roeder's first ever Manager-of-the-Month award didn't have the same effect it had on most of its recipients and would see the good run come to a crashing end.

# 17. Fallin'

**Charlton Athletic 4 West Ham United 4  19.11.01**

The good run came to a crashing end. A home game against Fulham is best forgotten, although things could have been very different if Fredi Kanouté's first half effort had gone in and not crashed against the post. As it was, the game ended in a 2-0 defeat and the curse of the Manager's award had struck again. I wasn't too disheartened. It's a bizarre fact – the poisoned chalice of the Manager-of-the-Month award always has that effect, it was a case of getting the game out of the way and concentrating on Charlton away, a week on Monday.

Uncle Rupert had selected this fixture for his Monday night slot for the second season running. And for the second season running, it was hugely inconvenient. The South London clubs are difficult to get to at the best of times, even when starting from the comparative proximity of East London. Starting from Bradford wasn't on for a Monday night match. I began to wonder if my enthusiasm was fading a little bit.

But it had nothing to do with fading. I still loved West Ham for better or for worse but I had other commitments now. Commitments I felt deserved more of my time and energy and, frankly, money. It simply wasn't fair, when money was already tight, to spend £100 on a trip to London to watch a football match. Particularly when it was available in The Great Northern for the price of a few pints. It wasn't right to take a day's precious holiday to go and watch that lot kick a ball around for 90 minutes, then come home and moan about how crap we were. It didn't make sense. Shauna, to be fair, was always in favour of me going to any game I wanted, she was fully aware of the fixture list and knew when West Ham had a game coming up. But I felt it was only fair to be sparing with them.

I had calculated that the 1997-98 campaign, the last time I attended every match in a season, together with a few reserve and youth team games and a not inconsiderable number of friendlies, had cost me something in the region of £5,000.

The previous season and the following campaign I had missed one or two games and they had cost roughly the same. I wasn't earning the sort of money to justify that sort of expense. With ticket prices now averaging around £28 and things like credit card booking fees creeping into the equation, attending every game was not an option.

I still loved my football. England's game against Sweden may have been only a friendly and may have been at a really awkward time of day but I still watched with enthusiasm as Trevor Sinclair, despite making noises about wanting a move, made his England debut and won the penalty that earned us a 1-1 draw at Old Trafford. If anything, I loved my football even more than when I did go to every game. In those days, it could become a chore. You felt obliged to go in case you missed something. Now it was a pleasure to be savoured.

Uncle Rupert had kindly brought the game into my own local pub lounge, so I didn't have to shell out £30 for a ticket to see the game in real time. But paradoxically, it was partly due to this over-exposure on satellite television, and the huge millions now available to pay the players, that tickets for 90 minutes of dubious entertainment cost such ridiculous sums of money.

I could think of no other sphere of entertainment, where the tickets cost so much for an hour-and-a-half which might be great, or might be a pile of sh*te, with no redress if it turns out to be the latter. As it happened, Charlton Athletic v West Ham United on Monday, November 19th, 2001 turned out to be entertainment and drama of the highest order, without a dry seat left in the house.

I watched the game in The Great Northern with Shauna's brother, Andrew. I was surprised and a little concerned to notice, in the corner, a small group of Charlton fans. They're not that prevalent in South London, so it was a shock to see more than one of them in West Yorkshire. It made for an interesting atmosphere. Paul Kitson, starting his first game of the season, raced onto a through ball in the opening minutes and fired an unstoppable shot in off the post to make it 1-0. He should have made it two shortly afterwards but a good, one-handed diving save from Charlton keeper Kiely somehow kept out Kitson's low, predatory strike. Pity Shaka hadn't been watching and learning.

A poor clearance from Dailly it may have been but Shaka should have dealt with it more effectively. Instead, Euell latched on to the loose ball to equalise. Within a couple of minutes, Charlton were 2-1 up, Tomas Repka hitting the self-destruct button in spectacular fashion. Instead of belting the ball out of the stadium, he presented it on a plate to Euell in a way that would have made Rigobert Song puff out his chest with pride. It looked like another costly defeat was on the cards, as at this stage but, just before half-time, Scott Minto broke down the left and played the best pass of his Hammers career. He bent the ball superbly around a Charlton defender and into the path of the onrushing Kitson, who couldn't miss. And he didn't. Two each at half-time and it took a while to get my breath back. I did so over a pint and a chat with the Charlton fans in the corner. I've never had a problem with Charlton Athletic, I've always found their fans to be generous in victory or defeat and, on the whole, nice people. Not this lot, though. What a bunch of tossers.

The gloves were off. "Come on you Irons!" I yelled at the screen as they reappeared for the second half and the Charlton fans yelled whatever it is they yell at their team. It was getting a little tense. The Sidcup Massive in the corner were taking this seriously and, with it being as close to the big match experience as I was going to get on a Monday night, and knowing the chances of a kicking were pretty slim, I revelled in it.

Charlton went 3-2 up, Johansson catching the defence asleep (again), and my heart started beating hard again. Having scored twice already it was clear Charlton's defence was no better than ours and therefore we had every chance of getting more. Sinclair knocked the ball back from the by-line and Kitson grabbed his third. I punched the air and expressed my delight, together with some Leeds fans who, uncharacteristically, had decided to take the side of the underdog.

Jermain Defoe took to the pitch to a chorus of boos and cat-calls from the Charlton fans, both at The Valley and in the corner of The Great Northern. They knew how good he was. They knew how capable he was of pinching a goal out of nothing. They knew better than most, because West Ham had nicked him from Charlton's youth team and they were still bitter about it.

Even more so when he volleyed West Ham into a 4-3 lead from 12 yards with only a couple of minutes to go. I felt like dancing provocatively in front of the glum faces gathered in the opposite corner of the pub (they say segregation is a bad thing – opposing fans should be allowed to mingle – but given the chance, these things always take a natural order). Tempted as I was to rub their noses in it, I knew taking the lead in the last minute didn't guarantee anything. In fact, with Repka and Dailly playing like Curly and Mo in defence, the only thing it guaranteed was a draw. And that's exactly what we got.

Fish beat Hayden Foxe to a header (unremarkable until you consider Foxe was the tallest player on the pitch by about a foot at the time) and Johansson dispatched the ball into the net with a spectacular overhead kick. If we were going to be robbed of victory, it was a goal worthy of doing so. I was glad I had remained circumspect when we had taken the lead. I could have made a fool of myself. After such an eventful game, my head was buzzing and I'd had a few – not a great idea on a Monday night. I rolled in at home at gone 11.00pm. Shauna had already gone to bed.

"Did you win?" Drunken memories raced around my head. I wanted to tell her all about each of the eight goals, which ones were great attacking, which ones were poor defending. Who had a good game, who had a bad game, where we go from here. But I looked at the bed and fatigue got the better of me. I drew up alongside her and whispered: "It was a draw." And fell soundly asleep.

In my dream, I imagined a West Ham squad without that ludicrous liability Rigobert Song. I woke up, rubbed my eyes and guess what? My dream had come true! Song had been packed off on loan to German side FC Cologne, where he could allegedly improve his chances of a World Cup place in the Cameroon national team and pick up some cheap after-shave. Meanwhile, David James had finally recovered from the injury he'd sustained playing for England in August and was due to make his West Ham debut. Steve Lomas was also due to return after a lengthy absence.

The following Saturday we met Tottenham at Upton

Park. With an England international between the posts of the West Ham goal for the first time since Phil Parkes hung up his gloves, with Lomas returning to drive the midfield bus and with Song not to be seen within a 100-mile radius of the stadium, I felt we'd get a result. We did – a 1-0 defeat.

Les Ferdinand's goal was scrappy and James wasn't completely blameless. Lomas limped off with a recurrence of the same injury and Song was still on the same continent. More than anything the whole month had been a reflection of the way things had been for the last few seasons at Upton Park. There was no consistency, no fluidity and no confidence in the team from the fans. We had some fantastic players but we also had some truly f\*\*king awful players. It was a highly uncomfortable period to be supporting West Ham.

Meanwhile Shauna and I prepared to feather our love-nest, drawing up audacious plans to completely gut the bedroom and start from scratch. Having selected a colour scheme, I rapidly found out what it meant to live in a converted mill – complications mainly. The windows were sashes and a real bugger to strip down, prepare and paint. The original walls were bumpy and uneven. And as for coving . . . don't even talk to me about coving. But we got stuck in and gave ourselves a deadline of December 21st to have it all ready in time for Christmas. In the meantime, my football would be restricted to Saturday afternoons in the bedroom with a paintbrush in my hand.

I didn't complain. It had been my idea to get started on the decorating. It was what I wanted, to be part of a couple that did things together, to feel a sense of belonging, to create my own environment, to regain a bit of control over my life. For the first time since I attended only three games in 1991-92, football was starting to recede in the importance stakes. One thing bothered me, though. It was the notion that when life is going well, things go badly for West Ham. With months like November, and only one point taken from nine available, two shocking home performances and conceding away from home like it was going out of fashion, decorating seemed like a better deal all round.

# 18. Gotta Get Thru This

## Manchester United 0 West Ham United 1  8.12.01

December kicked off with a 1-0 defeat at Sunderland and with me sanding down walls ready for papering. It didn't sound like I had missed much at the Stadium of Light – Michael Carrick had hit the bar, Phillips scored a second half winner for the Black Cats. That's a funny nickname, isn't it? Black Cats? As I understand it they held a poll of Mackem fans asking them what they wanted to be known as and that was the best they could come up with. It was something to do with miners coming out of the pit and looking like black cats. My old Panini sticker album from 1980 has them down as "The Rokerites" which I suppose they couldn't use any more after moving from Roker Park and "Stadium of Light-ites" was out of the question. I'd have been interested to see what the other suggestions were for the red and white striped Wearsiders. "The Deckchairs" would have been mine. One of the printable ones, anyway. "The well-organised-but-dull-ites" might have been more appropriate. Wouldn't it have been better to keep their traditional name, to give them a reminder of their roots, their history? To my knowledge, in these days of sophisticated electronics and gadgetry, they stopped using Hammers or Irons to build ships long ago. But we are still called the "Irons" or the "Hammers", because it's the reason why we exist. Where would we be if we changed our nickname every few years? I suppose we could become the "Soldering Irons."

The Wednesday evening saw me finally able to get a coat of gloss on those sash windows and even if I say so myself, they looked the dog's doo-dahs. The evening hadn't been all plain sailing, however. Aston Villa had taken a first minute lead at Upton Park and looked like hanging on to it, especially when Parlow missed a second half penalty. It was a bit daft letting Parlow take a spot-kick against Villa – his record wasn't fantastic but Frank Lampard wasn't there to argue the toss and no-one else was brave enough to attempt it. The pictures filled my head as I peeled the masking tape off the panes of glass (you have to do it while the paint is still wet, otherwise it dries and peels the paint off the frames when you remove it – Rob's handy hints from painful experience number 223). I could see a third home defeat in a row and doom and gloom descending. Jermain Defoe had made his first Premiership start against Tottenham but was now back in his more familiar role, warming the bench. He stepped off it to grab a 90th minute equaliser and earn West Ham a point they fully deserved. Villa had proved a tough nut to crack once again.

The following Saturday, we were away at Old Trafford. I tried to blot it from my mind and concentrate on coving. Although we had won there back in January, it was inconceivable lightning could strike twice in the same place, particularly given our recent form. We'd only managed two points from the last 15 available. Not the sort of form that was going to send shivers running down the corridors of power at the Theatre of Screams. I tried to ignore it and wrap my head around the problems involved with cutting coving to fit an angle other than 90 degrees. What happened at three o'clock? I ran out of adhesive. Off I went to Focus to get some more. On went the radio. Manchester United, therefore, it must be the main commentary match. The pulse of the game was throbbing away and while it didn't appear to be end-to-end stuff, West Ham were more than holding their own. I arrived home shortly after half-time and decided it wouldn't do any harm to have the radio on while decorating, even though the same tactics hadn't worked against either Sunderland or Villa.

Then a beautiful thing happened. An inspired Parlow floated cross and the glorious prospect of not one but two West Ham players lining up to nod it home. Defoe took his chance and looped it over the ever-popular Barthez's head into the net. I wobbled at the top of the stepladders, partly through excitement but partly because having heard the cross described so lucidly on the radio, I was physically trying to head the ball home myself. Instead, all that happened was the coving I had been struggling with so manfully, came crashing down around my ears. "Stay up!" I yelled. "Stay up, you arseholes!" Shauna had been making a cup of tea and had no idea what had been going on. She popped her head around the door. "It's no good shouting at them," she said. "West Ham can't hear you from here."

Working in Manchester gave me a good opportunity to revel in our victory and I did just that while knowing how quickly these things can go sour. I had once again landed on my feet with my colleagues. I worked in a team of guys with a great sense of humour and fine knowledge of football. Duncan and Steve were Burnley fans; Nick had come up from Nottingham just before me and was a Villa fan (a lot of claret and blue going on there). Phil supported Manchester United but didn't whinge too much when I taped an A4 size picture of Defoe to his computer terminal. In slack moments we would enjoy football trivia quizzes and with fans of clubs like Manchester City, Preston North End, Bolton

Wanderers and Oldham Athletic dotted around the office, it made for interesting Monday morning conversations.

At lunchtime we'd have the usual chats about who was the greatest player of all-time, the best-ever England team and dream up lists of greatest-ever sportsmen. Phil would scream his objections at the inclusion of Phil Taylor. "Darts isn't a sport!" he'd protest. I'd baulk at the idea of Michael Schumacher. "It's down to the machine, not the man," I'd say. Duncan hated Steve Redgrave. "Bloody rowing!" was his argument. It was all good fun.

Despite winning at Old Trafford there was still work to be done on the home front and the next Saturday, the fixtures got no easier with the visit of Arsenal. Our win over Manchester United had been their sixth defeat of a season that wasn't even halfway through yet and Arsenal, as United's only serious rivals, could smell the scent of victory already. They came to Upton Park brimming with the confidence of a side that had lost only once there in 14 years. The returning Kanouté, however, clearly wasn't aware of that tradition and he swept home a Schemmel cutback to put us 1-0 up. We were playing well. The confidence gained from the second successive win at Manchester United had clearly paid dividends and the team was starting to believe in themselves again. It was a shame this only ever seemed to happen against the bigger teams but I wasn't complaining on this occasion. Unfortunately the lead only lasted a couple of minutes, Ashley Cole swept home an equaliser and despite playing well for the remainder of the game, neither side could find a winner.

It was a period of consolidation for West Ham. After getting battered at Everton and Blackburn, then putting together three successive victories, things had started to go decidedly pear-shaped again. Now, with four fully deserved points taken from Manchester United and Arsenal in successive games, it was a time to put the defensive frailties behind us and concentrate on moving forward.

The defensive frailties may have started to fade but the character flaws of the squad remained. Quite why professional football clubs insist on having a Christmas party every year is beyond me. It nearly always ends in tears. To me it seems so out of place, for a team of professional athletes to go out and get wasted with the full blessing of the management. It's a joke and an insult to the people who pay their wages. On this occasion Hayden Foxe let the side down. The gangly Aussie proved his head wasn't the only ginger nut he possessed and showed a great deal more accuracy passing water in public than he ever did passing a football. It was a pity, because a few days before, in Zurich, Parlow had collected the 2001 FIFA Fair Play award for his display of sportsmanship at Everton in December 2000. These two events in the space of a few days, for me, did more than anything to highlight the essential difference between players from the continent and those from Britain and the Commonwealth. The difference in attitude to fitness, diet, training, lifestyle and the people who pay their wages was remarkable. Talk about chalk and cheese.

Parlow might push over the occasional referee but you'd never catch him getting so pissed he feels compelled to water the plants in public. It's a culture thing.

With the bedroom successfully completed and finished with a very tasteful claret coloured carpet (I was over-ruled on pale blue skirting boards), I had a free Saturday before Christmas to take in the game at Leicester City. It was a cold day to be hanging about outside, so I didn't. Filbert Street has in recent years been a relatively good venue for us but, even so, I've still seen us lose there more often than I've seen us win. Leicester were in a perilous position. Not only were they bottom of the Premiership, they had Dave Bassett as their manager. There could be no more positive guarantee of relegation.

I have to admit I felt a little bit of sympathy for Leicester City. Two years previously they'd been Worthington Cup winners and enjoyed a European adventure. Their manager, Martin O'Neill, was widely acknowledged as one of the brightest managerial talents in the Premiership. In the likes of Neil Lennon, Emile Heskey and Matt Elliott they had the backbone of a side that could have gone on to achieve better things. Then, overnight, it seemed to fall apart. Heskey, Lennon and O'Neill all departed. Peter Taylor came in after performing miracles with the England Under-21 squad. When he showed the first signs of failing to emulate O'Neill, the Leicester board took the absolutely bizarre step of getting rid of him and bringing in a manager who had already been relegated with Watford, Sheffield United and Nottingham Forest.

Once the game got under way, of course, all that sympathy disappeared. I forgot the bitterly cold conditions and urged us on towards three points. We started to look much more composed and soaked up most of the aerial bombardment Leicester could throw at us but a 20-minute headless chicken spell in the second half saw Izzet score and left us staring an underserved defeat in the face once again.

Joe Cole had been having a good game but had failed to really light up any of those he'd played in so far that season with a meaningful contribution. This afternoon, though, his trickery was too much for Elliott to handle. He chopped Cole down in the penalty area. It happened right in front of me, I'd never seen a more clear-cut penalty. Elliott, though, reacted like he'd been falsely accused of rape and murder and reacted by head-butting Trevor Sinclair. Nice man. With Elliott sent off, Parlow dispatched the equalising penalty and West Ham should have gone on to win. We should have but I am always happy to come away undefeated, so I was satisfied with a draw.

I wasn't so chuffed at having to wait half an hour in my car while all the people blocking me in meandered their way back – didn't they have homes to go to? At least it gave me the opportunity to listen to the exciting finale at Elland Road, where Newcastle United beat Leeds United 4-3.

I spent Christmas away from my parents for the first time in my life. No matter where I have been living or who I have been living with, I have always gravitated back there for Christmas. It was a strange feeling to be phoning mum and dad on Christmas Day but I wasn't sad about it. There comes a time in everyone's life when it has to happen. Shauna was cutting herself up about it, thinking my parents would think she had stolen me away from them, but I knew that wasn't the case at all. My two sisters and I have our own families now – we have to put them first.

It was also a strange feeling not to be going to a football match on Boxing Day. Instead I went for a meal with Shauna and her mum at a local pub set up on the moors. When we returned home from a great feed, I checked the ever-faithful Teletext to find our run of good form on Boxing Day had continued. After stuffing Charlton Athletic 5-0 last year, Derby County were thrashed 4-0. Sebastien Schemmel got the opener and his much deserved first goal for the club. Despite having the number of marbles in his possession questioned by his manager at FC Metz, Seb was proving to be a bargain buy. Only his crossing left a little bit to be desired but he had a great pair of lungs and would scamper up and down the touchline all day long. He happened to be in the right place at the right time to sweep in a deflected free kick in the opening 10 minutes. The scoreline suggested a rout but it wasn't until the last 15 minutes that West Ham cut free. A beautiful curling cross-field pass from Carrick opened up the way for Parlow to score the second. Sinclair, with his traditional Boxing Day spectacular volley, and Defoe came on to bag a last minute goal in similarly traditional fashion. It was becoming something of a trademark.

We put our little black and white cat, Delia, in the cattery and set off for London the next day to visit my folks. The combination of poor weather, New Year sales and general holiday traffic made the journey a complete nightmare. It took us over seven hours to get to London from Bradford, a trip which, on a good day, with a following wind, normally takes about four-and-a-half. We just had time to get changed and go out again for a meal with the whole family. It was quite a stressful experience and since that time I have opted, whenever possible, to take the coach or train. It's a lot less aggravation.

We had, effectively, one full day in which to relax. That was spent at sister Sylvia's house, via a trip to MFI to buy bedroom furniture. Now the bedroom had been so tastefully completed, it was time to stop living off those clothing rails you see at boot fairs and go up market a bit. Only a bit. It was MFI, after all.

The next day I took Shauna to a game for the first time. I was a little bit nervous about it. In a way it was like introducing her to my family. It was important to me she liked them and they liked her. I was introducing her to my club and saying: "This is the lady who's been keeping me away from you". The club took one look, nodded sagely and said: "We understand".

129

It was the first time I had sat in the new Dr Martens Stand and although I had many happy memories of the old West Stand, I have to say it is a vast improvement. There are no pillars obstructing the view, the facilities have improved beyond all recognition, although the accommodation is somewhat cramped. It is, on the whole, a lot more comfortable. I should think so, too, at £42 per throw.

Before taking our seats we took a walk around and I showed Shauna the sights. The Central, The Millers Well, The Boleyn . . . and Kev's fantastic new haircut. I hadn't seen Kev for ages. He looked a bit different. His hair had grown and he was wearing a floppy sun hat. I had to admire his style, if not his optimism – It was December 29th after all.

My sister, Lynn, had just returned from a trip to EuroDisney with husband Alan and her three kids. She had told me how it had cost them £20 to buy a round of hot dogs and drinks and I had gasped with incredulity. When I looked at the prices of the food at football, though, I realised I would have been left without at least two limbs if I'd had to buy more than two of anything. Extortion, daylight robbery, call it what you will, it's bloody expensive going to football these days and it's no wonder those who used to frequent Upton Park and many other Premiership or first division football grounds are now forced to watch from a distance.

As for the game, it was enjoyable but hardly worth its £84 plus sundries. A Trevor Sinclair strike looked like being enough to beat Liverpool but they had England stars Owen and Gerrard on the bench and Owen grabbed his 100th Liverpool goal. I wasn't sure if it was his 100th Liverpool goal against West Ham or not but it certainly felt like it. The first one I had seen had been in the first leg of the 1996 FA Youth Cup final. He'd come a long way in five years.

West Ham had come a long way since losing 7-1 at Blackburn in mid-October. The recent run had seen them end the year in 11th place on 25 points. Being me, I was still thinking we were 17 points away from safety but the more optimistic Hammers fans were thinking more in terms of it being 30 points away from Europe. We were now unbeaten in six games (I know, but it's a lot for us) and had played Manchester United, Arsenal and Liverpool in those six matches. There was every reason to be optimistic for 2002.

# 19. My Sweet Lord

**Chelsea 1 West Ham United 1   26.1.02**

A word or two, if I may, about smoking. It's not big and it's not clever. This is big confession time for me, as I have smoked, in varying degrees of seriousness, since the age of 16. I always kept this fact from my parents but I reckon they had a pretty good idea. I always thought I would have stopped by the time I ever needed to confess and I always managed to go without when I had to, so I figured I could give up any time I wanted to. The death of one of my biggest heroes, George Harrison, prompted me to finally do something about it.

What I hadn't accounted for was that it wasn't nicotine I was particularly hooked on. It was the act of smoking and certain triggers always made me crave one, like one of Pavlov's dogs hearing a bell ring. I would start to ache when I saw the motorway sign on the M62 saying "Highest Motorway In England" because it was always the signal for me to spark up. Getting in from work was another, as was finishing a particularly filling meal. Shauna smoked, too, so we egged each other on and comforted each other and promised we'd give up soon. In the meantime, I'd nip to the shop and get 20 Embassy No.1 for myself and 20 Silk Cut Ultra for Shauna.

This New Year's Day was the first day of quitting. The first day of freedom, the first day our money jar would miraculously start to overflow. It was also the first day of tetchy arguments, aching limbs, short tempers and going to bed early.

I'd already decided not to go to Leeds. Yes, we were on a good run and, yes, if we could win at Old Trafford we could win anywhere. But it seemed like such a waste of time seeing as we'd won there the previous year. The law of West Ham away matches means we are unlikely to win there again until around 2020. Add to that the fact my seat was No.13 in row M (13th letter of the alphabet) via entrance 13 and you'll understand why I chose to flog the ticket on to a mate I bumped into at Leicester. Oh no, I'll have the rozzers round now. It was face value, honest Guv. I didn't even take the f**king extortionate £1.50 booking fee off the guy. What is the booking fee for exactly? A stamp cost 28p last time I looked.

Whatever, I decided not to go well before giving up smoking and it turned out to be a decision vindicated after 10 minutes, by which time Viduka had already put Leeds 2-0 up. What wasn't such a great idea was to sit and watch an interminably slow British film, *The English Patient*. That's what you had to be to watch the bloody thing; English and patient. And aching all over through nicotine withdrawal. I went to bed early and for the first time in 17 years of smoking, wished I'd never picked one up in the first place.

West Ham lost 3-0 at Leeds. Normal service was thereby resumed. I can't remember who caved in first but by the following weekend Shauna and I had started sharing a packet of 10 of an evening and by the weekend after that, we were back on to 20 a day. Oh well, it was worth a go. It was my first attempt and everyone is allowed to fail at their first attempt.

Look at West Ham for example. They failed at their first attempt to win a cup-tie on far too regular a basis for my liking. Maybe they were hooked on it, too? Despite everything, despite playing Macclesfield Town away in the third round of the FA Cup, despite our record against lower league opposition, despite the fact the BBC vultures had chosen to circle over the Moss Rose Ground, I decided to go. Again it was handy living in Bradford. I was able to get to Macclesfield in an hour or so and met up with Gary, John the Seller and Liam and Sean, our Wakefield contingent. There was a bit of a 'couldn't care less' atmosphere outside the ground, the majority of fans more concerned about the destination of the unsettled Parlow rather than the result of the game.

It seemed ever since Parlow had joined us, speculation abounded over where he was going next. As he had never settled at a club for more than a couple of years at a time, such speculation was not entirely unreasonable. But having settled at West Ham and constantly proclaimed his love for the club and his general contentment with life, you'd think the press would have left this particular bone alone.

Since his referee-pushing days were over, the press had struggled to find anything to write about Parlow. There was his handbags-type spat with David James while the keeper was still at Villa and his tantrum in the 5-4 Bradford game, when he demanded to be substituted and wrestled the ball from Frank Lampard to take that penalty. Such displays of emotion, even the infamous decking of referee Paul Alcock in his Sheffield Wednesday days, showed nothing more than a deep passion for the game and a desire to be a winner. I would say that – I'm on his side.

But in January 2002 it looked for all the world like Parlow was after one last hurrah, one last payday before he retired from the game. It would be hypocritical of me to say 'who could blame him?' I've said in my introduction most footballers are over-paid and have a stinking attitude. Parlow was very well paid at West

Ham. It was plain greedy to consider a move to Manchester United at that stage of his career.

And that's how the majority of West Ham fans saw it and called it that miserable Sunday lunchtime in Macclesfield. The BBC predators were to be disappointed once again. As at Wycombe in 1994, the expected giant-killing in front of the *Match of the Day* cameras failed to materialise and West Ham ran out comfortable 3-0 winners. Defoe scored twice and Cole bagged a third. John Moncur received a yellow card, said something to the referee and promptly received an instant second. Parlow was nowhere to be seen. The fans made their feelings very clear on the matter. "Who needs Di Canio?" they sang: "We've got Jermain Defoe." Whether they meant it or not, was another matter.

The fourth round draw paired us away at either Chelsea or Norwich City, who still had to settle their tie in a replay at Stamford Bridge after it ended goalless at Carrow Road. Meanwhile, we played Leicester City at Upton Park, still managed by Dave Bassett and still rooted firmly to the bottom of the table. This time, Parlow was to be seen and grabbed a first-half winner. I never thought he would leave and, of course, he didn't. He might talk a good transfer but he knows which side his bread is buttered.

Chelsea provided the league opposition the following weekend in another pay-per-view game I should have left well alone. The MFI furniture had arrived on the Saturday, so I was grateful the game had been moved. Even so, I only had time to build two wardrobes and one bedside cabinet – the rest would have to wait.

As I sat in The Great Northern watching the first half unfold, I felt a great sense of unease. We were holding on reasonably comfortably but didn't show anything much in the way of attacking flair. I knew if Chelsea scored it was game over. They did so just before half-time. I returned to the bar for a re-fill, thinking if we were going to lose, I might as well have a drink and promised myself a pint for every goal Chelsea scored. That being the case it was well after six by the time I got home, as Chelsea spanked us 5-1. I excused myself a pint for Defoe's consolation goal. I expected Shauna to be furious and tried desperately to walk in a straight line when I got in but she'd seen the score on Teletext and had a warm bed waiting for me. As I say, when life is going well, West Ham are sh*te.

It was a bizarre twist of fate. No sooner had we been beaten out of sight at Stamford Bridge than we were expected to return there to play an FA Cup tie. This happens a lot more frequently than it should. I remember it happening against Sheffield Wednesday in the late 80s and by the time we were done I was sick of the sight of them.

Admittedly, it didn't take much to get sick of the sight of Chelsea. It certainly didn't take much to get tired of the sight of that miserable teddy bear, Jimmy Floyd Hasselbaink, particularly when he scored a goal of such breathtaking brilliance that even David James had to stand back, admire the view and admit he was beaten. West Ham, though, refused to do the same. There's nothing like a good hiding to galvanise the spirit and Chelsea found to their cost we wouldn't roll over like the good boys we had been the previous Sunday. Vladimir Labant, a new Slovakian signing from Czech side Slavia Prague, played on the left and looked dangerous when attacking and scary in defence. His superbly taken free kick was beaten out just far enough for Fredi Kanouté to bang home the rebound and send us all into raptures. Game over, 1-1. You could see Chelsea were gutted. Having already beaten them at Upton Park in the league, and with a good record against higher-ranked (supposedly) opposition at the Boleyn, I had no doubt Herr Roeder would be Francis Drake to Ranieri's King Phillip and unleash a cunning plan to undermine the Chelsea armada.

First, the small matter of Southampton away in the league. Although we had won on our final visit to The Dell, a repeat performance was not likely to happen on our first visit to St Mary's. Having sacked manager Stuart Gray after their 2-0 defeat at The Boleyn in October, Southampton had opted for the debatable skills of Gordon Strachan to guide them to safety. I like Strachan. He has an honesty and openness about him that seems rare in Premiership managers these days. He's from a similar school to Harry Redknapp in that way. Sometimes though, you get the impression he's putting it on a bit.

Debatable his skills may be but that night they were better than Herr Roeder's and Southampton exacted revenge for the October defeat with an identical 2-0 win. It seemed the season was developing along similar lines to 1997-98, when Hartson and Kitson enjoyed their first full season at the club. Great at home but pants away. It was all very well but as it was mainly away games I went to, it didn't fill me with optimism for the rest of the season. And what if the home form disappeared?

## 20. Nothing

**West Ham United 2 Chelsea 3  6.2.02**

They say April is the cruellest month. Whoever said that clearly wasn't a West Ham fan. February – what a waste of time that month is? Why do we even bother with it? In these days of modern technology surely there must be a way of skipping it and going straight into March. I wouldn't miss it, would you?

The month started well enough, with a 2-0 win over Blackburn Rovers. Scant consolation after the 7-1 mullering they had dished out in October but consolation nonetheless. Although Blackburn had won the Premiership seven years previously, they had since been relegated and we were probably considered to be the 'bigger and better' team. Blackburn's tumble out of the Premiership taught us all a salutary lesson. If you sell your best players and bring in untried, second rate management, you'll get no more than you deserve. They got that when they were relegated at the end on the 1999-00 season but after bringing in a quality manager in the shape of Graeme Souness, they were starting to build again. It had been widely acknowledged that fateful day in October that the average third division side would have beaten us convincingly, we were that poor. Souness, to his credit, acknowledged the fact ahead of anyone. He's a man who calls a spade a spade. This time, though, it was Blackburn's chance to be poor. Goals from Fredi and

Trevor Sinclair extended the unbeaten home run to six games.

The FA Cup tie against Chelsea was a heart breaker. Not because we got beaten at home. Not because we led twice and had a real chance of progressing. Not because we had the prospect of Preston North End in the fifth round at Upton Park. Not because it was Chelsea. It was all those things and more. I was really pissed off by it all.

It all started brightly enough, Jermain Defoe bagging a goal out of nothing with a shot that beat Cudicini at the near post. But sloppy defending at the other end cost us an equaliser. That constant thorn in our side, Hasselbaink, was on hand again to fire home from a free kick while the wall were still arranging themselves in a pretty pattern. To be fair, it probably wouldn't have mattered if we'd had six weeks' notice in writing, it would still have flown into the back of the net.

Defoe put us back in charge but it seemed to be a game we were hell-bent on losing. A suicidal back-header from Don Hutchison gifted them another equaliser and with the game seemingly heading for extra time, Terry stole in at the far post to nick an undeserved winner for Chelsea. Not just undeserved, because some of his arrogant off-the-field antics have dragged the name of English footballers through the dirt. I mean undeserved, because Chelsea didn't show enough to warrant a fifth round berth. I suppose that is cup football.

I was gutted and as the season progressed the enormity of the cup defeat grew on me. We could have played Preston in the fifth round, got revenge over Spurs in the quarter-finals, an easy win over Fulham in the semi-final and met Arsenal in the final. Piece of cake. We'd have won the cup and played every club we've already beaten in an FA Cup final in the process.

Except I don't think it works that way. We would have played Preston, because the draw had already been made, but would we have played Spurs in the quarters? Does it follow like that or are the balls re-numbered for each round? Does it matter our name begins with a 'W'? Does any of this paragraph make any sense at all? It's one of those little things, like a dripping tap. It has bothered me for years.

But it didn't matter now anyway, because we were out. Now we only had the league to worry about and even then there was more worry of relegation than there was optimism about qualifying for Europe. The bubble had burst on the season in a pretty big way as far as I was concerned. I began to wish the whole season had been played out on an Etch-a-sketch, so I could give it a bloody good shake and start again.

That was certainly the way I was feeling as I headed toward Bolton's Reebok Stadium the following Saturday. I wasn't in the best of moods following our cup exit to Chelsea and I was a little hung-over after we'd had friends over the night before. But the good news was there were plenty of cold snacks, such as quiche and samosas, to make my journey interesting. Unfortunately, they were nearly all gone by the time I hit the motorway. Princess Margaret had died and the radio was droning on and on about her tragic life. I wasn't overly excited about going to Bolton at the best of times. Today, I wished I'd stayed in bed.

Despite visiting The Reebok the last time we'd played there and despite asking for directions from people who lived in the area, I still managed to get comprehensively lost. I ended up pulling up by a burger van and asking directions. I was bloody miles away. So I had a burger. No wonder I was heading for 14 stone! After eventually finding the stadium – it shouldn't be so hard to find, it looks like a space ship that's landed slap bang in the middle of town – I managed to bag one of the final parking spots. I knew what a long walk it would be – upwards – to my seat, so decided to make a start at about 2.20pm, setting up base camp on the mezzanine floor at 2.45pm and eventually reaching the summit at something approaching 3pm. I felt like sticking a f**king flag in my seat, not sitting on it. It felt like I was on the top of Mount Everest, too. It was freezing. Another good reason to hate February. I'd forgotten how high up and windy it gets at The Reebok and I only had a light jacket on over my Hammers shirt. Silly boy.

With my teeth chattering away I watched Defoe screw an early chance wide before Gardner scored what turned out to be the winner in the first half. Richard Garcia was making his full debut in midfield and had a competent enough game but didn't blow my socks off. Another product of the youth team, he had earned the right to have his chance. It was unfortunate for him. On the biggest day of the Aussie's career to date, none of his colleagues seemed to give a XXXX.

Sometimes you can tell after about 10 minutes of a game how it's going to turn out. I had Bolton Wanderers v West Ham United on February 9th, 2002 sussed after about 25 minutes. Yet I couldn't leave my seat, frozen though I was, until the final whistle had sounded, just in case. It's what makes football such a brilliant spectator sport. You might think you know what's going to happen next, then something amazing happens to prove you wrong. On this occasion, however, I was spot-on. I could quite comfortably have left at half-time and not missed anything. Instead I stayed, half froze to death and sat in the car for almost an hour after the game waiting to get away. The fun was starting to disappear. It seemed they only ever won when I wasn't looking.

I don't know what it is about West Ham that makes us, on the whole, play so badly away from home. Is it simply because we are biased and criticise every tiny mistake, every pass that goes astray or every missed opportunity? Why is it teams that come to Upton Park never play as badly as we do when we go away? Why do referees always seem to have it in for us? Why do we rarely receive any positive coverage in the media? Is this me displaying my paranoia, or do the rest of you feel the way I do? Is it just us or do fans of other clubs feel similarly persecuted? Sometimes, being a West Ham fan is too much like hard work.

The following Saturday I returned to Nottingham, this time with Shauna, to attend Chris and Christina's wedding blessing. They had got married out in Sri Lanka in December and now had a gathering for all those who couldn't make it. We decided to make a weekend of it, travelling down on the Friday afternoon, staying at a small farm guest-house on the outskirts of the city. We went into town on the Friday evening and I showed Shauna all the things that I felt made Nottingham one of the prettiest cities in England. Saturday involved a bit of shopping. Shauna spotted a dress and bought it, which was just as well, as when we returned to the guest-house we discovered she'd forgotten to bring her outfit for the wedding. Fate, that is. West Ham, meanwhile, were winning behind my back again. Kanouté scored the winner at home to Middlesbrough.

It seemed we were starting to become somewhat invincible at home again. Our record of P13 W7 D4 L2 F18 A7 meant we had the best defensive record at home in the whole of the Premiership and, overall, our home form was more than comparable to that of Manchester United, Arsenal or Liverpool. It was a pity our rank away record was only a little better than rock bottom Leicester City. That read P14 W2 D3 L9 F12 A35. We weren't going to win anything by conceding 35 goals on the road – other than a place in division one. While we continued to win at home, it was fine. But if that went bandy, we were definitely up sh*t creek. We ended February, however, on 34 points and in 11th position. A small clutch of four or five teams leapfrogged each other every weekend and we zipped between 15th and 11th depending on whether we'd played at home and the likes of Charlton Athletic, Sunderland, Blackburn Rovers and Fulham had been away.

## 21. Me Julie

**West Ham United 3 Manchester United 5  16.3.02**

I drove to Villa Park on autopilot. It's one of those Premiership grounds I seem to have visited more often than the others. Maybe it's because when I lived in London, although it was considered a 'Northern Away Trip', it was nice and easy to get to and you could be home in time for tea. It's about the same distance from Bradford as it is from London – but you don't have to deal with the M25.

Word outside the ground was Herr Roeder was fed up with the spineless displays away from home and had altered the formation, playing Joe Cole in a central holding role in midfield, similar to the one Gerrard plays for Liverpool. That would have made total sense, if Cole hadn't been our most creative and tricky player. I would have put Carrick in the role but Herr Roeder is in charge, not me. It all seemed to be working pretty well, for the first half-an-hour anyway, as Parlow made up for his penalty miss against Villa back in December and put us 1-0 up from the spot. We'd been playing well enough for me to confidently text my Villa-supporting colleague, Nick, and give him a bit of stick.

When will I learn? How many times have we been cruising along only to be hit by a thunderbolt and see it all fall apart like a clown's car at the circus? I have, after all, seen us lose a game 4-3 to Wimbledon from being 3-0 up – and lose it comfortably. Villa equalised through

Angel – not Brett this time, but Juan Pablo. It puzzled me why Premiership managers persisted with South American players. With the exception, possibly, of Ossie Ardiles and Ricky Villa at Spurs and, um, er, well, they're sh*t on the whole, aren't they? So Angel had scored against West Ham. Well, big deal, so had a million other players on their home patch this season (well, 35 had anyway). While the pay they receive would knock spots off what they could earn in Montevideo or Caracas, the average South American doesn't perform well on an icy January afternoon in a cup-tie at Grimsby. If they want big bucks they are better off in Spain or Italy. I don't think they do anything to improve or glamourise the game in this country. They sit there like leeches draining huge wages from clubs who can ill afford it and complaining about the weather. Why Manchester United pursued Ronaldinho and Kleberson with such fervour after their experience with Veron is quite beyond me. Anyway, where was I? Oh yes, Angel scored and it looked for all the world like the game was going to end in another Villa-West Ham draw. This time I was wrong.

Vassell had other ideas and scored a winner for Villa in injury time. We hadn't run down the clock and I was gutted. We'd had a chance to stem the flow, to find a new formation that would stop us being rolled over every time we did a left out of Green Street, and we'd failed to take it. It seemed, more than anything, lack of concentration for the full 90 minutes was to blame. Like the cup replay against Chelsea, a lapse of concentration in the last minute cost us big time. I could see Herr Roeder pacing the technical area with his index finder pointing at his head. I thought he was trying to tell the team to be sensible and concentrate. In reality, he was miming the act of shooting himself.

It didn't help when I left Villa Park and wound up on the wrong carriageway of the M6. A sarcastic text message from Nick compounded my misery. It had been one of those days. West Ham could take a hike.

Shauna and I braced ourselves for another attempt at giving up smoking. This time we would not be alone in our efforts, nicotine patches being the preferred method. Shauna got on well with them but I found if you rolled them up too tight, they wouldn't light. Once I'd got to grips with them, though, I found they helped me a great deal and I sailed through all the usual tests, such as a trip to the pub, a large and hugely enjoyable meal and large and hugely enjoyable sex. The biggest test, though, was yet to come – a home game against Everton.

Cole again took centre stage and was credited with the winner by Teletext even though his shot from outside the box took a massive deflection off Sinclair. Cole's finishing was something of a worry to me. It was possibly the reason why Herr Roeder had selected him for the midfield holding role, to keep him out of mischief up front. He seemed to love to shoot at every available opportunity but nine times out of 10, the ball would end up in the stand. If Sinclair was credited with the goal, it would have meant our Joey was still without a Premiership strike to call his own all season – not a good return for a creative, attacking midfield player. Especially when you look at the number of goals scored by similar players like Scholes at Manchester United, Parlour at Arsenal or Bowyer at Leeds United. He still had a lot more in his range of skills than all of those players but he needed to add finishing to his list to make him a world-beater.

His goal or not, it was enough to beat Everton and I managed another day without a fag as a result. We'd made radical plans to ensure we didn't want to smoke at the weekend – decorating the kitchen. I say decorating, it was a quick tart-up job but it still absorbed most of the weekend after failing to start until noon on Saturday due to two stinking hangovers. The patches seemed to be working now I had worked out how to use them. There were no aching limbs, no tetchiness, no dry mouth or lack of sleep both of us had experienced before. It bothered me though, that while we were not smoking cigarettes, we were still pumping nicotine into our bodies. Not only that, we were both eating and drinking for England and thinking of anything we could do to keep ourselves occupied rather than think about cigarettes. It didn't work, of course. Every time I'd get in from work the main topic of conversation would centre on how our day went without a cigarette. Pathetic. To paraphrase John Lennon, I wished I could get hold of Sir Walter Raleigh and give him a good kicking.

Shauna and I were starting to argue quite a bit. While the initial romantic glow had started to fade, I knew I loved her and I wanted to be with her for the rest of my life but arguments were occurring more frequently than was healthy. We had planned to get married on December 1st but very few concrete plans had been made and it was now the middle of March. Although it was only to be a small gathering of immediate family, it would take longer to get sorted than nine months. We'd also been together for almost eight months and not once had I suggested planning anything, other than our next bottle of wine, next packet of fags or next night in front of the telly.

It takes two to argue but, I have to admit, most of this was my fault. Maths has never been my strong point, you see – and I'm not brilliant with money either. When I have it, I spend it – and that's where it was all going horribly wrong. I didn't make plans, because I couldn't see how I was going to pay for them. I couldn't admit I was skint, could I? How would that look? So whenever Shauna asked what we were going to do about the wedding, or when we could go away on holiday, I would snap back at her. It wasn't fair on her and it wasn't like she was demanding Caribbean cruises – a week in a caravan somewhere would have done. She needed a break as much as I did. We'd both been working hard, doing a lot of travelling and making sacrifices. The strain was starting to show. I knew It was in my hands but I was so afraid we'd split up if I revealed the extent of my predicament, so, like a fool, I kept quiet about it.

Meanwhile the Manchester United bandwagon rolled into town. A trip to London was out of the question. In fact, I looked at my financial situation and wondered how I would ever be able to afford to go to a football match ever again, it was that tight. There were things needing attention in the flat and for the first time in my life I had to think about someone other that myself when it came to money. Not only that, I still had to pay off the debts that had been run up and re-financed again and again since the age of 18. If there is one thing I would have changed about my life it would have been never to have had a credit card. They are the work of the devil. If someone offers you one, do yourself a favour. Tell them to f**k off.

So I missed the Mancs at home for the first time in 10 years. I wasn't bitter about it – I'd had to spend the last of the week's money on carpet tiles for the kitchen, which was a higher priority and I was glad to do it. I also knew that had the money been available, Shauna would have had no problems whatsoever about me going to the match. I simply didn't have the cash. Even if I'd forgotten all about carpet tiles, the money I would have saved wouldn't have been enough to buy me a ticket, travel and food, which I estimated at around £75, so I might as well have carpet tiles and listen to the game on the radio.

Although we lost a fantastic game, 5-3, it was one of

those matches you didn't mind losing. We were beaten by a far superior team, yet showed enough skill, courage and determination to score three goals against them and, towards the end, with the score at 4-3, threaten an equaliser. Steve Lomas had opened the scoring, only for Beckham to equalise with a side-footed lobbed volley from the corner of the penalty area. Kanouté restored the lead and with the defensive record we enjoyed at Upton Park, it seemed entirely possible a first home win over United in the Premiership was on the cards. Wrong. Butt equalised with an uncharacteristic overhead kick to make the score 2-2 after 21 minutes, then Scholes showed Joe Cole how it should be done before Solskjaer added a fourth. Although Defoe pulled it back to 3-4, Beckham added a fifth from the spot two minutes from time. I was still happy at the end of the game. Although we had conceded five goals at home, we had not been disgraced. We had put up a decent fight and showed why we were a force to be reckoned with at Upton Park. The carpet tiles looked great, too.

With three players in the full England squad and a game against Italy being played around the corner at Elland Road, it seemed daft not to go and watch, particularly as I had stumbled upon a pair of free tickets. I could also take the opportunity to wear my Hammers shirt at Elland Road and not worry about having my head beaten to a messy pulp. I was nervous for David James, Trevor Sinclair and Joe Cole. All three had a great chance of making Sven-Goran Eriksson's squad for the World Cup in June but I was worrying about Phil Neville syndrome. Was it better to have no Hammers in the squad and then blame everyone else when it went horribly wrong? At first it seemed my fears would be unfounded as Cole battled doggedly to slip a pass through for Fowler to open the scoring. But then Joe lost possession in his own half and Italy equalized, while

James gave away an injury time penalty. I did my coat right up as I left Elland Road, just as I would for a league match. I wondered how enjoyable the World Cup would be if any of the three were selected and played and, for once, felt grateful for not having been born in 1966. I don't think I could have handled the pressure.

Ipswich Town were rather like my carpet tiles – blue, on the floor and getting walked on by everyone. By the time they arrived at Upton Park on Easter Saturday they were in serious danger of relegation and had seen a disastrous change in fortunes from the previous season. It was important for us to bounce straight back from the Manchester United defeat but I had no doubt we would do it – it hadn't been a demoralising humiliation at home, we'd simply been out-gunned by a better team. Whoever came along next was likely to be taught a lesson. Unfortunately for Ipswich, it was them.

With 20 minutes to go, however, it looked like, for all their superiority, West Ham would only get a point. Bent equalised after super-striker Lomas had put us 1-0 up just before the break. It was the Irishman's second goal in two games and he was clearly enjoying his comeback from injury. Parlow's last act, before being substituted, was to win the game with a 25-yard drive that visibly knocked the stuffing out of Ipswich. It was hard to believe this was the same team that had come to Upton Park and won comfortably the year before. The same team that had finished fifth in the Premiership last May, the same team that had been rubbing shoulders with the likes of Inter Milan in the UEFA Cup. I made a mental note as Defoe scored the third goal, guaranteeing three points and virtual safety from the dreaded drop. No West Ham side would ever experience such a sharp decline. Never. Would it?

## 22. One Step Closer

**West Ham United 3 Sunderland 0  20.4.02**

The Easter weekend concluded with a remarkable 1-0 victory at Craven Cottage. It was remarkable for many reasons. Firstly, in a season that had seen West Ham rise from relegation candidates to potential top-half material, it was only our third away win of the campaign. Secondly, despite being under the cosh for most of the game, Fredi Kanouté's header right on the stroke of half-time was enough to win the game. Thirdly, it seemed the only person connected with West Ham who left the match unhappy was Parlow. I love Parlow, don't get me wrong. But by this point he was starting to test my patience.

Parlow was a player who wore his heart on his sleeve, something fans of any club will appreciate. It shows a certain type of loyalty, a determination to do well, a disappointment when things go wrong. I like that in a player. Nothing irritates me more than seeing players laugh and joke as they leave the field after a heavy defeat. It is unprofessional and takes the piss out of the paying public. From that point of view, Parlow has had few equals. But it's a double-edged sword. Such passion and verve, coupled with an unquenchable self-belief, meant Parlow could never accept he might sometimes be wrong. Sometimes, he might have to be sacrificed for the good of the team. There could be few who would question his status as our most talented player.

But sometimes talent alone isn't enough. Away from home, work-rate and good old-fashioned blood and guts are needed to get results. At Fulham, Parlow wasn't showing that level of commitment and Herr Roeder was right to substitute him after 67 minutes to protect the lead that, although hard-earned, was also somewhat fortunate and needed to be guarded with 11 fully committed players.

Parlow always talks about being a professional. Part of being a professional is to accept the manager's decisions and not to go spouting off to the press about how it would have been better to substitute a team-mate because they weren't working as hard as you.

To be fair, the press were always after a decent quote and a story from Parlow. Any player with a history as colourful as his was always going to be the subject of newspaper speculation either from a transfer perspective or from a controversial comment he'd made. They would no doubt twist anything he said to suit themselves but after all the will-he-won't-he? speculation at the turn of the year and now this, I wished he would play his football, show his talent, accept the manager's decision and shut his f**king gob.

Herr Roeder, meanwhile, was demonstrating a fine ability to play the diplomat in such situations. Let's face it, he had to be stoical when faced with a character like Parlow. He was a handful for more than just opposition defences. I'm almost certain Parlow's petulant "play me or release me" plea to the club would have been met by a wry smile from Herr Roeder, a brief rolling of the eyeballs and a mental note to buy a new packet of Rennies.

The rest of the squad continued to trundle along nicely. The tendency to be spanked out of sight away from home had now been largely eradicated. The central defensive partnership of Dailly and Repka, while still frightening, was starting to show signs that it might yet form a decent understanding. It was a good-cop/bad-cop partnership, with Repka the bully and Dailly taking the softly-softly approach. Dailly would ask opposing forwards nicely to surrender possession. If that didn't work, Repka would sneak up behind them and garrotte them with a length of piano wire.

Winterburn and Schemmel formed a reliable pairing at full-back and although we were acutely aware this couldn't last forever, there was Labant waiting in the wings. Minto and Ian Pearce could also do a job at full-back. It seemed Herr Roeder was sold on the idea of 4-4-2 and so was I, to an extent. I'd seen far too many three-man West Ham midfields get torn to shreds under Redknapp as he watched on helplessly. Both systems have their merits but it seemed neither manager was prepared to change. It would have been nice, for example, to play 3-5-2 at home occasionally, just as I would like to have seen Harry try 4-4-2 away, to give us a little more rigidity. The defence we had at last seemed to be getting it right, so I wasn't too concerned. I wished it was August, not April, and we could start again.

Cole, Carrick, Lomas and Sinclair formed a balanced quartet in midfield and in Parlow, Kanouté and Defoe, Herr Roeder had access to three of the finest strikers in the Premiership. Parlow apart, everyone seemed happy to put pen to paper and secure improved deals. Herr Roeder had won over the majority of his critics and now 43 points had been achieved, mathematical safety meant we could concentrate on finishing as high as possible and end the season with a flourish.

They say when it doesn't matter, the luck goes with you and I think it would be fair to say that's what happened in the next game, at home to Charlton Athletic. The Addicks played well and did everything but score, even missing a penalty. It wasn't their day. Parlow showed them how it should be done with a penalty before half-time before Kanouté wrapped it up with a second half strike. It was professional and workmanlike. We took our chances, they didn't, end of story. It wasn't like West Ham at all. There was a serious risk of it all getting rather boring. Did you know that Charlton are called the Addicks because the owner of the local fishmongers used to stand on the corner on match day and shout: "Come and get yer addick!" No? Neither did I.

A third London derby in a row saw us travel the short distance across town to White Hart Lane. It was my sister Sylvia's 40th birthday, so Shauna and I drove down from Yorkshire to take part in the surprise party arranged for her. It meant the nearest I could get to being at the game was to tune into TalkSPORT and listen to their appalling 'live' commentary. Presumably they call it 'live' commentary because they shout loud enough to wake the dead. It's painful to listen to and anyone who moans about BBC bias should take a listen to that shower. It makes your ears bleed.

The last few visits to Tottenham had been nothing to shout about and it seemed this wouldn't be either. A Sheringham goal had put Spurs 1-0 up and it looked like it would stay that way until a rocket of a volley by Pearce late on levelled the game at 1-1. It didn't matter how many times I heard it described, by people who were there, by the over-excitable types at TalkSH*TE or by the newspaper hacks who largely ignored it anyway, I didn't realise what a fantastic strike it was until I saw it for myself on video. I often champion the cause of Ian Pearce and this gave me further ammunition. A 1-1 draw at Spurs was a creditable result. They were in the group of clubs vying for seventh place with us and any points we could pick up away from home bucked the season-long trend of winning at home and losing away.

It also prompted me to note another useless statistic. No one had managed to do the double over us in the league so far. We'd lost at home to Manchester United, Tottenham and Fulham but gained seven points on our visits to their respective grounds. I always saw that as a benchmark for success. No one managed the double over us in 1985-86 either, our "championship" third-place season, or in the promotion campaign of 1992-93. It's a rare feat for a club like West Ham. Sunderland and Bolton Wanderers still had the chance to dent that record but, given our impressive home form, I saw no reason to expect it to happen.

Sylvia's party passed by and mum and dad arranged to come up and visit us in Yorkshire at the end of May. Shauna and I were still experiencing some problems, mainly centered around my refusal to open up on a variety of subjects, particularly the financial situation. It was also becoming blindingly obvious a wedding wasn't going to happen in December if we hadn't done anything about it so far. Bearing in mind the amount of fighting going on, we thought it best to put those plans on hold anyway.

Sunderland were put to the sword the following weekend. It was becoming dangerously predictable – there was surely a danger of becoming complacent. Joe Cole had a goal struck off for no apparent reason other than the fact Joe Cole doesn't usually score goals but strikes from Sinclair, Steve 'Pele' Lomas and another late one from Jermain Defoe finished off Sunderland and left us sitting pretty in seventh place with 50 points. Seventh was the highest we could achieve. The most optimistic of West Ham fans could not have predicted that in August, after the departure of Harry and the apparent instability at the club. The natural order to things prevailed inside the top six – who finished seventh was more of a lottery, emphasised by the fact only four points separated seventh place from 15th.

Midweek, Shauna celebrated the exciting news that she had been successful in her application for a new job, working as PA to the managing director of the local newspaper group. She had trained as a journalist in the early 90s but, rather like me with property, had drifted out of it and wound up doing something different. This was her opportunity. While it was news we could both celebrate, she went out with her mum for a few drinks, while I joined her brother to watch the Arsenal game in a pub in Baildon.

It had been a hard task finding a pub showing the game. Manchester United were playing a Champions League game on ITV and the majority of pub landlords I phoned mid-afternoon were showing it. Eventually I stumbled upon a landlord with a London accent, who confirmed he would be showing the West Ham match in the snug at the back of the pub, while, to satisfy the majority of customers, he'd be showing the United game on the big screen in the main bar. That suited me fine, or it would have done if I hadn't arrived and sat down in the snug with Andrew to find the place teeming with Arsenal fans.

It was a real case of *déjà vu*, watching West Ham at Highbury among Gooners. I had promised myself I wouldn't repeat the experience after last year. The added bizarre twist this time was the fact I was watching among Arsenal fans in a pub in West Yorkshire.

Arsenal were flying and every man and his dog expected us to lie down and take our medicine but it didn't quite work that way. Kanouté's shot from a tight angle clearly crossed the line before Ashley Cole hacked it clear. That's the luck of the champions, I suppose. (That's if you believe luck has anything to do with it and it's not just the fact referees are so petrified of making controversial decisions at the home of big clubs, they would rather have their eyes gouged out than award a debatable goal to the visiting team in front of the North Bank.) That's my theory, anyway. The linesman must have already had his eyes gouged out. You didn't need the eyesight of Steve Austin to see the ball had crossed the line but we were little West Ham, playing in the big boy's back yard and they needed a win to keep their title challenge going. Which way do you think the decision was going to go?

Ljungberg, the man with the most ridiculously outdated 'hairstyle' in the Premiership, scored twice late on and that was curtains. The Landlord at The Angel wandered across and gave me a wink: "That's better, eh?" he said, full of chirpy Goonerness. Dramatically, I looked him in the eye, put down my glass and withdrew my custom. I was quite pleased with myself. It looked almost hard.

We had two matches left, away at Newcastle United and home to Bolton Wanderers. Three points from those two games would probably be enough to secure seventh place and I knew which game my money was on but I went to Newcastle nevertheless. Despite things being a little strained at home, I decided to come home on the Friday night after playing in a football tournament in Gateshead organised through work. I hadn't played properly for years and fitness, for me, was becoming a thing of the past. Too much beer and good living, see? I had a 'mare and wanted to get home. It seemed daft to come back all that way to turn around and go back the next day but I'd done stranger things in my time. Both Shauna and I had long since dumped the nicotine patches and were back to sharing a packet of 10 Marlboro lights every evening for the sake of our sanity. I needed that as much as anything.

I drove back up to Newcastle, alone this time. All the

trips I had ever done to the north-east before had always been with *OLAS*, or satellite groups of *OLAS*. I felt quite lonely and detached – not only from my friends, most of whom I saw when I got there, but from the team as well. And I don't only mean detached from the team because I was back up in the gods and watching the game on a radar screen. It could have been anyone down there.

Something very familiar happened, though, to make me feel at home. Jermain Defoe scored a cracking opening goal in a first half that West Ham dominated and should have underlined their superiority with more goals. But Shearer equalised before half-time and the familiar sight of shipping three goals away from home appeared before me for the last time that season. It had been an average game overall – good first half, poor second. David James could have done better. But we were safe, so it didn't matter and we couldn't finish high enough for a European spot. Newcastle could, their motivation was greater. That's my excuse and I'm sticking to it.

## 23. Come Back

**West Ham United 2 Bolton Wanderers 1 11.5.02**

The year 2002 was a significant one for many reasons. Whether you are a fan of the Royal Family or not (I am ambivalent about the whole thing), it was HM Queen Elizabeth's Golden Jubilee year and we were given the excuse to party. That factor alone makes them okay with me. The Queen, a well-known Hammers' fan, visited Upton Park in early May to officially open the new Dr Martens Stand. It meant Lou and Doris had to get the Mr Sheen out to give the cardboard turrets a quick once-over and the stadium manager had to beat the moths out of the old red carpet, which hadn't seen the light of day since King Olav V of Norway dropped in for a plate of jellied eels.

It was an honour, though. The Queen had come to us and not to either of our poor relations in north London. Joe Cole was introduced to Her Majesty – quite a day for him as he celebrated his inclusion in the England squad for the forthcoming World Cup. David James had also made it through to the final 22 but Trevor Sinclair had narrowly missed out.

I was more surprised by Cole's inclusion than Sinclair's omission. Sven had been bold in his early selections but it seemed he had fallen into the age-old trap so many international managers stumble into, of trying plenty of new players but when it came to the crunch, sticking with the tried and tested losers. I didn't expect to see Joe featuring in any of the games in Japan and South Korea that summer.

The fans had their chance to wish them luck in the final Premiership game of the season against Bolton Wanderers. In a carnival atmosphere, Steve Lomas opened the scoring, only for Djorkaeff to wipe it out and a draw seemed likely even though West Ham had dominated. Ian Pearce popped up with a late winner, though, to secure seventh place and a creditable 53 points for West Ham, something we could only have dreamed of in the darkest days of September and October.

Herr Roeder seemed to have things under control. The defence, while still suspect, had stopped shipping silly numbers of goals and with the midfield and strike force we had, there was every reason to feel optimistic for the 2002-03 campaign to come. He clearly didn't feel the need to reward Steve Potts, one of the club's most loyal servants, with his 400th league appearance. If he'd just put him on with 10 seconds to go it would have been a nice gesture. It seems there really is no room for sentiment in sport these days.

Meanwhile there was a World Cup to enjoy and England were managed by an exciting new Swedish manager with radical ideas. With the competition being played in Asia for the first time, there was no true advantage to any of the European or South American sides. It looked like being the most open tournament for years and one England had every chance of winning.

It's been a recurring theme through all my books – when things go well for West Ham, they tend to break down in my personal life and this was proving to be no exception. I simply couldn't cope with the demands of a relationship, while holding on to all the angst bubbling up inside me over my financial problems. Having kept them to myself and having struggled to cope with them for far too long, it seemed I had two options. I could take the easy option, split up with Shauna, run away and bury my head in the sand and let it go on and on for the rest of my life. Or, I could be a man and look my problems squarely in the face and tackle them. It was one of those soap-opera moments, when you find yourself shouting: "Just tell her, she'll understand!" at the screen. But that wouldn't get the ratings up and the hero packs his bags and disappears off into the sunset – or the Queen Vic – or wherever.

That's exactly what I did. While it's very easy to tell a soap-opera character what to do, it's quite another to have to live your own little existence, where every action has a consequence you can touch. I packed a bag and sloped off to a local hotel for the night to gather my thoughts. Thoughts gathered, I decided to leave.

My decision coincided with my parents' visit to Yorkshire. They had taken a cottage up near Brimham Rocks, about 15 miles from my home, so I took the opportunity to take some time off and take a break. I'd made tentative arrangements to move back to Nottingham, get my old room back and, hopefully, my old job, too. I didn't need the stress involved with opening up to Shauna and admitting I was actually a born loser. Once I told her the truth, she'd probably kick me out anyway, I reckoned. But after a few days away I started to miss her terribly and realised, although miles away from my place of birth, the little mill-conversion flat was my home. It was where I belonged.

Shauna asked me to go and see her and I told her the whole story. We sat and cried for an hour. I told her how sorry I was and how much I loved her. She said the same, although what she had to be sorry about I'm not sure. I'm the one who had dug a great big hole for us both. I had come along with huge debts, made them worse while we'd been together. Admittedly, I hadn't run up much more, as I hadn't been able to obtain any more credit, but I'd spent most of my money on having a good time, when I should have been strong enough to say no. I should have been firmer with myself and turned down the odd football ticket here and there. I should have been more responsible and learnt to say no a lot more.

We'd both been in relationships before but this one was for real. This one meant working hard for each other, not running away when the going got tough. I was starting to realise what I had got myself into. I had the chance to walk away and forget it. I had the chance to behave like a child for the rest of my life if I wanted to. It was time for me to grow up. I gave Shauna a huge hug and promised her things would get better. I made it my mission. I needed to cleanse myself of everything that had been wrong in my life until then, my sloppy attitude with money, my sloppy attitude towards relationships, my sloppy attitude towards my appearance, my health. Everything needed a complete overhaul. Until this point it had seemed like a hopeless task but I knew, with Shauna's love and support, I could achieve it.

I spent the remainder of the week with my parents and we all met up for a Chinese takeaway on the Friday evening before they ventured back home. The World Cup was about to start in Japan. My new life was about to start in Bradford.

## 24. A Little Less Conversation

**England 1 Argentina 0  7.6.02**

England's preparations for the 2002 World Cup finals in Korea and Japan had been patchy to say the least. For poor Trevor Sinclair they had been chaotic. Called into the squad as a stand-by for Dyer, he made a second half appearance as a substitute against South Korea in a warm-up game. But it seemed Sven had his heart set on Hearsay reject Dyer and even if he had to send him out on crutches, he'd do it rather than play Trevor. 'Sincs' is no mug and he could see the writing on the wall. With his wife expecting a baby, he decided his best option was to come home.

Who could blame him? But no sooner had his flight touched down in London, than Danny Murphy picked up a knock and Sincs was heading back out to the Far East, digestive system complaining at the stresses of airline food and body clock so f**ked when he got there he was convinced it was a week last Tuesday. At least he was part of the squad now. There were three Hammers in the squad for the first time since 1966 and despite indifferent performances by England in the friendlies, confidence at home seemed to be building.

Unlike the summer tournaments of 1996, 1998 and 2000, there were very few current or ex-Hammers featuring in other squads. Rigobert Song had laughably been made captain of Cameroon. It was even rumoured Bayern Munich were interested in signing him. Was this the same Rigobert Song who couldn't make a tackle to save his life? Was this the same Bayern Munich who had won the Champions League in May? Someone, somewhere was pulling my leg, big style. The Cameroon squad also included the ill-fated Marc-Vivien Foé, a midfield player we missed more than I thought we would.

Matt Holland was playing for the Republic of Ireland but as he'd never actually played a first team game for West Ham, that was scraping the bottom of the barrel. Apart from Matty, West Ham interest was thin on the ground.

With the tournament being held in the Far East, it was clear the timings would be something of a problem. It wasn't so apparent when England's opening game against Sweden was scheduled to kick-off at 12.30pm on Sunday 2nd June. It gave the new, improved Robert Banks time to wake up, make love to his new, improved girlfriend, make her breakfast and drink leisurely cups of coffee while studying the Sunday papers, get showered and dressed, get to the corner shop for four cans of dodgy Stella, then settle down for the match. What could be more natural on a Sunday morning?

The game itself was a huge anti-climax. After being in control and taking the lead in the first half, England took to the field for the second half looking like a group of players who had just been introduced to each other. Sweden should have won the game in the end. It was more due to luck than judgement that Sven's men emerged with a point. Joe Cole had come on as a second half substitute but hadn't had much of a chance to shine. Sven's faith in players like Hargreaves (okay, he played for Bayern Munich but they were in for Rigobert Song, so what the hell did they know?) Dyer and Ashley Cole seemed unshakeable. While I acknowledged he was at least giving youth a chance, unlike many managers before him, I had to question the youth he was selecting.

Still, we survived to play another day but Argentina's 1-0 win over Nigeria meant we'd probably have to beat them to stand any chance of qualifying for the second phase.

Argentina was another midday kick-off but this time not so conveniently placed on a Friday. They'd been very good at work, allowing most of those people who lived and died football the time off to watch the games if they wanted (from their holiday entitlement, of course). But they also put up big screens in the basement so everyone could watch the game and return to work in the afternoon if they so wished. In a way I wish I had gone for that option now, as I witnessed one of England's most memorable World Cup performances sat at home. Alone.

It might have been better, on reflection, to watch the game surrounded by people leaping up and down in the air when Beckham coolly slotted home the first-half penalty that won the game. It might have been a more memorable experience to have been surrounded by friends and colleagues when the final whistle went and the whole country celebrated. But for me, there was a very personal moment within the game, a moment which, if I couldn't share with West Ham fans, I didn't want to share with anyone.

Sinclair came on after 18 minutes for the injured Hargreaves, who could now spend the rest of the tournament trying to prevent Rigobert Song joining his club and ruining it for everyone. You could see Trev bursting with pride as he crossed the touchline. He played very well and when Beckham scored the penalty it was Trevor who was first to congratulate him. That was the image which kept flickering across my TV screen, the image that kept a smile on my face for the next few days. I couldn't have been more proud if it had been my own son playing for England.

After the feelings of pride had subsided, I spared a little thought for Phil Neville and the Romania game two years previously. I remembered then my thoughts about West Ham players being involved and whether it was a mixed blessing. The positive emotions experienced when it goes well by far outweigh the negative ones when it all goes wrong. But then, Phil Neville was a Manchester United player and crap. Trevor Sinclair was a West Ham player and tremendously gifted. Hardly a comparison.

The Republic of Ireland had done well, getting 1-1 draws against Germany and Cameroon (not hard if Rigobert was playing, admittedly) and they needed to beat Saudi Arabia in their final group match to guarantee qualification for the knockout phase. I went across with Nick to the Arndale Centre in Manchester during my lunch hour to watch the game on the big screens there. The waif-like figure of Gary Breen drifted in to score the third goal to give the Republic a 3-0 win. The last time I'd seen Breen he was on his arse in the net at the Bobby Moore end of Upton Park. Either he'd improved a lot or Saudi Arabia were seriously sh*te. I knew which option I was prepared to believe.

It seemed FIFA were determined to make it harder and harder for the fans to watch their national side. Trevor was to keep his place for the game against Nigeria but kick-off was set for the ridiculous hour of 7.30am on a Wednesday morning. I'd had the chance to take the day off but decided to save holiday in case England progressed any further. I therefore had the quite unreal experience of getting up at five in the morning to get to Manchester in time to watch the whole game on television.

The local pubs and bars were taking the whole thing

very seriously. Over the whole period of the World Cup there was a terrific atmosphere in the city, a feel-good factor that would carry on into the Commonwealth Games being staged in Manchester. The local Henry J Beans had teamed up with the radio station to provide a limited number of tickets to watch the Nigeria game in the bar, with the lure of a free breakfast and bottle of Budweiser to ease the pain of such an early start. We snapped up the tickets at work and that Wednesday morning, a small corner of the bar was filled with CIS staff from a broad range of backgrounds, all supporting England. I was there representing West Ham, Duncan and Steve (Burnley), Simon (Bolton), Nick (Aston Villa), Clare (Chelsea) and Phil (Manchester United). We tucked into our free breakfasts but I passed on the free beer, in case any of my bosses are reading. The game was, again, an anti-climax but a 0-0 draw was enough to see England through to the second phase. The biggest cheer of the morning came from the other group match, in which Sweden drew 1-1 with Argentina. Another of the tournament favourites had fallen at the first hurdle. Holders France had been eliminated the day before. Maybe it would be England's year at last?

We didn't have long to wait until the next game and this time it was as sensible kick-off time on a sensible day. I watched us beat Denmark 3-0 at home with Shauna, a ham and cheese sandwich and a few cans of beer. I say it was a sensible time for kick-off, forgetting of course that once you start drinking on a sunny Saturday afternoon, unless there is something pressing to stop you, it's hard not to continue. We could have done without the expense of spending the rest of the day and most of the evening in the beer garden of The Great Northern. But it's not every day your country reaches the quarter-finals of the World Cup and certainly not every day one of your club's players helps them get there and one of your former players (Rio Ferdinand) scores the first goal.

There had been a lot of speculation in the press that the Denmark game would be tough. They had, after all, qualified as winners of the group containing France, Uruguay and surprise package Senegal. It had been a pleasant surprise when England raced into a 3-0 lead.

Now I had confessed my sins to Shauna and she had vowed to help me, we were stronger than ever. There was only one thing missing in our relationship: the pitter-patter of tiny feet. And before you say anything, I'm not talking about babies. Shauna's cute little black and white cat, Delia, had sadly passed away at the end of March after a short illness. At first we decided not to replace her, because, frankly, she could not be replaced. But as the weeks wore on we missed her presence so much and with cats having been the main topic of our first-ever conversation, I felt it was important to have one around. We took on a hyperactive tortoiseshell called Phoebe who wrecked the joint after 48 hours and so we took her back. Then we settled for an all-black tom cat who didn't have a name. Call me a softy but I fell for him straight away and we brought him home. After being over-ruled on names like Sincs, Shaka and Fredi, we settled on Charlie. After spending 12 hours scared stiff under the dining table, he finally plucked up the courage to see what was for tea and he's been with us ever since.

Meanwhile a quarter-final beckoned against Brazil. It was a stupidly early kick-off again and while I had enjoyed the experience of the Nigeria game, I opted to watch from the comfort of my front room. The previous evening the BBC had shown the full 90 minutes of England's last World Cup encounter with Brazil, in 1970. Here was a prime example of nostalgia blurring the vision. I had never seen the game the whole way through

– I was only two when it took place – but speak to anyone who knows anything about football at the time and they would say it was a classic. I decided to watch. There were four incidents of note: Moore's tackle on Pele, an exquisite example of anticipation. Then there was Banksy's save from Pele, world class indeed but probably not the finest save ever made in the history of the world. Astle's glaring miss is best forgotten and Jairzinho's goal was waiting to happen. Apart from that, the game was dull, as you might expect for a match played in 100 degrees' heat and the rarefied atmosphere of Mexico. Classic? My arse.

Unfortunately the 2002 re-match was no better and had the same end result. Owen gave England the lead but 10-man Brazil equalised just before half-time and Ronaldinho, the man with the comedy teeth, floated in a debatable free-kick over the head of Seaman a minute or two after the break. Most of the England players looked ineffective, a measure of the level of skill of the Brazilians. Trevor looked tired and drawn and was substituted but I was proud of him. Two of the three West Ham players had won World Cup finals caps. That in itself was a compliment to the way the club had progressed and credit, too, to Herr Roeder, that these players had continued to warrant international places under his stewardship.

With the World Cup over, there was nothing left to do, except try to encourage the South Koreans to turn over the Germans, which, of course, didn't happen. Despite losing 5-1 at home to England back in September, the Germans yet again had dug deep and found the resources to drag themselves into their seventh World Cup final. Remarkably, it was the first time they had ever played Brazil in a World Cup match. Unsurprisingly, Brazil won.

The tournament had been spoiled a little, for me,

because FIFA had picked a location that made it impossible to have reasonable kick-off times and made it hard for English and other European people to enjoy the games without taking holiday or wiping out the rest of the day through being drunk. FIFA should be applauded for taking the game to those areas of the world still developing within the game. The fact South Korea got further than England, Argentina, France or Spain says a lot. But it was noticeable the hugely wealthy Japan was chosen to host the tournament ahead of a more deserving country in, say, Africa. Africa – who will now get the 2010 World Cup – had been providing quarter-finalists since 1990. But they didn't have pots of cash.

Shauna and I didn't have pots of cash either but we muddled through and by sitting down and working out exactly what I owed, I'd already started making inroads. The time was clearly right for me to stop smoking. As I had got us into something of a financial muddle, I found it hard to justify spending £25 a week on fags. I had hoped to see something for it – an extra treat every week – but we kept pummelling the credit cards and that in itself had its own satisfaction. By the end of July, with Shauna's help, I had got rid of two store cards, a credit card and checked out my credit history. I had grasped the nettle and finally started behaving like a grown-up. I smoked my last cigarette on July 20th and needed no patches, no substitutes – just the knowledge I was doing us both a big favour.

I also realised I wouldn't be able to attend as many matches in the coming season. That, also, was a cross I was happy to bear. I knew things would soon start to improve and I'd be able to start going again. For now there were bigger and better priorities.

Herr Roeder had been busying himself in the transfer market ahead of the 2002-03 season, looking to build on the success of a seventh place finish. It seems odd to talk about seventh place as success but you have to put it in perspective. West Ham, even playing to the best of their ability, with all players fit, are unlikely ever to finish in the top four. In modern-day terms it was the equivalent of finishing third. Mind you, if you apply the same criteria to our fifth-place finish, we won the league in 1998-99.

I wasn't sure how I felt about the coming season. All the doubts I'd had about Herr Roeder had been dispelled by the seventh place finish and terrific home form, which saw us lose only three matches at Upton Park. If we could maintain that and keep our strength and shape away from home, then maybe even a small improvement was on the cards. Having said that, there was a very thin line between success and failure in the Premiership. A couple more adverse results and we could easily have finished 15th, not seventh. But we had finished seventh. Herr Roeder was certainly progressing well with his jigsaw. He'd got most of the sky done and was about to finish all the boats in the harbour when someone knocked it off the table and it all went wrong.

He signed Gary Breen.

I know, I know, I'd watched, along with everyone else, as Breen scored against Saudi Arabia in the World Cup. Following that goal, knowing he was out of contract at Coventry City, and hearing there were a lot of big European clubs sniffing around him, filled me with fear. I knew we'd try and sign him. What the 'big European clubs' hadn't made clear was they were sniffing around him in order to bolster their teams of ball-boys and programme-sellers. I thought he was a pile of crap the first time I saw him play for Coventry City and I had seen nothing since then to change my mind. When we signed him on a free transfer, allegedly at £30,000 a week in wages, I hit the roof. The only consolation was we'd only given him a one-year deal. But you can do a lot of damage in a year. Just ask hapless keeper, Allen McKnight.

I found out about the transfer through Shauna. Now she was working for the local paper, she had her finger constantly on the pulse of local, national and international news and that included sport. "Who's this Barry Green you've signed, then?"

Barry Green was the only major arrival of the summer and it didn't exactly fill me with optimism. Sure, we now had established England internationals in Trevor Sinclair, David James and Joe Cole and, in Michael Carrick and Jermain Defoe, we had two U-21 regulars who would surely soon make the breakthrough to the senior squad. Our midfield and strikers were awesome but our defence, on paper, looked shaky. On grass it looked abysmal. Tomas Repka had improved and steadied himself since his two early dismissals but he still showed suicidal tendencies away from home. Christian Dailly, now nicknamed 'Dilly' by the fans, was equally worrying when the ball came in his general direction. It wasn't like the days when Rio was in the side and you didn't worry if he was marking the likes of Shearer or Owen. He had pace, technique and agility. These two were simply in the way. The addition of Barry Green did nothing for me. He was like the other two, only more so, and I hadn't even seen him play in a claret and blue shirt yet.

Full-backs were another area causing concern. Sebastien Schemmel had deservedly won Hammer-of-the-Year for his tireless running up and down the right wing but, again, away from home he was no Julian Dicks or Frank Lampard Snr. He was just another Tommy McQueen. The other full-back options of Scott Minto, Ian Pearce, Nigel Winterburn and Vladimir Labant – soon heading back to Prague with 'Return to Sender' stamped on his forehead – were either elderly or ordinary. The more I thought about the season to come, the more I prayed our home form would hold out. If it didn't, we were in serious trouble.

Progress was at least being made in some areas. At Chadwell Heath, a new sports hall had been constructed, with state of the art facilities including a swimming pool and an artificial playing surface, new offices and a medical centre. The new away kit also looked the mutt's nuts. White, with a claret pin-stripe, it took me back to my first days as a regular on the road, when we had an away shirt of very similar design. Having said that, I saw us take some colossal beatings wearing that shirt. I hoped it wasn't an omen. Apart from those two areas, I was struggling to find anything to be optimistic about for the new season.

## 25. Crossroads

**West Ham United 2 Arsenal 2  24.8.02**

The pre-season friendlies had been going okay, nothing more. I never read too much into them anyway. I've seen years when we haven't strung two passes together in pre-season and we've gone on and played breathtaking football. I had also seen us go into a season undefeated and get relegated. You take them for what they are, fitness-testers. Having said that, a 5-4 defeat at Reading was still a concern. The defence was showing its frailties early on. A 1-0 victory over Vitesse Arnhem in a game played at Roots Hall, Southend did lift the spirits briefly, as did the signing on loan of French midfielder Edouard Cissé from Paris St Germain.

But it was clear we didn't need midfielders, we had bags of them. We needed quality defenders, of which we had, er, well, none.

Shauna and I put Charlie in the cattery for a few days and took a trip down to my parents' house on the south coast. It was all we were going to be able to afford in terms of a holiday this year but it was pleasant, nonetheless, to have day trips out dodging the showers and be waited on hand and foot when we returned. Money was still too tight to enjoy it properly but we were starting to make progress and get on top of things and I hadn't had a cigarette, or felt remotely like smoking, since I had stopped on July 20th. The main benefit, obviously, was the extra money that went towards reducing my credit card bill.

But other little benefits came to light which I hadn't considered. I had more energy, for a start, and while I had read that I would suddenly be able to taste things, it didn't quite happen like that but I did start to enjoy my food a little more. Possibly too much, as I started to roll worryingly towards 14 stones. But for me, the two biggest benefits were that I didn't stink like a pub and I got an extra half an hour of flex-time every week at work. I started playing five-a-side football on a Monday night after work to try and keep the weight down a bit. It was a hopeless exercise but enjoyable nonetheless.

On Saturday, August 17th, 2003, the Premiership season got underway but we had to wait. Our game against Newcastle United at St James' Park had been selected by none other than Uncle Rupert for live transmission on, you've guessed it, Monday night. And so West Ham fans were screwed once again and made the long trip to Newcastle on a Monday, probably having to take two days holiday in the process. For me, it was a case of remaining sensible. Newcastle wasn't very far, I could have easily made it on a Monday night, but petrol, parking, match ticket, food and other associated costs were prohibitive. With the game also being shown live on Sky, I played five-a-side football that Monday night proudly sporting my West Ham shirt, drove home like the clappers and got showered and changed. Shauna had tea ready for me to gulp down and I made it to the pub just in time to park my bum on a prime seat, pint-in-hand, ready for kick-off.

We held on for about an hour. Looking back, it was hard to see how we managed to hold out so long. When Dailly and Shearer duelled on the edge of the box, there could only be one outcome. The fact the goal was struck off for a foul on Dailly was highly debatable, somewhat fortunate and merely delayed the inevitable. We showed some brief flashes of inspiration, Cole going on a mazy, jinking run before slamming a shot just past the post but those incidents were few and far between.

Opening games are often like cup-ties – both teams are well up for it and keen to show the fans, media and management alike they are a force to be reckoned with. Not so for West Ham. The Tuesday papers said we competed for an hour, then gave in. I beg to differ. Having seen the game from a sensible distance (i.e. not perched up on the Moon), I could see we were struggling from the first whistle and it was more by luck than judgement that we stayed level into the second half.

The fact the roof caved in and we conceded four in the last half an hour was typical. Had Newcastle been 2-0 up at half-time and finished the game at 4-0, you would have had to say it was fair. The fact all four goals came in the space of 25 minutes left a little bit of a bitter taste. Still it was the first of 38 games and there was plenty of time to put it all right.

But I was painfully aware that the last time we lost 4-0 on the opening day, we ended up relegated.

Home form would, no doubt be our saviour. There was every reason to believe that would be the case. A few more changes had taken place at Upton Park. To add to the MDF turrets hastily put up by Handy Andy in his coffee break (my, how the opposition must have cowered when they saw those imposing icons), a new presence had appeared pitch-side. The pitch itself had been moved the year before, to take account of the new stand. On the perimeter track, by the players' tunnel, there sat a huge West Ham badge bearing the legend "The Academy of Football, Founded in 1895."

Now I don't know about you but if I was a visiting supporter to Upton Park and saw that, I would piss my pants. The moment we lost our first home game it should have been removed. We are not in a position to crow about anything at West Ham. We do, of course, crow all the time about producing three World Cup-winning players. It's something to be proud of. But it's something to be proud of in an understated, modest way. Even the museum, opened the day we faced Arsenal, is a bit, well, in yer face. When a club the size of West Ham starts standing up and beating its chest, it just begs to be taken down a peg or two.

The other change I didn't like was the moving of the cameras from the rickety, old cradle in the roof of the East Stand, to the comfy confines of the new Doc Martens Stand. It confused everyone. Showboaters like Cole and Sinclair didn't know where to place themselves to show their best side and anyone watching on TV, who hadn't been to Upton Park for a while, was totally lost. What was the point?

The moving of the cameras and the stupid badge on the perimeter track didn't seem to distract the team as they set about destroying champions Arsenal. In a breathtaking display of one-touch, slick, fast-moving football, West Ham took a 2-0 lead through Cole and Kanouté and seemed destined to end Arsenal's unbeaten run stretching back to the previous December. Henry (or Terry 'Enry, as they call him in Yorkshire) scored a belter from the edge of the box and it was game-on again. Unfortunately, I was confined to watching the game on Teletext – possibly the most frustrating way to watch football.

The sight of a grown man sitting in front of a TV screen, urging a pixelated score to change, is not a pretty one. The score flashed up "West Ham 3 Arsenal 1 – scorer to follow." Then a couple of seconds later it read "West Ham 3 Arsenal 1 – Kanouté missed pen." This confused me. I wondered if he'd missed a penalty and then someone else had knocked in the rebound.

Then reality struck. "West Ham 2 Arsenal 1 – Kanouté missed pen." I wondered if I could sue Teletext for providing duff information. I knew at that point we would not win the game. Call me a pessimist but I have been a West Ham fan for far too long to be anything else.

As the final whistle approached, it looked as though we might do it. Against my better judgement I switched off Teletext and went to Final Score on *Grandstand*, where Ray Stubbs' cheery little mug informed me Arsenal's unbeaten record looked likely to remain intact, as Sylvain Wiltord had scored an equaliser. I cursed openly but knew there were still a couple of minutes of injury time left – still time for West Ham to f\*\*k up even more. They did their best, David James bravely diving at the feet of Kanu to prevent what would have been a real morale-sapping defeat.

I look upon this game as the one that changed the course of the season. Even though it was only the second game in, we were 2-0 up and then should have been 3-1 ahead against a team who hadn't lost since December. Our brand of football was impossible to combat when it was played right. To play that kind of football requires supreme confidence – not only in your own ability but also in the ability of your team-mates. Missing the penalty seemed to drain the confidence away. It was a poor penalty. Seaman had time to nip down the road for 20 Rothmans and come back in time to collect it with one hand tied behind his back.

One other item worthy of note: Barry Green came on in the 68th minute to make his debut. With the score delicately poised at 2-1, I had to question the wisdom of making such a fundamental change. I don't know if Nigel Winterburn was injured or not but what a situation to throw a player of questionable talent into? Herr Roeder obviously thought he was a superstar, or he wouldn't have given him a contract reportedly worth 30 grand a week. But I hadn't yet spoken to anyone else who thought he was anything other than an expensive liability. The sound heard as he took the pitch wasn't applause. It was the sound of 35,000 hands slapping 35,000 foreheads.

So, two games played, one point gained. Same as last season. Same results against the same teams – defeat at Newcastle and a draw at home to the Gooners. More goals conceded after two games but then, more scored, so swings and roundabouts, nothing to worry about. Charlton Athletic at home next – we beat them easily last year, so let's call that four points from three games. We're on our way.

Except, of course, it didn't quite work out that way. Once the Charlton players had composed themselves after falling about laughing at our 'Academy of Football' badge, they took a 2-0 lead into the half-time break that we didn't even look like denting, let alone overturning. It was real Keystone Cops stuff. James managed to miss a throw-in, for God's sake, and had it not been for Winterburn on the line to head clear, he could have kissed goodbye to England's No.1 spot. Our finishing was laughable, although I suppose we could console ourselves in the knowledge we had been making chances. It was a reversal of the game back in March, when we won 2-0 and Charlton couldn't score for toffee. It goes to show what goes around comes around and you should be humble in victory. Be nice to people on the way up, because you never know if you'll meet them on the way back down again.

A streaker ran across the pitch to provide the most entertaining incident of the afternoon. It was a game we should have won. "The two goals we conceded were our undoing," said Herr Roeder after the game. Really Glenn, is that so? You ever thought of going on *Mastermind*? I was prepared, still, to give everyone the benefit of the doubt. Only three games in, still everything to play for but, worryingly, we were bottom of the Premiership.

We'd been there before, I knew that. We were never usually the best of starters, so I wasn't too concerned but something was nagging away at me. Home form was our rock and so far we only had one point from six. We hadn't strengthened our defence. If anything, we had weakened it and we couldn't do anything about it until January because of this brilliant new idea of the transfer window. Quietly, I started to panic.

## 26. Starry Eyed Surprise

### Chelsea 2 West Ham United 3  28.9.02

A friendly international against Portugal at Villa Park meant there were 11 long days to wait before we could do anything about wrenching ourselves off the bottom of the table by beating newly-promoted West Bromwich Albion at Upton Park.

The Portugal game provided caps for James, Sinclair and Cole but provided nothing in terms of a spectacle. The locals in The Great Northern were much more interested in the inclusion of Leeds players Bowyer and Smith. Is it me, or do you think Smith wears lipstick? Go on, tell me you haven't noticed. I swear he used to play the part of a nurse in Casualty. He scored in the 1-1 draw but it was a waste of a Saturday afternoon.

Despite, in my eyes, having such a sh*te defence, four of them were on international duty that weekend. Unsurprisingly they all got bad results. Apart from James playing in goal for England, Dailly 'starred' in Scotland's 2-2 draw against the mighty Faroe Islands, Labant played for Slovakia in their 3-0 thumping in Turkey and Barry Green was instrumental in securing a 4-2 defeat for the Republic of Ireland in Moscow against Russia. Tremendous. How on earth did these players all get to be at the same club at the same time? I asked myself. They must be talented to have got this far, you don't get to such a high level without talent. But there was clearly something missing, be it drive, determination, concentration, something. It couldn't just be bad luck. Could it? .

Herr Roeder, meanwhile, kept morale up by looking forward to the opening of the transfer window due in January. "If I can get this particular target it will be a brilliant signing," he said confidently. Was he so desperate to sign Les Ferdinand? We needed signings now, not in January. Our lack of transfer dealing in the summer had left us desperately short at the back. It was no good having England class between the sticks and up front if the four defenders picked every week played like a bunch of schoolgirls.

West Bromwich Albion at home on a Wednesday evening meant we'd never have a better chance to get off the mark. Upton Park in midweek still provided an intimidating atmosphere despite the cardboard turrets and the joke badge. West Brom were new to it all and still had the decency to be impressed by the whole set up. It had been a good 11 years since we had played them in a competitive game at the Boleyn Ground and things had certainly changed a bit in the meantime.

What hadn't changed, though, was West Ham's ability to irritate and antagonise. Having blown Arsenal aside for the best part of an hour, we now struggled to get through against very average sides like Charlton and West Brom. The fit-again Parlow made his first start of the season, alongside Kanouté. The midfield of Cole, Carrick, Sinclair and Cissé should have been good enough to see off the majority of Premiership threats, particularly at home, but it was the middle two at the back, Repka and Barry Green, who were causing me the most concern. Was I the only person who could see their lack of ability sapping the confidence of everyone else in the team? I knew it wasn't only me because I still read the fanzines, still spoke to people whose opinions I respected and I still had eyes in my head. I could see something was terribly wrong but no-one seemed prepared to do anything about it. Certainly the two centre-backs didn't seem bothered as Jason Roberts scored in the 28th minute to notch West Brom's winner. I couldn't believe it.

As if being rooted to the bottom wasn't bad enough, we knew even a win at Spurs the following Sunday, on Uncle Rupert's super highway, wouldn't be enough to drag us up to 19th spot. Herr Roeder's response to the shocking display by our defenders had been to drop Carrick and reward all three doddering, clumsy incompetents with starting berths against Tottenham.

A West Ham side sporting a 4-4-2 formation, with Green, Repka and Dailly as three of the back four, did not exactly have me rubbing my hands with glee and expecting three points in the bag. I was not to be proved wrong. For the second away game running we held out for an hour before the roof caved in. Davies barged Dailly out of the way to nip in for their first. To his credit, Christian Dailly does have something about him in the opposition's half of the field and he headed on Parlow's pass for Kanouté to score an equaliser.

At this point of the game it would have been fair to say a draw would have been deserved. Neither team was exactly showing world-class defensive skills. Ian Pearce, back at the scene of his tremendous volleyed equaliser back in April, turned villain as he fouled Keane and got himself sent off in the process. Sheringham scored from the spot. So we were 2-1 down and with only 10 men, three of whom were Dailly, Repka and Barry Green. The odds didn't look good. Parlow, however, had other ideas. Sensing he may be about to be substituted, he took the game by the scruff of the neck and flighted a superb free-kick through the centre of the Spurs' defence. Trevor Sinclair had to stretch for it but as long as he connected, he would score. And score he did. I was delighted. I felt a point was deserved and would do morale the world of good.

I had forgotten though, about our suicidal defending and with two minutes to go, saw Gardner dancing his way through the West Ham half, with the ball at his feet but not under control. West Ham defenders chased but did nothing. No challenge came. By the time he reached the edge of the box it was too late. "Is someone going to challenge him or what?" I could hear myself shouting. I heard myself because I really was shouting out aloud. The eyes of the entire pub now stared at me in my West Ham shirt. They looked up at the screen in time to see Gardner let fly with a pathetic 20-yarder. It wouldn't have troubled James if it hadn't taken a wicked deflection off the shin of none other than the hapless Barry Green.

I wanted to cry. Shauna had joined me by this point and try as she might, she couldn't work out why it was so important. How could this football team have such a profound effect on me? Why was it, for instance, I felt compelled to point out every West Ham shirt I ever saw when I was out in town? Why did I go all misty eyed when I heard Irene Forsyte playing *I'm Forever Blowing Bubbles* in a 1920s Paris nightclub on TV. And why was it I got so excited when I saw Alfie Moon or Billy Mitchell on *Eastenders* with a West Ham scarf on? Why was that? It was a question I had asked myself many times and had never been able to come up with the answer. So how was I going to explain it to someone who didn't understand? She wanted to understand, bless her, and I wanted to make her understand. But it's not easy.

It certainly isn't easy to explain why, as a grown man, you want to cry because your football team got beaten. It's not the fact we lost – we had done that often enough in the last 28 years for it not to hurt any more. It was the way we were losing, the fact the club seemed to be haemorrhaging, lying in agony on the street. People were passing by and saying: "Oh, they'll be all right" but I could see we were not going to be okay. We needed help and we needed it fast. It was like a bad dream. I was watching my best friend waste away and no one could hear my pleas for help.

At least we had Manchester City next, at home. With Kevin Keegan now at the helm, they had predictably been leaking goals and scoring them at the same rate. As we had been doing the same, I expected a goal feast at Upton Park. As always, though, this game is impossible to predict and it ended 0-0. Repka and Barry Green continued in defence, this time with Minto and Schemmel as full-backs, but I didn't see that combination of four doing anything on a long-term basis. Perhaps it was time to try something else – three centre-backs and two wing-backs perhaps? Both Schemmel and Pearce had proved they could play this system and I'd seen Steve Lomas play right wing-back at Anfield once and make it look as though he'd been doing it all his life. But Herr Roeder said it would be 4-4-2, so 4-4-2 it was. I was grateful for the point but we had now played four games at home and garnered a pathetic two points. That had to change if we were going to haul ourselves anywhere near safety.

It wasn't looking good for the trip to Stamford Bridge, where Chelsea were once again shaping up as contenders for a top four finish but lacked the consistency required to allow them to make a sustained challenge for the title. Despite consecutive heavy defeats at The Bridge, it has, over the last 10 years or so, been a comparatively rich source of points for us. I didn't hold out much hope, though, when I turned on the TV to see we were 1-0 down thanks to that man Hasselbaink again. I didn't want to know. I turned it off and went out. But it's never easy when you know West Ham are playing and you have access to the scores if you need them. I turned on the TV again, stunned to see we were 2-1 ahead with goals from Defoe and Parlow. No sooner had I tuned in, than Zola equalised from a free kick and, again, I waited for the inevitable.

When I first started supporting West Ham – I mean regularly supporting, going to games both home and away, in the early 80s – there used to be a Saturday afternoon football show on LBC Radio. I used to love LBC. All my friends listened to Capital or Radio One but I used to like LBC because it was talk radio with a sense of humour. They had good football coverage, especially of the local London teams. On Sunday nights there was a show called *Nightline* hosted by Tommy Boyd – he of the curly hair who used to present *Magpie*. It was a great show and appealed to my imagination, because despite the fact there were phone-in competitions, he always made you feel you were the only person listening – his 'avid listener'. There is a point to this, bear with me. On Saturday afternoons, the presenter of the sports show would say something along the lines of: "There's been a goal at Upton Park . . . which way has it gone? . . . Let's go over to Steve Tongue to find out...." Then there would be a pause, during which you would have time to produce a whole litter of kittens before being put out of your misery.

That's exactly what happened on this Saturday afternoon in September 2002. I was transported back to my bedroom in Clockhouse Road, Beckenham and my little silver Hitachi stereo was tuned to 97.3 FM and there was this voice saying: "Goal at Stamford Bridge – which way has it gone?"

I closed my eyes and lived the dream for a split second. "It's gone to West Ham," the reporter stated dramatically, as though San Marino had scored the winning goal against Brazil. That's how it felt. There were still seven long minutes to go. I knew how good West

Ham were at throwing it all away at the best of times, let alone in our present state. Barry Green and Tomas Repka were at the back so you can understand my pessimism. I watched, waited, turned the TV off, turned it on again, paced up and down, wanted to smoke, made a cup of coffee, poured it away, then made another, before the final score flashed through and we had won. "Make a point of watching *The Premiership* on ITV tonight for Parlow's first goal, it's a bit special." Never mind, I thought. Pipe LBC Radio to Yorkshire.

## 27. Down 4 U

**West Ham United 1 Birmingham City 2  5.10.02**

Parlow's goal had indeed been a bit special. Teeing up his own volley from 20 yards out, more like 25 to allow for the angle, it was the only true candidate for the September Goal of the Month. Had it not won, there would have been riots in Green Street. Mainly started by Parlow himself. It had been pretty much a one-man show. Kanouté had gone off injured after four minutes and Defoe equalised just before half-time but from then on it had been the Parlow show. It proved how important he was to West Ham United. Worryingly so. He was out of contract at the end of the season but, at 34 years of age, how much longer would he be able to put in sustained performances like that? All the time the defence kept playing the way they were, the more we needed his talents to get us out of jail.

At home in Bradford, things continued to improve. Having concentrated hard on clearing debts, it was time to give ourselves something positive to look forward to, so we got some holiday brochures and picked out a two-week break in Zante for the middle of June. Working for the Co-operative group had its bonuses, including a low-deposit and a staff discount, so I tucked the brochure in my bag, ready to go and make the booking at Monday lunchtime.

I was about five minutes away from leaving the office for the travel agents when I got an urgent phone call from Shauna telling me to hold everything. Her brother had announced he was marrying Terri in Cyprus in May. The holiday decision had been made for us. It was a close-run thing. There was no way we could have afforded two holidays, so it's as well Andrew decided to tell us 10 minutes *before* I made the booking for Zante, not 10 minutes after. Cyprus is a bit dearer than Greece, so we could only afford a week and we couldn't afford the five-star prices of the Grecian Park Hotel in Protarus, where they would be staying. But we figured they wouldn't want us under their noses anyway and opted for some studio apartments about 10 minutes down the road. The dates, May 4th-11th, meant being away for the last game of the season. I didn't care. I needed a holiday.

I also needed to see my West Ham. It had been a while since I had last been to a game. The last time I had been to so few games was in 1991-92. when I had to work most Saturdays. Back then, having found it was possible not to go, I made that choice more often than not, even when I was free to see the Hammers play. That year, I went to only three games and saw us win all three. We were relegated. I began to wonder if my absence was making the lads play so poorly now but, as I had been to loads of games the previous season and only seen us win once, I reasoned my presence had very little effect on anything. I was still keen to get to a game though.

As a reward to myself for managing to clear two store cards, one credit card and seriously reduce the balance on another, I allowed myself to go to Chesterfield for the Worthington Cup tie. Chesterfield isn't far from where I live and I was able to make it quite comfortably in time for kick-off. I settled down to watch the game expecting a renewed confidence to flow through the West Ham team following their exploits at Stamford Bridge at the weekend.

It didn't quite happen like that, although Jermain Defoe did score early on to settle any nerves. Tomas Repka and Barry Green continued to play like headless chickens at the back and it was by no means certain the game would be won in the 90 minutes. And it wasn't. At first hand I got to witness what had been going on in what I considered to be a shambles of a display. Shortly after half-time, Chesterfield equalised with a well taken shot after the defence had been split in half with a well executed pass. It shouldn't have been that easy against a Premiership side. Suddenly everyone got the jitters. David James fumbled a simple cross and almost pawed it into his own net. It was laughable, I found myself watching the last half-an-hour and penalties through my fingers, like a six-year-old watching an episode of *Dr. Who*. Michael Carrick deserves particular praise. Many fans in the early part of the season had singled him out after a dreadful drop in form. He was outstanding in midfield and scored the winning penalty to silence his critics and signal his return to form.

I drove back up the M1 having not quite satisfied my need to see West Ham back to full strength and in the peak of health. We had won the tie but not convincingly. Having said that, there have been many occasions when a more confident West Ham team might have lost the tie. With the first league win in the bag and through to the third round of the Worthington Cup, the next match, at home to Birmingham City, would be vital as an indicator on the way the season was likely to progress. It seemed impossible in early October we could be facing such a make-or-break game but that was the way I viewed it. It was vital we followed up our great win at Stamford Bridge with a home victory, especially as we then faced fellow strugglers Sunderland a fortnight later.

Birmingham City had arrived in the Premiership following a play-off final victory over Norwich City in May and were expected by many to make the journey straight back down. But any side managed by Steve Bruce is likely to be well organised and he had assembled a good squad of players. Love him or hate him, Savage is a good player to have on your side and he'd been acquired from Leicester City following their demise. Stan Lazaridis was well known to West Ham fans and many, myself included, felt we were wrong to let him go at all, let alone for just £1.5m. Other players like Stern John (what a great name that is!) and Morrison had made their mark at first division level and were acclimatising well to the rarefied atmosphere of the Premiership.

They had adapted far too well for my liking. They clearly had a stomach for a fight after netting a 90th minute equaliser at Anfield earlier in the season but on this occasion, they didn't need to fight, they simply had to turn up. Repka and Barry Green started their third game in a row as the centre-back pairing. This was fine as long as Birmingham decided not to come out of their own half. After four minutes, they scored. John passed Barry Green like he wasn't there, dribbled unchallenged along the by-line and drilled a low shot in at the far post. What was going on? Surely it would be disallowed? Surely everyone had stopped playing after a linesman's flag? No, we were simply crap.

The midfield and strikers were doing their best to overturn the situation. Cole equalised to take his personal tally for the season to two, doubling the number of goals he'd managed in the whole of the previous campaign. He'd obviously been practicing his shooting in his back garden over the summer. West Ham were playing well enough going forward – a beautiful free-flowing move saw a Parlow diving header whistle past the wrong side of the post by inches. We looked magnificent up front but you can't spend the whole game attacking and every time Birmingham came at us, they looked likely to score. John again did the damage just before half-time, bringing down a cross from Lazaridis and turning brilliantly to make Repka look like a statue before toe-poking the winner past James.

It wasn't so long ago I'd been locked in conversation with Stan Lazaridis outside St James' Park, Newcastle. He'd scored the winner in a tremendous 1-0 win for West Ham and he was telling me how petrified he was of flying and he didn't fancy the trip back to London by plane. I offered him my seat in the *OLAS* 4x4, which he politely declined. Still, I thought he might have remembered the offer before going and setting up the winner like that. Ungrateful sod. Strange, though. How can a man who comes from Australia and plies his trade in England get along in life if he's scared of flying? He must spend half his life on a plane.

Anyway, none of that mattered. What did matter was that West Ham were in serious, serious doo-doo. Five points from eight games set the pulse racing for all the wrong reasons. We'd lost at home to two of the teams tipped for relegation and scored only three goals at 'Fortress' Upton Park, as PA announcer Jeremy Nicholas had always referred to it the previous season. The cardboard turrets and Academy badge were starting to look somewhat tired already. The Sunday papers slaughtered us. They loved every minute of it and stuck the boot in at every opportunity. Uncle Rupert's Sky TV were only too keen to put us on the pedestal of live television. His newspapers were equally keen to rip us to shreds. Heads he won, tails we lost. "Repka and Breen produced shameful displays that were unacceptable at this level" wrote the *News of the World*. They may have been sticking the boot in but they were right and it could have been any paper making those comments. It was awful.

I was learning a lot about life in general now I had established my home in Yorkshire. The Yorkshire people have a very pragmatic view on life and don't suffer fools gladly. Therefore it would not have been prudent for me to start moaning about not having any money if I still smoked 20 fags a day and ran two cars. Shauna and I held regular money meetings in which she would shame me into making sure I was keeping my eye on the ball. That may sound a little cruel but it's the kind of treatment I needed to get out of my current rut. I suggested we cut a significant monthly outgoing by getting rid of both our cars and buying a new one to share between us. I agreed to get the train in to Manchester every day. Although it would cost roughly the same as petrol, I wouldn't have to park anywhere, I could read, write, or, as it turned out, mainly snooze on the train and wouldn't be putting 84 miles a day on the milometer. Actually, that wasn't quite right. The speedo had broken about six months ago. I must have done 5,000 miles in the car without the milometer budging an inch. Still, as it was on 134,000 already, I figured it could do with a rest.

Shauna handed her Ford Ka back to the finance company, I traded in my Mondeo and we got ourselves a nice, little black Fiesta. Much cheaper to run, insure and maintain. God I was getting sensible. And not before time, either. If we were both going to achieve what we wanted out of life – nice house, wedding, kids, for Shauna to have the time to pursue her interior design and soft furnishing dreams and for me to go to football again on a regular basis – we would both have to make sacrifices in the meantime. It was hard, though, and I felt particularly guilty about making Shauna give up so much, especially as she hadn't realised the mess I was in when she met me. It made me love her all the more and be more determined to put it all right.

Having taken out a train season ticket loan through

work for £1,500, it might not have been the best time to start looking around for another job. It probably wasn't a good idea anyway. I loved the job I had in Manchester, it was something I could do and do well. I took a pride in my work and enjoyed the daily banter with my colleagues. But although the pay was reasonable, promotion chances were limited and I was aware I could do more to try and ease the financial situation. If I could get a job in Leeds earning roughly the same money, then I'd save £160 a month at a stroke in train fares alone. I started to look around, even though it would probably mean working with Leeds fans and being thoroughly depressed all the time.

Of course, money troubles never entered the head of Barry Green. His only problem was how he could spend the ridiculous salary he'd reportedly been put on. It was enough to make you weep. He earned more in a week than I did in a year and he was making a complete mess of his job. If I'd performed like that in my job I'd be looking for a new one on Monday morning. The whole thing stank.

They say that after the Lord Mayor's Show comes the Corporation dustcart. That was certainly the case for the England team, who had come home from Japan on the crest of a wave after beating arch-enemies Argentina and being considered a bit unfortunate to be eliminated in the quarter-finals by the eventual winners. In Slovakia, the first qualifier for the next major tournament, Euro 2004, England struggled to find any rhythm or consistency but still somehow managed to win 2-1. They were not so fortunate against lowly Macedonia the following Wednesday, when a 2-2 draw was all they could muster at Southampton. Of the West Ham trio featuring in the Far East, only James made the squad for these two qualifying games. Sinclair had withdrawn through injury and Cole had been unfortunately dropped back to the U-21 squad.

I had told myself the game against Birmingham City had been an important indicator of the way the season would progress from here on but as we had lost it, I had decided it wasn't so vital. What really mattered was the game against Sunderland at the Stadium of Light. The result would determine whether we had the courage and determination to stay up. As it happened, we won the game 1-0, so I was pleased to report to myself West Ham were back in rude health and well on the way to mid-table security.

Parlow had again been instrumental, swivelling on a sixpence to ping a 50-yard pass diagonally across the pitch and right into the path of the onrushing Sinclair. Brilliant though the pass was, Sincs still had a lot to do but, without thinking too much about it, rifled a rising shot into the roof of the net from the edge of the box. Pleasing though it was to see, it was irritating to know he was capable of such brilliance, when on so many occasions I'd seen him shoot and miss instead of laying it off to a better-placed colleague.

I was prepared to let this one ride, however. This was important psychologically. The three points lifted us off the bottom of the table and gave us our second win of the season. Not only that, it was the first game Howard Wilkinson had taken charge of as the new Sunderland boss after the sacking of Peter Reid.

This often happens to us. I think Premiership chairmen must deliberately time the sackings of their managers to coincide with West Ham's visit. Coventry City's first game under Ron Atkinson resulted in a 2-0 win for them at Highfield Road. Southampton's first match under Glenn Hoddle ended in a 2-1 win for the Saints at The Dell. The impetus of a new manager often produces such performances – when a team might not have won for months, a new gaffer comes in and suddenly they look like world-beaters. I fretted that Wilkinson might have the same effect on Sunderland. He was a scary man indeed but was also old school and didn't have the backing of the fans. We weren't to know it at the time but Sunderland were possibly the worst team in Premiership history. No, not possibly, they were the worst team in Premiership history, as their final tally of a meagre 19 points would illustrate. It was also easy to forget Niall Quinn had come within a whisker of equalising 15 minutes from the end, when his lob hit a post. But a win is a win and we weren't in a position to be picky. The three points shot us up to 16th place in the table and gave us the opportunity to re-group.

Premiership wins are a bit like buses. Nothing for ages, then two come along one behind the other. Away again, this time in a rearranged fixture at Fulham. Or rather, a re-arranged fixture at QPR. Fulham were playing their home matches at Loftus Road while Craven Cottage was being redeveloped. While West Ham turned up looking somewhat bewildered and still trying to pick up the threads of their season, Fulham were already well into their stride having started the season early playing in the Intertoto cup.

In the end, another 1-0 victory was only gained thanks to a last minute penalty from Parlow but victory should have been secured well before then. Parlow's uncharacteristic miss in the first half was followed by a typical Sinclair scissor kick that Van der Sar had to tip over the bar. Sinclair was playing a league fixture back on his old stamping ground for the first time since leaving QPR in January 1998 and he was loving every minute of it.

It might have been significant, it might not have, but in the 180 minutes of football played against Sunderland and Fulham, Barry Green was on the pitch for only 22 of them (including the bit when Quinn hit the post). I was starting to see a pattern emerging here. Herr Roeder had placed a lot of faith in Green by making him the club's major summer signing, just as Harry Redknapp had placed a lot of faith in Rigobert Song and Titi Camara. He'd trusted them with being the players purchased with the Rio money. He couldn't cast them aside as surplus to requirements. That would have shown him up to be a poor judge of a player, a man not to be trusted with the club's family silver. He had to keep the players he'd placed so much faith in involved without giving them enough responsibility to do any permanent damage. So, despite knowing deep down he'd made a f**k-up that made The Charge of the Light Brigade look like a typing error, Herr Roeder possibly knew he had to keep Barry Green in the squad and give him little tit-bits of action to justify his exorbitant wages and his very existence at the club.

Without him the team was doing okay, thanks very much. But at Premiership level there is a very thin line between success and failure and to succeed you need to put together longer and more frequent unbeaten runs. We didn't know it at the time but the win over Fulham at Loftus Road on October 23rd would be the last of 2002.

Uncle Rupert's empire had seen fit, for some reason, to show our home match against Everton on live TV the following Sunday. After two consecutive away wins, it was reasonable to suppose we could banish the demons that had haunted us in east London and finally secure a home victory.

The search for a new job had taken me to an open day with Yorkshire Bank on that very same Sunday. It was an informal gathering – for a general chat, brief interview and aptitude test – to see if it was the sort of thing that would suit both parties. I went along not expecting too much but was shocked to see so many familiar faces, people I had worked with in some capacity or another over the last couple of years. I had always thought CIS was a good company to work for. The only reason I wanted to move was a logistical one. I hadn't realised so many people wanted out. The job looked interesting but if I was being honest with myself, I didn't want to move. I was happy in my current post. It was costing an arm and a leg to get there and back every day. I was also spending up to four hours a day traveling. But when I thought about it, most people who live in the suburbs of London and commute into the West End or the City probably face a similar journey time, particularly if they have to travel into Liverpool Street. I decided to count my blessings but go along for the ride anyway with Yorkshire Bank to see what they would offer. If it was meant to be, it was meant to be. *Que Sera*.

Clearly a first home win of the season was not meant to be against Everton, that much was clear from the opening half an hour of a dour display. Whoever picked this one for live transmission was going to be back working on *Dream Team* on Monday morning. It is not a fixture renowned for its high levels of excitement. In fact it was a fixture renowned for Everton winning. Like Aston Villa, they always seemed to be a team we found hard to beat at home. Sinclair's deflected winner in the previous campaign had been only the third win over Everton in 10 attempts. Under David Moyes, Everton were a much more organised outfit all round and, in Wayne Rooney, they had one of the most prodigious young talents to hit the Premiership, probably since Michael Owen. He had succeeded where we had failed, in ending Arsenal's unbeaten run with a spectacular goal launching his career with a bang. It was to be hoped, for his sake, he would keep it up – but not for the moment.

Rooney's appearance, however, did change the

course of a game that was heading for a stale 0-0 draw. David Unsworth, the rhinoceros who had played for us during 1997-98, put in a deep, hanging cross, which was met powerfully at the far post by Carsley's head. As far as I could see, that was it. We'd not shown much in the way of attacking flair, pumping a lot of high balls up the pitch, by-passing our most talented players and asking the likes of Parlow and Sinclair to battle it out in the air with growlers like Unsworth and Stubbs. It wasn't going to happen. Joe Cole had formed a worrying habit of beating three men, drifting inside and unleashing an unstoppable shot – wide.

For the first time, the Upton Park faithful began to show their discontent. They had given Herr Roeder the benefit of the doubt in the earlier matches at Upton Park but after six games without a win, it was getting ridiculous. The home crowd at West Ham had got used to seeing their team win more often than not. Now they weren't seeing them win at all. Although 16th place in the Premiership was not a disaster for a team that hadn't won at home all season, the mutterings of disapproval were beginning to become audible. It wasn't prudent for any team, let alone West Ham United, to rely on away form. We'd already had our allotted three away wins for the season anyway – and Anfield was coming up next.

## 28. It's All Gravy

**West Ham United 3 Leeds United 4  10.11.02**

I might never see my beloved West Ham win at Anfield but no one can ever tell me it was for a lack of effort on my part. I had been to Anfield each and every year since promotion to the Premiership in 1993 and had made a few more trips before then. The nearest I had come to seeing us win was a 2-2 draw in February 1999. Had Trevor Sinclair squared the ball instead of blazing over, we might have won 3-2 and the name of debutant striker Gavin Holligan would be forever enshrined in Upton Park folklore. Thanks a lot, Trevor. Gavin, now wandering anonymously at Wycombe, sends his regards by the way. Because of that terrible effort, I found myself trailing over the Pennines once again towards fortress Anfield, looking for the Holy Grail of a West Ham victory. Having won our last three away games, there was every possibility – but then 'This is Anfield', as their much more tasteful and intimidating sign says – and we hadn't won there since late September back in '63 when Gerry and the Pacemakers were at number one. I wasn't born then, so I was determined to be around when it happened again, and I will keep going to Anfield at every opportunity until I see it happen. It will, one day.

Not today. Owen was once again proving to be a bit of a pain in the arse. On a wet, slippery pitch, England's top striker made his ambitions clear early on by pouncing on a slip by Repka and driving a terrific shot in from the edge of the box that James did well to tip over. It seemed Repka had also made his intentions very clear – to play like a complete wan*er. I didn't see what rating he got in the *News of the World* the following day but it couldn't have been much more than the resounding zero he got for the game against Birmingham. How embarrassing was that? I had never seen anyone get a big fat zilch before, although I stopped reading the paper too closely after that.

It made me wonder what Repka would have to do before Herr Roeder dropped him. Shoot someone? Score a hat-trick of own goals? This was a player who had cost West Ham United £5million. He was not some dodgy third division Bambi bought on a wing and a prayer. This guy was supposed to be international class. The true picture was starting to emerge in my mind. Fiorentina had to sell because they were facing bankruptcy. Repka hadn't wanted to come but Ludo had told him what a great club West Ham was and he'd relented. Cheers, Ludo. His sending off while playing for the Czech Republic against Belgium in a World Cup play-off match meant he was unlikely to ever represent his home nation again. His dismissal had cost his country the game and a place in the 2002 World Cup finals. And here he was, on his back-side, on the edge of the penalty area at Anfield, letting Owen skip through like it was a practice match.

To be fair to Repka, Owen was on fire and maybe Tomas was proving to be something of a scapegoat for West Ham's results, especially as Barry Green had largely been confined to the bench in recent weeks. Scapegoat or not, it didn't help that his performances were so far below the acceptable standard it was an insult to the people who had paid good money to come and watch. I knew for a fact there were two or three people sitting in the West Ham section of the crowd at Anfield who could, and would, given the chance, have played better than Tomas Repka at that moment.

Owen jumped over Repka's challenge on 28 minutes like he hadn't been there at all. A pity he hadn't made contact. It would have taken both Owen and Repka out of the game – one on a stretcher and one with a red card. We'd have had a fighting chance. Not only that, Repka would have been suspended for three games. Oh, hang on, Barry Green was there to take over. As you were, Tomas.

Steve Lomas is normally a reliable sort of character, the sort of bloke you want to have in your midfield. But you wouldn't put your house on him to score, even from three yards. He had a brilliant chance to equalise just after half-time but scuffed his shot weakly at Dudek in the Liverpool goal. Herr Roeder had stuck rigidly with a 4-4-2 formation and played Sinclair and Defoe up front. A bit of a luxury at Anfield, I thought, particularly as Sincs wasn't an out-and-out striker and, under the circumstances, it might have been better to play a target man up front on his own. But who did we have that we could genuinely call a target man, who was fit enough to play? The squad was wafer thin and couldn't cope with the growing injury list. Personally I would have played Repka up front on his own. He could have done less damage up there.

Liverpool's second owed more to the Harold Lloyd School of Comedy than the Michael Owen School of Soccer Skills. Having dragged the ball past James to a wide angle at the edge of the box, he hit a weak shot that defender after defender tried to keep out but seemed to be fazed by the lack of pace on the ball and missed it completely. Christian Dailly arrived at the last minute, like a cavalry charge in full flow. But instead of making a last-ditch clearance, he merely helped to carry the ball over the line. It was farcical.

Technically, the introduction of Titi Camara should have improved things. He was the target man we needed. If only he'd been any good. The word 'poncing' is over-used in football sometimes but, despite the motivation of being back at Anfield, Camara did just that, poncing about up front and making himself as useful as an ashtray on a motorbike. It could have been much worse. Liverpool were about to embark on a barren home run of their own – the signs were already there that they might lack the killer instinct needed to secure a Champions League spot.

The immediate future held few comforts for the Hammers. Home games against Leeds United and Manchester United beckoned but first there was the mild relief of the third round of the Worthington Cup and a home tie against Oldham Athletic. Oldham were flying in the second division and with former Hammers Iain Dowie and David Cross forming the management/coaching team at Boundary Park, the game had upset written all over it. My hopes of a place in the fourth round were further dented when I saw the team sheet included our old friend Barry Green.

Once again we played with no particular fluidity and with no confidence at the back whatsoever. The crisis that started with the defence was now spreading its malaise through the rest of the team and the midfield was starting to look decidedly dodgy. To add insult to injury, Camara made a rare start up front in another 4-4-2 formation showing no signs of adapting to Oldham's more flexible approach with wing-backs. It was only a surprise we waited as long as the 41st minute to concede the winning goal.

I hung my head in shame at work the next day. Sometimes you can shrug off a bad result, put it down to bad luck or an off day. This was bordering on pure incompetence and was making me very uncomfortable indeed. The fears I'd tried not to harbour following the 2-2 draw at home to Arsenal had faded after the three consecutive away wins but were now back in full view. I had thought incompetent defending had a limit. I had thought, after three, four, five or six similar displays, something would be done. Someone would be given a rocket that would send them to Mars and back by the time Leeds United showed up on Sunday. Apparently not.

Exactly what happened in the first 45 minutes against Leeds is hard to explain but it's significant that United themselves were experiencing a few problems at the time and had we been playing a side on their mettle we could well have been 10-0 down at half-time. You might think I'm exaggerating. If you didn't see the game, take a look at the video. On second thoughts, don't. I couldn't handle the responsibility.

Watching a game surrounded by opposing fans is an uncomfortable experience at the best of times. Add to the mixture the fact this was Leeds United playing at the home of MY team and you'll start to understand what an unpleasant afternoon this was. Add even further into the mix, a good few pints of alcohol, my inability to keep my trap shut or my hands in my pockets, and you've got double trouble. Now add the fact West Ham was playing possibly the worst football I had ever seen. I was in purgatory.

To say it was the worst football I had ever seen West Ham play is a bold statement and needs some qualification. I watched the Hammers struggle badly under John Lyall in 1988-89 and again under Billy Bonds in 1991-92. We played some awful football in those long, dark days. I saw us lose 2-0 at home to Oldham under Lou Macari and I thought I'd never see us score again. Some of the football we played in November 1994 under Harry Redknapp was utter pish. But there was no excuse for this.

The quality of player we had at the club was exponentially better than anything we'd had under Lyall, Bonds or Macari. The opposition on this occasion was not particularly brilliant. We certainly should not have been 4-1 down at half-time and had we been concentrating, we wouldn't have been. The Leeds fans in the pub were crowing. By now they had realised I was a West Ham fan - not just by my reaction to Parlow's 20th minute equaliser but by the claret and blue shirt I proudly, but foolishly, wore to the pub. I was on my own in there. The other Bradford-based West Ham fans had clearly decided they couldn't take it any more, or, even worse, had made the trip to London.

Barmby had given Leeds the lead with a diving header after a defensive mix-up between James, Dailly and Pearce. Parlow's equaliser turned out to be nothing more than a stay of execution. Each time Leeds scored they stroked the ball into an empty net. It was so humiliating, I wanted to leave – but in those situations something makes you want to stay. You feel so unwelcome and yet the game is being played on your turf, so it was the snarling Leeds fans who should have been made to feel unwelcome. So I stayed and ordered another pint in my broadest London accent. Comments like: "We could do with another one, 4-1 is a dodgy old lead in football," didn't deter me. I wanted to be there when the fightback came. Even though, in reality, I didn't think it would.

At last Herr Roeder made the change I had been dying to see and Repka was taken off at half-time. Without him or Barry Green the team started to splutter into life, pinning Leeds back in their own half. Parlow scored from the spot on 49 minutes after winning the penalty himself and it was game-on. Sinclair had injured a cheekbone and wore a protective mask. Looking for all the world like Biggles, he flew his Sopwith Camel in at the near post to narrow the gap to one goal with 16 minutes to go and suddenly it was nail-biting stuff.

By now the tension in the pub was so real you could have cut it with a knife. The Leeds fans didn't like this one bit and started venting their frustrations on me and Terry Venables. The "Little cockney wan*er" gave them an excuse to have a dig at me while staring at the screen and pretending it was aimed at the former England boss they adored after Euro 96. Leeds fans have a sense of humour similar to the average German at the best of times but now they were simply nasty. Half of me urged West Ham to equalise. Half of me urged them not to. It was getting heated. In the end, I decided an equaliser would be worth the risk. What the hell, I thought to myself. "Come on you Irons!" I yelled. "This lot are bricking it!" It all went quiet, which suited me fine. It shut up those mouthy little tw*ts but I reckon, had an equaliser gone in, I might have left the pub feet-first. In a box.

Despite going close in the last 16 minutes, the equaliser didn't come and I was able to leave without the aid of a paramedic. It was a frightening experience, though, and a damn sight more dangerous than simply watching a game in the wrong section of the crowd.

The experience of watching the game and the exhilarating display in the second half had made me forget the shambles of the first half. I couldn't understand why things were being allowed to continue. Why hadn't someone – anyone – been fired? I had sympathy for Herr Roeder, though. He was doing a difficult job but his refusal to budge from 4-4-2 had, I was sure, cost us a few games. His determination to stick with the likes of Repka, Dailly and Barry Green, when they were clearly off-form, was nothing short of suicide. Granted, he had few choices within the squad but with regular performances like that, surely he had nothing to lose by changing the shape, the personnel or both. Surely he could try something a bit different? The transfer window wouldn't open for another two months. We needed points now.

When Redknapp stuck like mud to a blanket with his 5-3-2 formations away from home, I was hollering for 4-4-2. All I wanted was a bit of variation. A bit of thought and planning being given to each match and the best combination of players and tactics to achieve a result other than a calamitous defeat. I'm sure Herr Roeder was as meticulous as the next man. But it wasn't showing. Not in late November 2002. West Ham were in the soft and smelly, big style.

Meanwhile, the subject occupying the thoughts of most Hammers fans over the last couple of years reared its ugly head again – that of Parlow's contract. It was due to expire in June 2003 but it seemed the club were in no hurry to start talks about renewing it. As ever, Parlow was very public in his thoughts and, to be fair, he had a point. This man was the darling of the fans. He had provided some cherished moments since his arrival in January 1999. It seemed the least the board could do would be to talk to him about a new contract.

But he was getting on. Thirty-four is pushing it a bit for a striker, although there have been notable exceptions, Parlow was starting to spend more time on the treatment table than on the pitch. Then there was the very real threat of relegation. It seemed unbelievable that contingency plans were already being made for the drop, especially as we now had go-faster cardboard turrets and a sign by the pitch to strike fear into the hearts of every opponent. But that was the way it appeared to me.

Another goal against Manchester United and a first home victory over them in 10 attempts might have strengthened Parlow's case. United arrived the following

Sunday and the atmosphere in the pub couldn't have been more different as the majority of Leeds fans present took the side of West Ham United. They were certainly looking smug, as the team they had stuffed so comprehensively seven days earlier put up a decent show against United, unfortunate to be trailing to a Van Nistelrooy goal just before half-time. This time, Hammers did not give up but pounded away until they got what they deserved, an 86th minute equaliser from Jermain Defoe. There was some speculation he had been offside, which spoiled things a bit, but then I'd thought Van Nistelrooy had been offside for his goal and no-one seemed to make much mention of that. It was frustrating West Ham always seemed to put on a decent display against United but when it came to games they should win, like against Leeds United at home, they always seemed to fail miserably.

Aston Villa were certainly a side we were capable of beating. They hadn't been setting the world on fire since Graham Taylor's return. Villa were often on a similar level to us and the games were always tight. We should at least have been able to get a draw, not the 4-1 mauling we eventually suffered. What upset me the most about this defeat was the fact it was probably close to what I considered to be our best team at the time. With James in goal and a back four of Schemmel, Dailly, Pearce and Winterburn. Dailly was without a doubt the best of the three dodgy centre-halves we had and I've always liked Ian Pearce. Winterburn was always dependable at left-back even if he was starting to show his age a little at times. Schemmel had been one of the biggest disappointments of the season so far. Voted Hammer-of-the-Year back in May, he was struggling to reproduce the form that had earned him that deserved accolade. Reports suggested his family had been struggling to adapt to the English way of life and he'd sent them back to France. It was hardly surprising this would have an effect on his form.

He seemed to be playing okay against Villa, though, as he put in a teasing cross Enckleman could only push into the path of Joe Cole. His finishing still needed some work. Had that gone in it might have been a different story but, instead, Villa opened the scoring on the half hour and it was the same script all over again. An almighty collapse with only a far-post diving header from Parlow to take home with us.

We were back on the bottom with not very much to look forward to. November had been a terrible month. December was not traditionally any better. With a mere 12 points from 15 games, there can be little doubt we deserved to be there. But just when we thought things were bleak, they got a whole lot worse.

# 29. Lose Yourself

**West Ham United 0 Southampton 1  2.12.02**

Southampton at Upton Park probably represented our best chance of a home win in recent weeks. I couldn't believe we had now reached December without a home victory. Not only was it unbelievable, it was highly embarrassing. Even those clubs around us, who we considered to be relegation fodder at the start of the season, had managed to win at home. West Bromwich Albion, Birmingham City and Bolton Wanderers had all managed to do it but not West Ham, the team with one of the best home records the previous year. It was scandalous. The longer it went on, though, it seemed the bigger the mental block and the harder it became. For the third time in four games Uncle Rupert sent along his cameras to capture the action live. Again, it seemed to be a strange choice but the TV people clearly liked us. The quality of the football might not be fantastic but there were always plenty of goals. The shambolic defending also always gave Andy Gray something to wet his pants over.

This game was no exception. Parlow had been struggling with his fitness for some time and it was starting to show. He dropped back into midfield and with Fredi Kanouté still on the long-term injured list, Ian Pearce surprisingly took an eleventh hour striking role up front. You could say it was indicative of the quality of the squad at the time that a defender had to play up front. Indeed, Titi Camara, supposedly a striker, was sitting on the bench and therefore was not considered worthy of a starting position. Honest. No one who had seen him play thought he was worthy of a starting position. So what was he even doing on the bench? What was he even doing at the club?

Pearce had started his career as a striker at Chelsea and then Blackburn Rovers (he scored the winner for Rovers at Upton Park in 1993-94) but he'd found his preferred role at the back and Harry Redknapp had brought him to Upton Park as a defender. I'd seen him take on most roles at the back and deal with them in his stride. Against Leeds United in 1997-98, he played at right wing-back and looked England class, scoring in a 3-0 win. When he came forward, he did so to great effect and he had quite a few goals to his name, so it wasn't a surprise – or a total disappointment – to see him start up front against Southampton.

It backfired though. We had one gilt-edged chance in the first half. It fell to Pearce – an incredible 33/1 to score the first goal – and although he got his shot on target, Saints' keeper Niemi, who was having a blinder, kept it out, much to the relief of the bookies facing ruin following a late avalanche of bets on the makeshift striker. Stuart the QPR fan was watching the game from a pub in Euston, waiting for a train back to Peterborough. It was as though he knew what was going to happen. I certainly knew what was going to happen. He sent me a text telling us to stay strong. I sent him one back. It's still on my phone to this day: "We lk doomed. Soton to score in last min. Put shirt on it. Spk l8er."

At 0-0 with a few minutes to go, I would have been grateful just to keep a clean sheet and avoid defeat. Herr Roeder prowled the technical area, tapping his head with his index finger, as he often did when drawing with a few minutes to go. He was either saying:

"Concentrate!" or "You're all f**king mental, you are!" Either would have been appropriate but I can't help thinking they were all too busy staring at him tapping his head to notice Beattie sliding in for the winning goal seconds from the end. It was a killer. I supped up and went straight home. Stuart the QPR fan rang me and we had a long chat. He could see what was going to happen. That was the point at which I knew for sure what was going to happen, too.

Pearce continued up front for the next game, against Middlesbrough at The Riverside. Not a traditionally rich source of points, he scored West Ham's second goal to give them a 2-1 lead with 13 minutes to go. Joe Cole had given us a first half lead, cancelled out by Nemeth just after the break. But Boro had been struggling as well and West Ham had more than matched them in every department. Pearce's goal was well deserved and it looked like a rare victory at Middlesbrough was in the bag. But although West Ham have been around as a football club for over 100 years, they have yet to learn that a game is played over 90 minutes. Not 87, nor 88. Ehiogu climbed high above the defence with three minutes to go to nod an equaliser and Cole's first game as captain ended in disappointment. Despite Barry Green coming on in the last minute, we still managed to hang on for a point and, in our perilous position, a point away from home was better than a smack in the mouth. But when it was so nearly the three that would have taken us off the bottom, it felt like a smack in the mouth.

Cole had been an interesting choice as captain. In the absence of Parlow and Steve Lomas there were, perhaps, more obvious, experienced options. But if you believe your best player should be captain and he should lead by example, then Joey Cole was the perfect choice. He did lead by example, too, scoring the opening goal and having one of his better away games that so nearly ended in victory.

The next game, at Old Trafford, was a case of damage limitation. With a goal difference already standing at a colossal minus 13, a huge defeat was not going to do us any favours in terms of morale, let alone our chances of survival. Our goal difference was significantly worse than our close relegation rivals, so, effectively, another point that had to be made up. Less said about Old Trafford the better. A 12.15pm kick-off suited no one. Even those Manchester United fans in the office who came from Manchester and went to games were starting to get cheesed off at their regular Saturday lunchtime slot. I had to admit, had it been us I would have been a bit miffed, too. It messes up the whole of the day and you haven't got enough time to get so pissed you can't clearly see the shambolic defending that was making your heart bleed.

I watched the game in the pub with Andrew, counting the seconds until the point we went behind. I didn't have to wait long. Solskjaer scored on a quarter of an hour and Veron added a second two minutes later from a well taken free kick, given away clumsily by reckless Repka. Veron is a funny looking bloke, isn't he? I always expect to see him wearing a cape and laughing menacingly. He belongs in a *Batman* film. It wasn't important when Defoe scored a perfectly good goal just before half-time but it was ruled out for offside. The replays showed the linesman had been wrong. But I hardly think a 3-2 victory would have followed had it been allowed to stand. It might have helped the goal difference, though, and scoring a goal at Old Trafford is almost as good as winning in terms of morale. I was upset that the officials seemed to be picking on us again. We were too weak and feeble to defend ourselves. Schemmel added an own goal on the hour and for a moment it looked as though the roof might cave in. But, mercifully, most of the United players clearly had plans for the afternoon and didn't want to over-exert themselves, so they settled for 3-0. A quick shower, then down to the golf course. It's a hard life.

The home game against Bolton Wanderers was taking on the significance of a cup final. Beating them was so vital for many reasons. It would have given us our first home win. It would have stopped us getting cast adrift from the other struggling teams at the foot of the table. And it would have allowed us to go into Christmas with a reason to be cheerful. Simon and Julie, Bolton fans at work, were diplomatic about the whole thing. But they must have fancied their chances.

They must have fancied them even more when they saw the dodgy Mr Repka lining up in defence and a makeshift striker in Ian Pearce playing up front. Pearcey had scored a late winner against Bolton in the final game of last season, so maybe he would be a lucky omen for us. Having run out of people to blame, I was now starting to think we were plain unfortunate. With Parlow and Kanouté still on the sidelines, Defoe and Pearce huffed and puffed away up front manfully. Pearce got his reward after 17 minutes. He took it like a natural striker, picking up a flick-on from Defoe, cutting inside and banging home a low shot from 15 yards. Makeshift he may have been, but he knew what he was doing.

It was vital to hang on. These three points were the most precious of the season so far, we simply could not afford another slip up. So what did we do? We slipped up. It was one of those can't-f**king-believe-it moments when no sooner had Michael Carrick hit a shot worthy of a goal and Defoe had spurned the rebound chance, Bolton raced up the other end and scored their equaliser.

The inquests had Ricketts marginally offside but that didn't give us three points. In any case, I don't think he was offside. The words straw, at and clutching sprang to mind. Herr Roeder's Ministry of Propaganda rolled into full swing. It was a well known fact no team bottom of the Premiership at Christmas had ever avoided relegation. It was such a well known fact, it was starting to piss me off big time. Herr Roeder declared this was the perfect motivation for the players, to prove history could be changed. The odds could be upset. He was missing the essential truth.

No team playing so badly over a five-month period had ever avoided the drop. That was the crucial point. Even if we turned into Brazil overnight, we were going to struggle to stay up. We needed points, not rhetoric. We needed players who could defend, not Tomas Repka and Barry Green. And we needed Parlow and Kanouté off the treatment table and back on the pitch. Not makeshift strikers. We needed the transfer window to open – and some inspired buys, not vicious and hurtful rumours about signing Les Ferdinand and Lee Bowyer.

I spent Christmas with the family in London. It was a wrench to be away from Shauna, who had opted to stay in Baildon with her mum, but it was only for a few days and our families are important to us both. We had our own mini-Christmas the day after the Bolton game, cooking a chicken instead of a turkey – there were only the two of us and Charlie – and exchanging presents by the Christmas tree. It was what I had dreamed about since the age of about 14 or 15. Me and the woman I love sharing a special Christmas together. It might sound stupid to you but all the years of heartache were finally being forgotten. I belonged and I loved it.

I was due back on Boxing Day, which meant I was able to take in the game against Fulham at Upton Park. They had been on a poor run and having won at Loftus Road earlier in the season (in fact it had been our last win of any description, if you've been concentrating), I had reason to be confident. With my talismanic presence, we would win the game. Games are labelled 'Must win' far too often in my view. The last six games had been 'must-win' with the exception perhaps of Old Trafford, which had been a 'must-avoid-a-spanking' game.

The afternoon started well enough with a drink in The Boleyn with Kev, the first time I'd seen him since last Christmas. He'd cut his hair and got rid of the fingerless mittens but I still struggled to believe he worked for a major insurance company by day. The game started well enough, too. Dailly had a header cleared off the line by Rufus Brevett but it was tight and Fulham ended the half on top. They took the lead just after the break and our world started to fall apart once again. It was such a bizarre and surreal experience. Upton Park, by now, was virtually unrecognisable to me. Three of the stands I stood in when I started going had been replaced. The team was littered with expensive superstars (and Barry Green). There were hideous cardboard turrets where the West Stand used to be and a stupid club badge by the side of the pitch telling the whole world how f**king brilliant we were. In reality, we hadn't won a home game for seven months, we were 1-0 down at home to Fulham and we were actually a pile of sh*te.

Sinclair equalised from the spot five minutes later but the surge in energy from the players didn't come. The must-win factor didn't seem to register with them. It was one thing among many others that I failed to recognise and I left Upton Park after the 1-1 draw wondering if it was now too late – I'd lost the club I loved so much. I don't mean I'd lost them in terms of going out of business. I mean I felt so strange to be there, like it wasn't my club any more. I had experienced the same feelings before a home game against Middlesbrough over Easter 2000. The seeds were definitely there. That day I hadn't seen one face in the crowd I recognised. On Boxing Day 2002, not only did I fail to recognise anyone in the stands, I failed to recognise the stadium and the team.

One good thing came out of the game. Repka opened his gob once too often in the dying minutes and was sent off. Three match ban – wicked.

There was one last hope. I dashed up the M1 and home to Shauna, persuading her to join me on a little trip to Blackburn on Saturday. I was going to give them one last chance to win back my trust. We couldn't afford it but I stretched and got us two tickets through work and we went along to the match at Ewood Park. It was the last game of 2002 and a chance to put the terrible start to the season behind us. I parked up in the usual spot and we went to the pub I always went to when visiting Blackburn. I knew we would probably lose but I was going to give them one more chance to prove me wrong, to show me why I should keep the faith, to give me one good reason why I shouldn't jack it all in. After all, Bradford City had a much more conveniently sited bunch of losers I could follow every week if I should so choose. I was like a Christian losing his faith and praying to God for a miracle.

The pub was full of familiar faces from away trips of old and it wasn't long before I was gassing away about old times and kick off was almost upon us. Blackburn always seems cold, even in August, but between Christmas and New Year it's bloody freezing, so we walked briskly to the away end and took our seats. I felt a warm glow I hadn't experienced before a football match for a couple of years. A tingle of anticipation, the thought, despite all that had gone before, we might get a result.

That all went out of the window after three minutes. David James has got hands the size of shovels but he couldn't manage to put one of them behind a Duff shot (quite literally) and allowed it to trickle past him into an empty net. The whole feel good factor started to dissolve, my heart sank and I found myself yelling "You're sh*t, West Ham!" at the top of my voice. Why? Why do I do this? Why spend all that money we didn't have on a game of football I knew, deep down, we would lose and then spend most of it yelling abuse at a team I was supposed to be supporting. I thought about it for a few minutes.

Joe Cole clattered down the left and fed Steve Lomas, whose shot was deflected into the net for a goal almost as stupid the first. I sat up. I'd been wrong to criticise. Anyone could make a mistake and, hey, it was Christmas. I decided to go with my original instinct – an upset was on the cards. West Ham played well, almost as well as the afternoon, in January 1995, when we led Rovers 2-1 at Ewood Park before finally succumbing to the champions-elect, 4-2. We were brilliant that afternoon in the face of adversity and although on this occasion, brilliant might have been pushing it, I was certainly pleased with the performance. We'd been hammered there 7-1 just over a year before and while those sort of scars take time to heal, they can galvanise a team into making sure lightning doesn't strike twice. It certainly didn't but Blackburn did, re-taking the lead through Andy Cole on 77 minutes. But now I had faith again. I had seen how well we had played and knew at the very least we wouldn't collapse.

The Pearce-Defoe combination up front was hardly going to win us the league but it produced more goals than people tend to remember. With four minutes left, Defoe latched on to a Pearcey knock-down, held off the defender well and slotted home from six yards. It was a wonderful moment. Okay, so the goal had done nothing more, in reality, than earn us a point. But it was worth much more psychologically. Blackburn was a venue where we traditionally got stuffed out of sight. The point meant we had drawn our last three games, four out of the last five. It was hardly European form but at least we were starting to pick up points. Maybe a turning point was around the corner. My faith had, to a large extent, been restored. I still knew our defence was about as much use as a condom machine in Vatican City but the transfer window was being unlocked and the hinges given a liberal squirt of WD-40. There was a light at the end of the tunnel. No team bottom of the Premiership at Christmas…. Yeah, yeah, whatever. Let's see.

## 30. Land Of The Living

**West Ham United 2 Blackburn Rovers 1  29.1.03**

The New Year recovery was supposed to start at The Valley, with three points against Charlton Athletic but the weather put paid to it and with it went my plans for an afternoon ensconced in front of the results service. I hate it when games get called off at short notice. Bottom lip out. Shauna had bought me a PlayStation 1 for Christmas – it got some hammer that afternoon.

It did at least mean we could forget about the stresses and strains of survival and concentrate on a good, old fashioned cup-tie. The home FA Cup third round match against Nottingham Forest had been eagerly anticipated both my former colleagues in Nottingham and myself since the draw had been made in early December. The barren run at home was now more than just an embarrassment, I was beginning to wonder if it was some sort of conspiracy.

For some reason Herr Roeder decided to stick with his tried but not-to-be-trusted 4-4-2 and made the even more baffling decision to start with Barry Green playing in central defence. The consequence, of course, was that we would concede goals but, as it happened, we were in the mood to keep up and it turned out to be a thrilling 90 minutes of football. David James made his contribution, proving his shocking lapse of concentration at Blackburn had not been a fluke by allowing a tame shot to wriggle under his body and

Forest were 1-0 up. Forest had a good side, challenging for a play-off place in the first division, and if anything, they might even have gone into the game as slight favourites. Their taking of the lead certainly came as no surprise but the teams were pretty evenly matched and Jermain Defoe stole an equaliser just before half-time.

But it seemed we were destined not to win at home again. Ever. Reid gave Forest the lead in the second half and not having scored more than two goals at home all season, it seemed a replay was the best we could hope for. But Joe Cole had other ideas and equalised again. Forest missed a penalty and it was left to Defoe to snatch a late winner, which was hard on Forest but meant so much to us.

Judging by the scenes after the final whistle, you'd think we'd won a quarter-final, not a third round tie against a side one division below us. But when you haven't won a game at home since May 11th and it's now January 4th, it was bloody important and it meant the world. It didn't matter it was a cup-tie against first division opposition. It was a win, our first of any description since October 23rd. I'd almost forgotten what it felt like.

In a reversion to tradition, which certainly got my vote, the draw for the fourth round of the FA Cup was held on a Monday lunchtime. There were several of us at work crouched over a crackly transistor radio, trying to hear who we'd got. I heard it all too clearly. Manchester United. Away.

Funnily enough, the United fans in the office were not too chuffed with the draw. The memory of Barthez directing the traffic in the six-yard box was still painfully fresh in their minds and they somehow felt lightning would strike twice. I wasn't so confident. Despite winning on two of our last three visits, I had to face the prospect of going out of the FA Cup in the fourth round for the second year running. No matter who we bought in the transfer market.

With the transfer window open once more the paper speculation turned out to be right and Herr Roeder unveiled our new signing, Lee Bowyer. I was underwhelmed. I'd heard the package he'd been promised, which apparently included a bonus of £1million if West Ham stayed up. I also heard he had been born in Poplar and had been a West Ham fan all his life. Funny, hadn't heard that before. Personally, I hated the bloke and I was ashamed to see him wearing the claret and blue. If this was the 'exciting transfer window signing' Herr Roeder had promised us back in September, then he was the only one getting excited.

This boy was Trouble with a capital 'T' and bother seemed to follow him around like a nasty smell. It wasn't necessarily his fault, some people have such an unfortunate disposition. I didn't want that unfortunate disposition at my club. Unimpressed as I was by Bowyer's signing, I still eagerly awaited the home match against Newcastle United, just in case he did make a difference. I wondered if my attitude would change if he proved to be the catalyst saving West Ham's season. I drifted off into a dream world where he played every game as though it was a cup final, scored 10 goals from outside the box and set up 20 more, did bucket loads of donkey work in midfield so Joe Cole could fully express himself and we ended up winning the FA Cup and finishing top half. Then I woke up.

Craig Bellamy put the Magpies 1-0 up and suddenly it was back to reality. You never see him and Lee Evans in the same room, do you?

To be fair, Newcastle's goal was somewhat against the run of play and Cole equalised a few minutes later, picking up a deflected Lomas throw-in and squeezing in a low shot. That took him to five for the season on my abacus. Maybe his finishing was finally starting to improve. Mind you, he was shooting enough. Too much, in fact. Still needed practice. Defoe nosed us in front just before half-time. And when James made a brilliant save just before the whistle, it seemed Newcastle would provide us with our first home win for the third season running. Bowyer wasn't outstanding in midfield but then he'd hardly played for five months. Not only did he look as though he'd stuck two fingers in the mains socket, he looked totally knackered as well.

Despite having some crummy results at home, we would end the season unbeaten at Upton Park by the top four, which makes the other results all the more bewildering.

A run of 12 home games without a win was never going to be easy to break and so it proved. Jenas scored his first ever Premiership goal – a blinder but it didn't make it any easier to accept. The goal knocked the stuffing out of us and although a point was enough to drag us off the bottom of the table, the more important factor had been the win. With a controversial signing like Bowyer making his debut, he had to be seen to be making an impact. I hoped, for his sake, he hadn't made too many plans for his £1million bonus.

I'd noticed towards the end of 2002 that I had something of a beer gut developing. I've always been chunky, for want of a better expression, but now, when I sat down, I had my own ready-made shelf to rest my dinner on. I weighed myself and, to my horror, found I was 14st 2lbs. It might not sound a lot but it's elephantine when you are only 5'5" in height. Part of it was probably due to stopping smoking up. But mainly it was down to being a lazy bastard and eating too much.

A free hot meal at work each lunchtime had not helped the waistline, particularly when nine times out of 10 it was pie and chips followed by evil sponge and custard. Something had to give. I changed my lunchtime eating habits and resolved to go running twice a week. Dr Atkins could take a hike – the Banksy diet was born.

The next game was another write-off. Arsenal away. It was one of those games we had won occasionally in the past but, these days, even a draw was out of the question. When Arsenal were mere pretenders to the crown we could sneak in there and f**k it up for them along with the best. But since they got their fancy French coach and the likes of Terry 'enry playing up front, a trip to Highbury was a different prospect. The game had again been selected for live TV on the assumption there would be a hatful of goals and it was a good chance to have a laugh at our expense.

I watched the game in the pub with Andrew and Paul, his best man's brother-in-law. It was a tenuous link but Paul was from Loughton and a big Hammers fan.

Officials used to give you the occasional break at Highbury, too, but not now. Steve Lomas' challenge on Pires was clumsy but nothing more than that. I wasn't even convinced it warranted a penalty, let alone a red card, but the referee gave both. The game was effectively over and I hadn't even finished my first pint.

It looked for a moment as though the floodgates could open. Arsenal could cut though us at will but just before half-time, Defoe gave us hope with an equaliser. He cut off a backpass from Edu and calmly netted. I half expected it to be disallowed but none of the officials was quick enough to think of anything, like: "Erm, you're not allowed more than one player in the Arsenal half" or "The ball didn't touch the netting" or "Sorry, I wasn't watching."

Normal service was resumed in the second half. Bowyer took a smack in the mouth from Bergkamp and was ignored by the referee. Maybe, like a lot of other people, he thought Bowyer deserved it for . . . being Lee

Bowyer. Or maybe, like a lot of people, he thought Beavis Bergkamp couldn't possibly perpetrate such a crime. He has a reputation for being an angel. Unwarranted, in my view. Remember his sending off for smashing Lomas in the gob in the 1998 FA Cup quarter-final? Anyway, Bowyer went crashing to the ground clutching his face and Bergkamp went on to cross for Terry 'enry to score the second and wrap up the game. The third goal was detail and meant we'd go crashing back to the bottom of the table.

Herr Roeder had at least tinkered with the formation in order to try and garner a result, taking Pearce out of the front line and returning him to the back to keep a terrified eye on Barry Green. Terry Venables might have called it a 'Christmas Tree' but I thought it looked more like 11 hopelessly outclassed footballers. Until Lomas got sent off, then we looked like 10 hopelessly outclassed footballers. I could see Herr Roeder's logic – keeping defence and midfield at four apiece, with Cole tucked in behind Defoe to help out in midfield when required (which, as it happened, was all of the game). Lomas being sent off rather messed up the game plan. It's tough being a football manager.

Herr Roeder then made the swoop of the century and brought in 84-year-old Les Ferdinand to spearhead the attack. I was devastated. Don't get me wrong, I like Ferdinand, he's a top bloke. When he played for QPR and Newcastle United he was one of the best strikers in the country. But then he was in his early 20s. I did not consider this a step forward. Andrew sent the news through to me in the form of a text message. I felt a tear welling in my eye. This was it. We really were going down.

At least it meant Ian Pearce could get back to doing what he did best, sorting out the mess made by Repka and Barry Green at the back. At Charlton, in the rearranged game, Teletext had West Ham's opener down as being scored by Edouard Cissé but it was later credited as a Rufus o.g. Now we were so bad we couldn't even score goals for ourselves. Charlton were in front by half-time and it looked as though a repeat of last season's classic 4-4 might be on the cards. Had it not been for the fact Paul Kitson, a desperately needed striker, had gone to Brighton a few months earlier, it may well have happened. Instead Charlton, and Parker in particular, ran riot and took a 3-1 lead. Teletext thought Trevor Sinclair had pulled one back but it turned out to be an own goal from Mark Fish. Even better! Now we could only get goals from aquatic animals. It was farcical.

The game ended 4-2 to Charlton and was not the confidence booster we needed before a televised trip to Old Trafford. Ferdinand had, however, played well and showed part of the problem had been with the strikers not holding the ball up properly. Sir Les showed how it should be done.

The other ray of hope to emerge from an otherwise miserable night at The Valley was the debut of young Glen Johnson. Johnson had been recalled from a loan spell at Millwall, where he had received rave reviews. An England U-20 international, he looked calm and assured in the right-back position and offered the chance of better things to come if he was given a decent run in the side. The most significant piece of transfer news, though, was a departure, not an arrival. We finally found a club stupid enough to take Titi Camara on loan. The fact they were Al-Ittihad from Saudi Arabia spoke volumes. He scored a hat-trick in his first game, although the rumour was it was against a local camel drivers XI.

Significantly, neither Ferdinand nor Johnson started against Manchester United the following Sunday. 'Sir

Les' had not been signed in time and Johnson was on the bench. Herr Roeder stuck with the 4-4-1-1 'headless chicken' formation that would have been the undoing of Arsenal if only that pesky referee hadn't got involved.

I'd had a ticket for the game for some time, so had Andrew and Paul. It had been my idea to get the train. I travelled by train every day from Bradford to Manchester and back and while I experienced the odd delay here and there, never suffered anything major. But there had been guard strikes at the weekend affecting the service, so I rang National Rail enquiries to make sure everything was up and running. As it had been my idea to get the train, I didn't want any embarrassing delays. "Are there any strikes on Arriva North West this weekend?" I asked. "No," came the reply. Unfortunately, the helpful soul on the other end of the line failed to mention engineering works between Todmorden and Rochdale, which meant we had to get off at Todmorden and board a coach. A trip that should have taken 70 minutes took the best part of two hours.

We could have taken the car but I'd said: "No, why do that, the train is easier!" So I wasn't exactly flavour of the month and a 20-minute wait for a tram to Old Trafford – followed by two changes – didn't exactly help matters. It was a wet day, a heavy day, almost surreal and what was to come could almost have been anticipated. We only arrived at our seats with about five minutes to spare but with five minutes to kick-off I would have expected the atmosphere to be a little more buoyant than it was. There wasn't the party atmosphere there had been before the January 2001 cup win.

It wouldn't have mattered if we'd been allowed to play a 4-4-4-4 formation, we'd still have lost.

To be slaughtered 6-0 was embarrassing. I'm not sure what made me cringe more – I thought them all through. First there was the scoreline. Losing by six is never nice but then this was Old Trafford and it wasn't the first time. Then there was the fact I'd have to face all my Manchester United-supporting colleagues on Monday morning. I thought about it and realised the supporters of other clubs would close ranks and make sure I didn't get too much grief. Then there was the way Barry Green got comprehensively turned inside out by Van Nistelrooy, Giggs and Solskjaer. This wasn't an unfortunate afternoon for Barry, it was a f**king disaster. ALL of the six goals ended with him flat on his arse in his own penalty area and could be attributed to him in some way. He was at the scene of the crime each and every time, shown up as being a waste of time, money and space. But then, if it meant Herr Roeder wouldn't ever let him anywhere near the first team ever again, a 6-0 cup defeat was a small price to pay. Then there was the way David James shared a joke with his England colleagues in the United team after the final whistle. Unprofessional, in my opinion.

There were only two things I couldn't reconcile. First, I felt I had let my friends down. Not only had I dragged them along to a match some of them hadn't wanted to come to, we now faced the prospect of a trek back by tram, coach and train that would have made Michael Palin think twice. The worst thing, though, and I'm sure many of you will agree, was the way Phil Neville danced merrily past three defenders, after a one-two with Forlan, and finished like he'd been a striker all his life. That was a killer.

I felt for Herr Roeder as he trudged off back to the dressing room after the game. I had a choice. I didn't have to watch that pile of sh*t week-in-week-out. He had a choice too, I suppose, he could have walked away and I half expected him to. I couldn't imagine who we would have got in to replace him but he must have been very brave, or very stupid, to show such a stiff upper lip.

I guess his thinking was there was only one direction we could go from now on – as long as he didn't pick Barry Green again. United did us a favour anyway. It would only have been Arsenal at home in the next round.

The best thing anyone can do after falling off their bike is to get straight back on again. Similarly, the best thing a football team can do after a 6-0 defeat on national television, is to have a home game against Blackburn Rovers three days later.

This really was a must-win game. Having been humiliated, it was important to bounce back and answer the critics with a convincing display and a home win at the 13th attempt. It turned out to be unlucky 13 for Rovers. Despite taking the lead through Yorke, Parlow was back from injury and scored the equaliser from the penalty spot. Jermain Defoe was in the habit of grabbing late goals and as he'd done at Ewood Park in the last game of 2002, he nipped inside to score from 12 yards and Upton Park went potty. The win against Forest had given us the first home victory. Newcastle United had been a well earned, if disappointing, draw. Now we had won our first league match of the season at home. Perhaps this was the turning point. It was such a major psychological boost and it had still come early enough, while we were still in touching distance of the other teams around us, to make a real difference. Even cynical and sceptical old me, who'd had us down as early as the second game, thought we still might have a chance.

## 31. Familiar Feeling

**West Ham United 0 Liverpool 3  2.2.03**

Herr Roeder's final fling with the transfer window before it slammed shut on his fingers was the purchase of left-back Rufus Brevett from Fulham. I had no strong opinion either way on this deal.

It wasn't a surprise, given our league position, that Herr Roeder hadn't been able to settle on a defensive partnership for a run of more than two games. Injuries and suspensions played a part but so did humiliating defeats. He'd tried virtually every combination of Barry Green, Dailly, Repka and Pearce but all of them looked shaky, to put it mildly. The transfer window had closed and a decent centre-half hadn't been purchased. I felt that was a mistake. We needed someone who could play with the grace and composure of Herr Roeder himself in his prime. I read somewhere that, while playing for QPR, Herr Roeder had been the unluckiest FA Cup final captain in history as he missed both the final AND replay against Spurs in 1982 through suspension. That sort of luck had followed him into management. He must have broken a hell of a lot of mirrors in his time.

If the home run was to continue, it would have to do so at Liverpool's expense. They came to Upton Park for another live Sunday match and I was so confident we'd give them a game, I persuaded Shauna, Andrew and Terri to join me in the pub to witness a fine display of attacking football. Unfortunately, they did but it came from Liverpool. By the time 10 minutes had elapsed, we were 2-0 down and looking like the Keystone Cops XI that had taken such a beating from Manchester United. It was a case of one step forward, two steps back. Baros, who looked like he'd come over secreted in the back of a lorry with 700 of his countrymen, started the rout on six minutes. It was poor defending from a Riise corner. We looked so vulnerable – I had to wonder what we did in training every day – before Gerrard added a spectacular second. We didn't even look like scoring. Brevett and Johnson looked solid enough down the flanks but every time the ball entered the central area Repka or Dailly were tested. It was a case of *'Apres-Vous, Claude'*, and 35,033 hands went over 70,066 eyes. It was shocking.

Fredi Kanouté had clearly got bored not being allowed to score goals and decided to try his hand at defending instead. I'm not exactly sure what he was trying to do. Heskey nipped in to set up Hyypia for the third and put the tin lid on it. It was snowing hard outside the pub. I didn't say much. All the optimism after the Blackburn game had disappeared as quickly as it had arrived.

Games were running out. We had to start winning.

We also had to avoid any more injuries and suspensions, although such a sensible thought probably didn't cross Kanouté's mind as he lashed out at Seth Johnson at Elland Road the following week and got himself sent off. I'm not sure what was going though his mind. Evidently not very much. Leeds United were 1-0 up at the time and there were still 20 minutes to go in a game that was definitely drawable, if not winnable. Leeds were struggling big time.

With Leeds only eight miles from my home, this was a game I felt I had to attend. I made sure I didn't have the same unlucky ticket combination as last year. The fact I had paid a lot of hard-saved cash to go to the game, and the fact Leeds were a bit on the sh*t side, made Fredi's rush of blood to the head all the more unforgivable. Leeds were well ahead of us at the time in terms of points but could easily be caught the way things were going. A defensive combination of Brevett, Repka, Pearce and Johnson appeared to be holding firm and not making the stupid mistakes that had plagued the side for most of the season. Had the Frenchman managed to contain himself, we may well have earned a point. We had a chance and we blew it. A damn shame.

It was a shame the FA had selected Upton Park to host an England international friendly match, only for Sven to turn up in baggy pants, a big red nose and a curly ginger wig, ready to pour a bucket of icy water down Tord Grip's pants. He clearly wasn't taking the game against Australia seriously. It seemed he was starting to cave in to requests from Premiership managers not to play their precious charges for more than 45 minutes at a time in case they got an injury.

Losing 3-1 at home to Australia was bad enough. The fact it happened at Upton Park made things a hundred times worse. We were being associated with losers enough as it was, without the national team about to our humiliation.

The break did at least give everyone at West Ham a chance to prepare fully for the crunch match at The Hawthorns against West Bromwich Albion. Sunderland had now firmly rooted themselves to the bottom of the table and West Ham entered the game just a point behind Albion but a mighty six behind Bolton Wanderers. Even at this stage, in late February, it looked like staying up was virtually impossible. The run we had needed to start in the New Year had failed to materialise and although we had only lost once at home in that time, we had drawn games we should have won and lost games we should have drawn. In our situation, that was not an option. If it was going to happen, it would have to start with a bang with a win over the Baggies in front of Uncle Rupert's lenses.

Despite everything we have to go through, I am proud to be a West Ham fan. Sometimes it's not a good idea to wear your colours in certain places but I do so at every opportunity. Even when we are at our lowest ebb, I don't think it does the team any favours to hide your colours. So I proudly donned my claret and blue shirt and strolled purposefully to The Great Northern, taking my position in the snug just before kick-off. The diet had been going well but my heart was thumping quite loudly. Louder, in fact, than it had in the morning when I had finished a two-and-a-half mile run. That was a measure of the tension inside me as I tried to watch the game.

To call it entertainment would be an exaggeration. It was the kind of entertainment you get from playing Russian roulette. Fine when you've finished and you're still in one piece but, at the time, sweat is dripping off you by the bucket. Albion were unfortunate to have a goal disallowed for offside. I tried hard to settle but couldn't. We were making inroads but didn't look like scoring. It was billed as the team that couldn't score against the team that couldn't defend. After watching the first 30 minutes, I couldn't decide which was which.

Trevor Sinclair missed the sort of chance that would have haunted him for the rest of his career if, two minutes later, he hadn't taken a much more difficult opportunity, firing in from a tight angle. We went in at half-time in the lead but the joy was short-lived. Albion came out punching and soon had their equaliser. Once again, Repka was beaten in the air from a corner and Dichio scored. West Brom could smell blood and went for the jugular but they didn't have the means to do anything more than look scary. Sinclair scored again after good work from Bowyer, Defoe and Ferdinand.

Parlow had stormed off in a huff after being substituted on 49 minutes. I thought he was struggling with his fitness. He wasn't a major influence on the game and Herr Roeder was right to show some strength, show who was in charge and take him off. I was surprised by Parlow's reaction. He's obviously a VERY proud man. Herr Roeder not only proved he had the stomach for a tough decision, he also showed he's got one hell of a sense of humour, too. He put Barry Green on for the last five minutes.

With my heart rate slowly returning to normal, I supped up and left the pub with my chest puffed out proudly. My joy was premature, though, as I turned on the TV at home to find Birmingham City were 2-0 up against Liverpool. Birmingham were rivals in the relegation zone, so it was vital they didn't pull away from us. Now we were three points away from safety but with a much worse goal difference. Everyone would start fighting for their lives now. The next few months would be one hell of a battle.

## 32. Move Your Feet

### Everton 0 West Ham United 0  15.3.03

The Totts at home is always good value and now George Graham was out of the way, replaced by Glenn Hoddle, there was a good chance of seeing some goals. The win against West Brom had put a smile back on my footballing face. I was cautiously optimistic. Despite publicly stating in December we were going down, I felt the team was starting to show some shape and determination. We certainly had the talent. This was what I had wanted to see from the very start. As I have said a million times, I don't mind losing, I can take defeat. It's about how you play the game. If you compete and do your best, then losing is no disgrace. If you make stupid mistakes, then you don't deserve any sympathy.

I couldn't say exactly where the sea change came from. Bowyer was playing okay but not starting any fires in midfield. It was an area where we had an embarrassment of riches anyway, so I still failed to see the point in signing him. Brevett, at left back, was proving to be a shrewd buy. Even at 33, he was younger than Winterburn and slotted into the side like he'd been there all his life. Ferdinand, up front, had been a signing I had cringed at but he held the ball up well and gave the defenders a much needed respite.

But for me, the player who made the biggest difference to the team was young Glen Johnson, at right-back. What a find this lad was proving to be. It was obvious after only three starts that this boy could play. His talent was to slot into the side and start berating the more seasoned professionals for their lack of effort and, with some justification, their lack of skill. That was incredible to see and something I thought might save us.

It's not normal behaviour for me to wear my Hammers shirt while listening to a game on the radio but that's what I did for the match against Tottenham. I was feeling excluded, like an outsider. Something I had once been so practically involved in now seemed very distant, yet the feelings hadn't changed in any way – I still desperately wanted West Ham to win every week and felt like I'd been cut in two when they lost. Why should I feel guilty about it though? I had earned my time off. I'd followed my team through thick and thin, home and away, since 1983. I was only sitting at home this very second, listening to the game on the radio, because my devotion to the club over the last 10 years had crippled me financially and I was having to take a year out to pay it all back, get myself back on the straight and narrow. I remembered how angry I used to get with people who never went to games when I used to go week in, week out. I dare say there are some of you reading this even now wondering what right I have to sit here writing a book about West Ham when I have hardly been to see them play in the last 18 months. Like I say, I've earned that right. I've got the scars. I'll be back when I'm good and ready. Not before.

Ferdinand had a few scars, too. Parlow's absence with gastroenteritis, no doubt brought on by a severe case of bruised ego at The Hawthorns, meant Les' partnership with Defoe was likely to be the key to keeping us in the Premiership. Our rivals were starting to thin out. Birmingham City had put together a run and were now fairly safe but West Brom and Sunderland had suffered appalling runs and were already as good as down. That left us to battle out the final relegation spot with Bolton Wanderers and three clubs – Aston Villa, Leeds United and Fulham – who were dropping quickly and unexpectedly into the relegation frame.

As we occupied 18th spot, our fate was not entirely in our own hands, although we did still have to play Bolton and Villa, so all we could do was try to win as many points as possible and wait and see.

Ferdinand struck the first goal against Tottenham and the tails were up. Carrick added a second just after the re-start and when Shauna came and joined me on the sofa. We bit out nails together for the last half an hour of the game.

It seemed the corner was slowly being turned. A second home win of the season, a clean sheet, back-to-back wins – it was all happening. There was still a chance. I knew, from past experience, West Ham tend to do this. They put on a show of excellence when it's simply too late and make you think they were so unlucky to go down. The fact of the matter is, we had been truly awful in the first half of the season. Herr Roeder and the players owed us a decent run.

The campaign I had been running to get myself into better shape physically and financially was also going well. Shauna and I had set ourselves targets to achieve in terms of paying off credit cards and loans and they were all being met. We had also both set ourselves weight-loss targets, which were also being easily achieved. Shauna didn't need to lose weight but she encouraged me and, in doing so, lost a few pounds herself. I was running four times a week, doing three miles each time, and had cut out all the pies, chips and chocolate forming the main part of my diet for the last few years. I'm 35 and should know better but I thought if I could hit 12 stone by the time we went out to Cyprus for Andrew's wedding in May, then West Ham would stay up.

I know. It's illogical and totally ridiculous but it's those little promises you make to yourself as you go through life that make the dull bits tolerable. Shauna was able to get me a pass for the local posh gym through her work. The following Saturday, as West Ham took on Everton at Goodison Park, I installed myself on a treadmill in front of Uncle Rupert's results service and prepared myself for a two-hour run, to see how far I would get.

Tony Cottee was watching the game for Sky and reporting back. Every time presenter Jeff Stelling introduced him, my heart raced a little bit more and my pace increased. Everton were having a great season. Having beaten us out of sight, 5-0, last season, I didn't hold out much hope of getting anything from the game. But, with half an hour gone, it was 0-0 and, according to TC, we were playing well. I cranked up the pace a little, deciding if I could keep going, then West Ham would keep going. Like *Forrest Gump*, I kept running. Still goalless at half-time. I was starting to get a little tired and my water bottle was running out. I stopped briefly, having been running for 45 minutes and wondering why I wasn't feeling totally exhausted. It was the adrenaline that came from feeling like I was making a difference.

This was how I could help, I thought. I topped up my water bottle and set the timer for 60 minutes as the second half kicked off. The harder I worked, the more I was doing for the boys. My positive mental attitude was wafting over the Pennines to Merseyside and was prompting the players in claret and blue to work as hard as I was. All those times I had stood on the touchline and yelled at players to work harder – now it was my turn. I yelled at myself to work harder.

All I wanted was a point – not a greedy request. I considered setting the speed higher and going for the win. That was unrealistic. While running, you have a lot of time to think, which can be very dangerous for a bloke with a mind as twisted as mine. If I set the speed higher, went for the win and it didn't happen, all my efforts would have been for nothing. I set my sights, worked hard and looked to achieve my goal. I ran for 47 minutes at 12km/h. The final whistle went – Everton 0, West Ham 0.

Thoughts raced through my head as I continued to run. A third game unbeaten. A second successive clean sheet. I punched the air and let out an involuntary "Yes!" just as the safety key popped out of the machine and my wobbly legs gave way, providing much amusement for the posh people all around me. I didn't care. West Ham had a point I hadn't expected. And I'd helped them to earn it. Yes, I had. Honest!

A third clean sheet followed next Saturday against Sunderland and, again, I set myself a goal to see it was achieved. I was helping Andrew to put up a new fence in Norma's back garden. The weather was unseasonably warm for March as we toiled away. I was determined to have the job finished by 3pm. If it could be done, West Ham would win.

As Andrew drove me home, Defoe put us 1-0 up and I began to relax a little. Shauna ran a bath for me and I asked her to let me know if Teletext changed. After five minutes, I was itching to get out of the bath and check for myself, she'd obviously lost interest. But then a knock at the door and her head popped through the gap. She wasn't smiling. Maybe my watch had been slow and we'd finished the fence at five past three. It was all starting to fall around my ears. This time we were going to drop points and it would be my fault. "Don't tell me, 1-1." Shauna looked at the floor and shook her head. "2-0," she muttered.

Very good, I thought. She was learning how to play

this game very quickly and very well. She knew what buttons to press to wind me up over football and I was pleased. It showed, even if she didn't understand how I felt about West Ham, she at least realised how much they meant to me and indulged me in my silly little superstitions. They were working – and running and putting up fences was helping me to lose weight and get fit. With April approaching I had a little over a month to lose another half a stone if West Ham were to stay up. For the away game at Southampton, I made sure I had a ticket – for a full work-out at the gym.

## 33. Out Of Time

**Bolton Wanderers 1 West Ham United 0  19.4.03**

At last, some sort of pattern seemed to be emerging. The early season inability to play the same defence two weeks' running had gone and now, every week, we were able to turn out with James, Johnson, Repka, Pearce and Brevett at the back. It was clearly working, as we had kept three consecutive clean sheets, conceded only two goals in our last five games and taken 10 points in the process. Repka's inclusion in a defensive unit that seemed to have half a clue made his game a lot steadier but, even so, I still winced every time the ball went near him, even when I was watching recorded highlights.

Not only that, a pattern had emerged with Ferdinand starting games up front with Defoe and being replaced after an hour or so by Kanouté. The system worked well. If only Parlow hadn't been sulking, he might have been able to play a fuller part, too.

The trip to Southampton was almost as daunting as the visit to Everton had been a couple of weeks before. We needed to take something from every game. Our Premiership survival depended on it.

Like most fans of teams needing league points to achieve something, be it safety, a championship, or a place in Europe, I was meticulous in my planning and drew up tables using my deep-seated knowledge of the sport to make predictions on the remaining games for ourselves and for the teams around us. We had 30 points as we entered the game at St Mary's. I had us down to win our remaining home games against Villa, Middlesbrough and Chelsea, a draw at Birmingham and Bolton and probable defeats at Southampton and Manchester City. That would put us on 41 points. My predictions for Bolton's results put them on 41 also but they had a far superior goal difference. West Brom and Sunderland were already down as far as I could see. Our other nearest rivals, Aston Villa and Leeds United, would get 42 by my reckoning. We needed a miracle to stay up – starting with some sort of positive result at Southampton.

I was at the gym early. It was Andrew's stag do and he was off to Hull. Quite why his best man should choose that godforsaken hole as a venue for a stag weekend, I don't know but everyone seemed keen. Finances dictated I should stay at home but I'd been invited along to have breakfast with them before they left. I went to the gym first – the diet was still going well, I was on course to make the 12 stone that would save West Ham from relegation. All I had to do was put in a little more effort and just have the one sausage.

I ran like fury for an hour on the treadmill, then rowed a couple of kilometres for good measure. Surely that would be enough for at least a point at St Mary's? I saw Paul, my fellow exiled Hammer, in the pub in Baildon over breakfast. He was positive and fancied our chances. I knew if hard work on my part had anything to do with it, we'd be good for at least a point.

And that was how it turned out. Is it any wonder football fans stick to these ridiculous superstitions, when time and again they produce the goods? This was better than the usual pair of lucky underpants. I felt I had control over this. I felt I was able to influence results – not just by making sure I had the right socks on, but I could actually turn a draw into a win if I worked hard enough. But I couldn't be greedy. I had to be realistic and not wish for too much, too soon. If I thought by running my nuts off we would win at Anfield, I mean, that would be crazy, wouldn't it?

No, the system I had was far more sensible and the 12 stone target to avoid the drop was another part of the deal. It gave me something real to aim for and I knew if I kept my part of the bargain, so would West Ham.

Beattie put Southampton 1-0 up but my hard work earlier in the day paid dividends when Defoe hooked in an equaliser eight minutes from time. It made me proud to feel I had done the best I could to ensure we got a point from a game I had previously labelled as a defeat.

The following week it was Villa at home. This, for me, was a bigger game than Bolton away would be the week after. Bolton were on a roll and I had them down to survive many weeks ago. I knew Villa were our most serious prospect of escape, so three points against them was vital. That being the case, I got to the gym early and went for a swim, before taking my position on the treadmill at 3pm. It was agony. It's never easy to watch a game based on reports alone at the best of times. Tony Cottee was at Upton Park and described the opening exchanges as I set the tempo on the treadmill. I was doing okay. Trevor Sinclair scored after 14 minutes, so I knew I must have the settings about right. The reports continued to come through but West Ham were losing control of the game. Villa were getting more chances so I started to run faster, urging the score to stay the same or increase in our favour.

Whether it was my fault for trying too hard, I don't know. Maybe my over-exertion was reflected in the way the players allowed Villa to take over. It seemed the harder I worked, the worse things got. Firstly, Villa equalised through Vassell, then took the lead through Leonhardsen just after the break. Repka's challenge on

Vassell wasn't combative or unfortunate, it was plain lunacy. His improvement meant nothing after his ridiculous shove. He is possibly the most irritating man ever to wear claret and blue. I'd seen him have okay games but I'd never seen him have a blinder. I wanted him to go away and take his rash challenges, stupid shoves and offensive back-chat home to the Czech Republic.

Not only was Repka a poor centre-half, he was messing up my superstition. This was not possible. Villa were supposed to be sh*t but they were playing us off the park at times. It was so frustrating as we struggled to get a foothold in the game.

After Kanouté's equaliser, I got back on the treadmill and ran my heart out for the last 26 minutes. Chance after chance went begging, Kanouté, Johnson and Defoe all being foiled by Enckleman in the Villa goal. This was another frustration. Here was a man who had expensively missed a throw-in completely against Birmingham City a few months before to become the pantomime joke of the West Midlands, yet here he was having the game of his life when all we wanted was one more goal to secure victory, make my predictions stand and keep my superstitious mind happy.

I left the gym drained, both physically and emotionally. My optimism after the way we had pulled ourselves together was totally shattered. We now needed not just a draw at Bolton but a win. I didn't think my aching body would be able to cope.

It was billed as D-day, winner-stays-up, all that kind of stuff. But in reality, Bolton had salvaged their season already and had the upper hand in the relegation battle right from the time they had walked away from Upton Park with a draw back in December. Sure, they still had some tough matches to come but if it came down to the last day, with us away at Birmingham and Bolton at home to Middlesbrough, I knew who my money would be on.

Having watched Sam Allardyce's side quite closely I knew their brand of uncompromising play, coupled with the skills of the likes of Okocha and Djorkaeff, would be hard to beat. And with the likes of Repka playing in the back four, there was always the chance of a red card before the afternoon was out. I felt a draw was the very most we could get from the game.

Ironically, the goal that sank us had nothing to do with Repka, Dailly or Barry Green. It owed more to a flash of individual brilliance from Okocha and you have to hold your hands up and say it was a terrific goal. It was out of character in a game littered with fouls and free-kicks. The tension was there for all to see, neither team wanted to lose but now Bolton had managed to gain the lead, they were not letting go.

Ian Pearce took out his frustration on Andre in the last minute, almost slicing him in half with a challenge reminiscent of Marco Boogers' effort on Gary Neville on his Old Trafford debut. Like Mad Clog before him, he got a red card. The scenes that followed were disgraceful but anything less and we'd be complaining the players didn't care. Rufus Brevett had been at the club only a short time but wore his heart on his sleeve. Joe Cole had shown his passion for the cause by being the only player appearing to try for the first six months of the season. When 6-0 down at Old Trafford, the amount of work he put in compared to the other players was almost embarrassing. Both players got themselves into bother after the final whistle. They both realised what this costly defeat meant, while Brevett subsequently incurred the added expense of the FA's £1,000 fine.

It was made a good deal worse by the fact Birmingham City, Villa and Fulham had all won. Fulham's win over Newcastle United was particularly galling, as they were the sort of games you would bet your house on them losing. Good job I am not a gambling man.

Naturally, I blamed myself for the inadequacies of my team. I'd found a winning formula in the exercise regime. I shouldn't have worried about the little blip against Villa. But as I sat through the Bolton game, unable to deal with the stress, I ate a whole walnut whip. I have to live with that guilt.

It had been a while since the world had seemed so empty. Although I was no longer attached to the club by the hip, I still felt every defeat as keenly as before. Even more so now, as each defeat nudged us closer and closer to the abyss. The Bolton game had been our first defeat in seven games, the sort of form that was needed if we were to avoid the drop but everyone around us was putting together a similar run. Birmingham had virtually guaranteed their safety. Bolton were matching us result for result and by beating us had put themselves a massive six points ahead with four games to play. Villa and Leeds were still in the reckoning but Fulham's win over Newcastle had given them a bit of breathing space, too.

We had four games left. We had to win them all and hope someone else slipped up. It was a tall order, perhaps taller than it should have been. In any normal season, the 32 points we already had in the bag would have been almost enough to guarantee safety. Two wins from the remaining four would probably have been enough. However, this was not an ordinary season. While the chasm in class between the top six and the rest of the Premiership appeared to be widening, the other teams in the division were bunching. It meant no one could put together a decent run, anyone could beat anyone else and only a handful of points covered seventh to 16th place.

That had been to our advantage the previous year and

the little run we put together over Easter meant we had been able to cement a seventh place finish. This season, it worked against us. With the abysmal run we suffered from October though to the end of January, we had too much ground to make up. This wasn't helped by the fact the two clubs below us, West Brom and Sunderland, were SO bad they allowed everyone to pick up points against them. It meant Hammers' six points gained at The Hawthorns and the Stadium of Light were virtually meaningless, as every other bugger had won there, too. The three points lost at home were equally, if not more, significant.

This Easter, our slip up would cost us dearly but it was a lot to expect to go from March to May without losing at least one game. It was an unreasonable ask.

It didn't stop us trying though. Middlesbrough came down to Upton Park on Easter Monday and were beaten 1-0 with a Trevor Sinclair strike. It was a tense afternoon. Tricky Trev brought the house down 15 minutes from the end, as, with Bolton's game at Blackburne Rovers still deadlocked at 0-0, he swept home Johnson's cross for the winning goal. Now the gap was four points with nine to play for – and Bolton still had to play title-chasing Arsenal.

As I idly flicked through Teletext after the match, my eye was caught by a headline about Herr Roeder. "Hammers boss collapses after game." I couldn't believe it. Herr Roeder was one of the younger and fitter managers in the Premiership and here was the TV telling me he'd had a heart attack. I guess it doesn't matter how fit you are, if you put yourself under such pressure, something has to give. As I revisited the pages later in the evening for updates, it appeared it was not a heart attack but a brain haemorrhage. My mate, Dobbo, had one of them when he worked in Germany. I knew they were not stress-related. I knew our manager had a serious health problem.

I don't want to be unfair to Herr Roeder but he's a stubborn so-and-so. It may be unkind of me to suggest he should have taken the opportunity to take a step back after undergoing brain surgery. The team had started winning again, no one would have been too critical of a man who was so ill if he had decided to call it a day, but from his hospital bed he kept going on about how he couldn't wait to get back to work. I couldn't help thinking it would be better for everyone concerned if he just forgot about it.

Trevor Brooking took over first team affairs in a caretaker capacity. This was a bizarre appointment in my view. I loved Trevor Brooking as a player (has there been anyone even close to being as consistently good as him since he retired?) but he had no managerial experience other than sitting on the *Match of the Day* panel with Mark Lawrenson and Alan Hansen umming and ahhing a lot. If I had been Paul Goddard or Roger Cross, I would have had my nose put seriously out of joint. But that's the way this club seems to operate. The appointment of Herr Roeder had been a surprise in the first place. The appointment of his temporary successor was no less so. The fact Brooking was on the West Ham board of directors, who were already coming in for some serious crap from the fans, made the decision all the more astounding. Nothing quite like putting your neck on the line.

It meant Brooking was either very brave to take on such responsibility and risk losing a lot of credibility with a lot of people who still worshipped him, or he was being used and his good nature was being taken advantage of.

Whatever the reasoning, he was put in charge for the trip to Manchester City, our last ever visit to Maine Road before the club's move to the new City of Manchester Stadium. I'd had us down for a defeat here but losing at

Bolton had meant this wasn't an option. Bolton's draw with Arsenal the day before had also upset the applecart somewhat and we now faced the prospect of still being two points adrift of safety even if we managed to beat City. Bloody Arsenal, eh? Always letting us down.

Brooking stuck pretty closely with the team Herr Roeder had used with such effect since March. Defoe started up front with Ferdinand and the midfield of Lomas, Cissé, Cole and Sinclair had bags of heart and a lot of talent.

It was clear after 20 minutes of the game that only one team was bothered about winning it and that was West Ham United. I'd seen enough to realise it would take a huge slice of bad luck for us not to win. But this is West Ham and if there is any bad luck around, we are likely to get it. Ferdinand went in for a 50-50 ball with their keeper, Schmeichel, and ended up being stretchered off with what looked like a badly gashed leg. That meant the usual trick of replacing him with Kanouté couldn't be done, because Fredi was already on the pitch for Cissé. So Hutchison came on for Ferdinand and the balance of the team was restored.

Chance after chance went begging. It seemed the breakthrough wouldn't come but then Hutchison hit a shot against the post and Kanouté bundled in the rebound to send everyone associated with the club absolutely bonkers.

The result put us on 38 points, two behind Bolton with two games to go. We had Chelsea at home and Birmingham City away. Bolton faced Southampton away and Middlesbrough at home. Leeds United were on 41, with Arsenal away and Aston Villa at home, and still represented a seriously catchable target. Our undeserved defeat at Elland Road and failure to come back to 4-4 in November were starting to look costly.

## 34. All Over

### Birmingham City 2 West Ham United 2  11.5.03

March April and May had been dominated by talk and plans for the holiday Shauna and I had booked in Cyprus. It represented many things for us, not least the wedding of Andrew and Terri. It was my first proper foreign holiday for 10 years, Shauna's first for four years and the fact we had managed to afford it at all showed we were making a good deal of progress.

The home game against Chelsea had been built up as the day Parlow would return to save us. For me, it had been billed as the day of last minute jobs and packing suitcases, as we were due to fly off to Cyprus on the Sunday. Obviously, I had hoped the matter would be finalised before going abroad. By that, I meant I hoped we would be safe. It had been playing on my mind from the day the holiday had been booked that I would be away for the final game. Now it was reality. Of course, if we lost to Chelsea and Bolton got a point at Southampton, our goal difference meant we were effectively down. But what a morale boost it would be if we could beat Chelsea and climb out of the bottom three going into the last match. For that to happen we would have to muster all our courage and hope Southampton weren't too bothered about preserving players for the FA Cup final against Arsenal.

I shamelessly donned my Hammers shirt as I trudged backwards and forwards from lounge to bedroom, packing suitcases and checking off lists. I had all three radios in the house tuned to Radio Five Live and the TV was on with Teletext up and running. I wasn't taking any chances. I had been out for a long run in the morning, in case that particular superstition wasn't quite dead yet. Seven pairs of socks and pants later, the stage was set for Parlow to perform his final act in front of his adoring home fans.

After 55 minutes of a tense and frenetic game, he came on to replace Les Ferdinand. It was like a scene from *Escape To Victory*. It was pure theatre and almost less believable than the thought of Sylvester Stallone playing in goal for the Allies against the Germans. Parlow pounced on 70 minutes, ran to the crowd with his shirt off and nowhere to be seen. The day was made for him. For all his posturing about a new contract and his open hostility towards Herr Roeder, I couldn't believe this man was going to leave us. In the four years he'd been with us, he'd become an institution. No matter what preposterous things he said in the papers, how other people laughed, he was always able to let his feet speak more sense than his gob. In the end, that's what matters.

With the game won there were emotional scenes, not just at Upton Park but in my front room, too. I allowed myself a moment of quiet contemplation having helped Shauna with the packing, mainly by standing there vacantly listening to the radio and saying "uh?" every time she spoke to me. Subsequently that evening, Bolton got a 0-0 draw at Southampton and sent us back to the dreaded 18th place. It meant a win at Birmingham next Sunday might not be enough. We could face the prospect of relegation having achieved 44 points and having lost only one of our last 11 matches. It was tough but the table doesn't lie.

As we set off to Cyprus the next day, the news filtered

through to me: Arsenal had let us down for a third time this season, by losing at home to Leeds United. Not only had they handed the title on a plate to Manchester United, they gave Leeds mathematical safety and narrowed our chances of survival still further. Nice to know who your mates are.

Cyprus offered me the chance, in a difficult week for my relationship with the club, to simply forget all about it. We arrived late on the Sunday night at our apartments and awoke on Monday morning to wall-to-wall sunshine and a beautiful hotel pool area, from which we took some shifting. We made the most of the sun and sat and relaxed all day. Very rarely did my mind stray to thoughts of Sunday and the game at St. Andrew's. When it did, my main concern was how I was going to get to see it.

We'd been out in the evenings and seen that while many of the bars and restaurants pandered to the needs of the English football fan by supplying Uncle Rupert, they assumed everyone would want to watch Everton v Manchester United or Chelsea v Liverpool.

Andrew and Terri were married on the Thursday. We were due to fly back late on the Sunday night. We had Sunday afternoon free to watch the match, all we had to do was find a bar that would show it to us. We walked miles. Shauna developed blisters and so did I. I asked in every bar if we could watch the West Ham game – to no avail.

In a way, the whole afternoon was indicative of the way my love affair with West Ham had gone and the way my life had developed in other areas. For the first time in my life, I took a holiday abroad with a woman. How grown up is that? I was approaching 35 and it had never happened before. I watched two people much younger than me get married. It made me feel plain old. Shauna and I had both scrimped and saved to ensure we had a fantastic week, which we did. It would have been so easy to go out and extend the overdraft, or prise out the credit card again. But I had vowed never to buy anything ever again I couldn't pay for up front. I was like a reformed alcoholic. The word 'credit' still sends a shiver down my spine.

The fact I had even contemplated going abroad, knowing I'd be away for the final game of the season, hinted that the passion for football, my team, might be dying out a little bit. The fact I had made only a handful of games this season was my choice – no-one had been holding a gun to my head – showed a certain sobering in some respects. I knew I would never fall out of love with West Ham. West Ham had to accept I had changed. West Ham as a club, as a team, as a thing, would never change – they would always break my heart. Maybe it was time to let go and make 28 years of pain go away.

I still cried real tears when we drew 2-2 at Birmingham. They were still my West Ham. It was West Ham that didn't love me any more – not the other way around. I hadn't quite made my target weight of 12 stone. I secretly felt a little guilty.

As we flew back into East Midlands airport, I felt like a huge weight had been lifted from me. Suddenly the burden of being a West Ham fan didn't sit so awkwardly on my shoulders. Suddenly, it seemed, I was free.

## 35. Misfit

It seemed that way but less than 24 hours later, I was fuming, as I learned of Jermain Defoe's transfer request. Call it bad advice, call it what you like, no-one is so naïve as to take such poor advice, surely?

I'd forgotten how plank-like the average footballer can be. I realise I may be making a gross generalisation, I know a lot of footballers and some of them are very bright but the majority never paid much attention at school, or anywhere else for that matter.

I was reminded of Manny Omoyimni, who, a few years back, 'forgot' he'd played in an earlier round of the Worthington Cup for Gillingham. Even if he hadn't forgotten, did he really think he'd then get away with playing for us in the quarter-final against Villa and West Ham wouldn't be punished? Honestly, I could swing for stupid people.

Fortunately, West Ham must have realised how stupid Defoe and/or his 'advisers' were and they told him to go back to his seat at the back of the class and stop making a noise. It was the last we heard of it. Fortunately for him, the fans, on the whole, forgave him. I haven't, though. What a stupid, stupid boy.

What had been bothering me more than most things during 2002-03 had been the fact West Ham had been struggling so badly, yet I hadn't been there for them. They had been there for me in my darkest hours and now they needed me, I was nowhere to be seen.

The reality of the situation, though, was that they didn't need me at all. Sure, they were always grateful for my affection and my cash whenever I went to see them but they never phoned, or wrote or anything – supporting West Ham was like having a series of one-night stands. Some were good, some – no, most – were bad. Sometimes you'd have three in a row, sometimes you'd go for months without one. While a lot of married people go on about how jealous they are of single people, they only have themselves to blame if they stay in a relationship that makes them unhappy.

I moved 150 miles to get away from an unhappy relationship, a job I loathed and a home life with no prospects. I couldn't do the same with West Ham. They followed me around the country. It might sound as though I wanted to be away from the Hammers, as though I wished I didn't support them. That's not the case at all. I wished I could call the shots, I wished I could wear the trousers in our relationship. For once, I wanted them to click their fingers and for me to tell them to piss off, not come running like a love-sick puppy.

I knew I could do it. Like all successful relationships, I'd have to work at it – even if we had passed our silver anniversary.

Shauna and I had been working on our relationship and were now happier than ever. I know what you've been thinking – Banksy gets himself shacked up and then doesn't go to football any more. I was always the first to poke fun at others when it happened to them. Deep down, though, I was poking fun because I was in denial – they had what I wanted, so it was easier to poke fun than to admit it. Even so, now I'd found it, I wasn't staying away because I couldn't be bothered to come to football. I stayed away because the last 10 years had cost me so much financially and emotionally, I needed a year or so out for my bank balance and my soul to recover. I knew I would come back fitter and stronger.

June was a month almost devoid of football. With the recovering Herr Roeder not due back at his desk until July 1st, it would be time soon enough for the bandwagon to start rolling again. I enjoyed the break. Herr Roeder's illness and Marc-Vivien Foé's untimely death during a match in the Confederations Cup created a little perspective. Football was, after all, just a game.

When the fixture list came out and tickets became available, I bought a ticket for the opening Nationwide first division game at Preston. After all the fuss over Defoe had died down it seemed we could well hang on to the majority of our key players. I started to relax and look forward to the new season. This time, it was going to be on my terms.

# 36. Finest Dreams

## Preston North End 1 West Ham United 2  9.8.03

There are many people, things or events I could blame for the demise of West Ham United in 2002-03. It would be unfair to heap all the blame on Barry Green but since when was life ever fair? At the end of the day, we were relegated on 42 points, a record number.

In any normal season, 42 points would have been more than enough to stay up, What cost us more than anything was the fact that the two teams finishing below us were so poor. West Brom and Sunderland were so, so poor, they allowed all the teams immediately above us to pick up points. Sunderland's relegation on a record low of 19 points was a case in point.

Add to that the fact Arsenal couldn't hit form when you would most expect it. They performed miracles to come back from 2-0 down at Upton Park with a display that would have deeply impressed Lazarus. Then they gave away a two-goal advantage at Bolton and failed to beat a struggling Leeds side when they were there for the taking.

In the final reckoning, there were more than three teams worse than us but the league table is compiled over 38 games, not 12. At the end of it all, we were the architects of our own demise. If you fail to win a league match at home until January 29th, you could argue you get exactly what you deserve.

There was one other factor I haven't mentioned.

Maybe the reason I don't mention it is because I am afraid to admit it, because absurd as it may sound, it may be true. As I have mentioned before, when life is going well for me, West Ham usually take a nose-dive. When life sucks, West Ham start winning and help me through my pain.

I've been having such a good time. I could blame Herr Roeder. I could blame Barry Green. I could blame the board. I could blame every other Premiership team except Chelsea, who graciously and ironically donated six points to a very worthy cause. At the end of it all, deep down, I blame myself. It's an interesting theory but I'm not going to deliberately look for misery just to prove it right.

Summers can be very long and very boring when there is no football around but in summer 2003 I had other things to occupy my mind. Apart from writing this book, Shauna and I had been designing our new kitchen. It's a bigger job than it sounds, planning out exactly in what order to do everything, arrange skip hire, get the cat put into the cattery for a week so he doesn't get cut in two by a moment of over-enthusiasm with a jigsaw.

Ah, jigsaws. Herr Roeder's jigsaw had been knocked on the floor over the summer and there weren't more than two pieces still left attached. He was sadly left with a headache of almighty proportions in more ways than one, as he returned to work on July 1st. It was clear sales would have to be made. There was no doubt about it but I crossed my fingers and hoped it wouldn't be too severe on a squad that would need to be bolstered, not depleted, to cope with a 46-game season and a decent cup run as well.

Promotion back to the Premiership had to be the priority. In days gone by, relegation wasn't such a financial catastrophe, players tended to stay, even if an immediate return didn't happen. These days, footballers come and go with the weather but I wanted to keep the nucleus of the team together, so they could re-pay us by undoing the mess they had landed us in.

The Board, the management team and the players must all accept their fair share for failing to act when the writing was on the wall. Yet the only people to suffer as a result of all the mistakes are us, the fans. Herr Roeder didn't have to go into work every Monday morning and get sniggered at by a dozen Manchester United fans. Tomas Repka didn't have to sit in a pub in Bradford watching abysmal football and hear Leeds fans calling him a cockney tw*t from the safety of their little crowd. There was something so unfair about the whole thing, because although it was the fans who were suffering, they were the ones who deserved it the least. They were the only part of the club that had performed to their capabilities in 2002-03.

It wasn't me who stuck rigidly to a 4-4-2 no matter what the venue or the opposition. It wasn't Gary who selected Repka every week when even a blind man could see he was struggling. It wasn't Paul who missed a penalty against Arsenal. It wasn't Liam who publicly fell out with Parlow and refused, point blank, to do anything about healing the rift. And it wasn't Kev who signed the woeful Barry Green. But we all continued to pay our money. I wasn't having any more of it.

As the 2002-03 season came to a close, it was clear several out-of-contract players would move on and wouldn't be replaced to keep the wage bill down. Parlow, of course, was the biggest name to go. I was devastated but had at least had plenty of time to get used to the idea. The first division was not a suitable arena for a player of his quality anyway and he ended up at Charlton Athletic. God bless you, Parlow. Sometimes you were an arse of the highest order but this club was so much richer for having you.

Lee Bowyer also left, for another big pay day at Newcastle United, and I have to say I didn't give a damn. Les Ferdinand went quickly back to the Premiership with newly-promoted Leicester City, which was a surprise and a disappointment. He had proved me wrong and I had hoped he would stay on to give us a push back to the top flight.

Other players released included retiring jester John Moncur, a great character and another I was sorry to see go into retirement, more for reasons of sentiment than ability. Scott Minto (Rotherham United), Edouard Cissé (AS Monaco), Raimond Van Der Gouw (retired) and Nigel Winterburn (retired) also left. But most importantly, Barry Green's contract expired and it was not renewed. This was a great relief to me, as I had been certain I'd read somewhere he was on a two-year deal. We may well have signed a World Cup defender for nothing but his wages had reportedly cost us over £1.5m. To me, it felt like his mere presence had cost us our Premiership status.

Of course there was more to it than Barry Green's ineptitude. But a football fan needs a scapegoat, he needs someone to focus the blame on and Barry Green fits the bill. He just looks like a scapegoat.

Trevor Sinclair, Joe Cole and Glen Johnson had all openly declared they were happy to stay at Upton Park and help to undo the mess they had contributed to. To be fair, of the three of them only Sinclair, with his World Cup hangover, can take any slice of blame. Throughout December and January he put in some shocking displays but Johnson and Cole had nothing to be ashamed of. Similarly, despite an early season wobble, Michael Carrick had come out of the campaign with a lot of credit and had declared his intentions to stay.

The board had very generously taken a 50% pay cut to reflect the drop in revenue that would inevitably follow as a result of relegation. They also stated the club would increase its borrowing to enable us to hang on to the best players and give us the best chance of returning to the top flight at the first attempt.

The thought of increasing credit would have made me wake up in a cold sweat and that's what must have happened to them. Either that or the bank looked at recent performances and simply told them to f**k off.

Now Herr Roeder was back at his desk, picking up the pieces and making a start on his new jigsaw, he was soon to realise that although this one had a picture on the box, it wasn't the right one.

The players we had been told we would be keeping were sold off from under his nose, one by one. Glen Johnson was the first to go and possibly this was the most astonishing piece of business of the lot. Roman Abramovic, had asked his son what he wanted for his birthday and he had replied "A cowboy outfit." So he went out and bought him Chelsea Football Club.

Frankly, the amount of money involved was obscene. Chelsea paid an undisclosed fee for Johnson, who had only just signed a four-year contract at Upton Park. That fee was reported to be around £6m. This was outrageous. I could understand it if the club wanted to cash in on established stars like Kanouté, Sinclair and James. But to sell off a player who had made only 14 starts in the Premiership, had steadied a shaky defence and proved himself to be a faithful, loyal and dependable servant, was madness. It was quite literally selling off the family silver.

The stress-free feeling I had enjoyed in late May and early June was starting to wear off. West Ham were crawling under my skin again. How they manage to achieve it time after time, I'll never know.

I bought myself a new mobile phone with WAP capability so I could keep a closer eye on what was going on. Sinclair had been due to join Middlesbrough for £2m but the deal feel through and Manchester City came up with £2.5m for his services. I've always thought of Kevin Keegan as a sort of a 'Jack and the Beanstalk' type of manager, going off into town with the fatted cow and coming home with a handful of beans. This time, though, for £2.5m I think he hit the jackpot.

Kanouté couldn't wait to join Tottenham. Good luck to both of them, they deserve each other. It had to be the comedy moment of the summer, when Fredi had to endure a two-day medical to ensure all his injury problems were behind him, Fredi was declared fit, a £4.5m deal was struck – and he broke down with a groin injury in his first training session as a Spurs player. Nice one, Fredi, it couldn't happen to a more deserving club.

I couldn't see Sinclair or Kanouté doing much in the first division. It wasn't their ball game. I'd seen Sinclair playing for QPR in the first division and he wasn't impressive. Maybe we were better off without him. At 30 years of age, it was a reasonable fee – not a fantastic one, but reasonable. As for Kanouté, well, he said nice things about the club when he left but I shall always remember him as being a bit like Slaven Bilic. He came on loan and played out of his skin. We signed him on a permanent deal and he got progressively less interested. Both were great players but neither were real West Ham players. They were only here for the money.

So with the matching candelabra and the silver salver had gone, no one seemed very keen on the knives and spoons at the back. I'd rather been hoping someone might come in for the ornate punch-bowl, Tomas Repka and the satin lamp-shade that was Christian Dailly. I wasn't so concerned about Dailly – he would be a lot more comfortable at first division level but I was uncomfortable with Repka at any level. Galatasaray were sniffing around at one point – they must have seen a video of the 4-3 Leeds game and changed their minds.

Matthew Etherington joined as a make-weight in the deal that took Fredi to Spurs. I wasn't filled with joy at the news. David Connolly, however, was another matter. I had seen him play for Wimbledon and for the Republic of Ireland and, as international strikers go, he cost virtually nothing at £285,000.

Robert Lee was one of those players always linked with a move to his native West Ham United but it never quite came off. There was talk of it when he left Charlton Athletic for Newcastle United, several times while he was on Tyneside and again before he joined Derby County. Now, at age 37, he became the obligatory aged but experienced squad member, following in the boots of Lee Chapman, Stuart Pearce and Nigel Winterburn to name but a few. I was pleased, though. I liked him as a player. He always reminded me of the old, fat bloke in your local five-a-side tournament. He looks like he can't play for toffee but you can't get the ball off him. If we were going to have to scrimp and save, then he was the sort of player I wanted to see, even if it was only for one year. It was hardly forward planning but we had to get ourselves out of a spot.

By the time the pre-season friendlies started it looked as though at least we'd have the spine of a very good side. David James was still there. Joe Cole was still there. And Jermain Defoe was still there. That's the key to any good side. We still lacked a presence at centre-back but if he could be found, we had every chance.

The pre-season tour of Sweden seemed to be going well, with games being won and drawn rather than being lost and few goals conceded. Perhaps Repka had found his level after all and we'd be okay. Other than Connolly, the signings we had made didn't fill me with excitement but there was something still nagging away at me. I totalled up the reported revenue from the sales of

Johnson, Sinclair and Kanouté. Maths has never been my strong point but I reckoned it came to around £12m. Reports widely suggested we had to find £20m to balance the books. Okay, so even after adding on the money being saved by not having to pay bucket loads of cash to the likes of Barry Green and Parlow, I was still some way off. Speculation still continued in the papers about Defoe and Cole and I knew one of them would have to go.

I was pretty much convinced it would be Defoe. Manchester United seemed keen at £10m and with Connolly on board, I could see him being the one to leave. I wasn't prepared for the sale of Joe Cole. The mobile phone I bought to keep me abreast of developments on the hour at least served its purpose but I wished to god it hadn't, as it flashed up "Chelsea agree £6.6m fee for Cole." I was gutted. It seemed one minute we were going to be keeping everyone at the club who was still under contract. The next, the place seemed like a ghost town. Tumbleweed blew across the training pitch at Chadwell Heath. A season that had looked like it might be quite a good laugh was suddenly looking like an almighty struggle.

It wasn't just the fact Joe had gone. It was the fee - £6.6m was a steal, a real kick in the bollocks to everyone who had watched him develop through the ranks from the age of 13. I could only put it down to the fact he only had a year left on his contract – how else could Chelsea get Cole for £6.6m yet had to pay £17m for Damien Duff. Is Duff a better player than Joe? I don't think so.

Joey was no doubt listening carefully to his 'advisers' as well. I nearly wet myself when I saw his quote on Teletext. "I used to watch from The Shed (at Chelsea)" I had pictures in my mind of him standing in his shed at home, watching Chelsea on the telly in the lounge through a crack in the wood. I'd always thought Cole was an Arsenal fan, anyway?

Herr Roeder was at last handed back control of the squad. "We've made a few adjustments," the board no doubt said as they handed over the reins. I've always said there's no point complaining about something unless you can offer a reasonable alternative, or offer a plan of action. Herr Roeder never criticised the board for selling off his best players but then I don't suppose he had any choice. What could he do about it?

As fans we have that choice. There is no one sticking a knife in our ribs and telling us we have to go to watch our team. (Although I notice the timing of the Cole transfer occurred a good while after season ticket sales had reached their desired level – or am I being cynical again?) We have the choice to vote with our feet. While I would not advocate going and supporting another side – it doesn't work that way anyhow – withdrawal of support is the only effective way of achieving objectives. In 1992, ticket prices were lowered after fans stayed away in their droves. If ticket sales, shirt sales, programme sales and all the associated spin-offs should take a nose-dive, then, maybe, at least the board of directors would feel the need to offer us an explanation for what had been going on. It's the only positive argument I can think of for going PLC. But I wouldn't want us answerable to faceless shareholders. As fans we hold an emotional stake in our club and our vote could count for so much more if we used it wisely.

It could never happen of course. For every pissed off fan who votes with his feet, there will be another who will take his place with a grin on his face, thinking how clever and how lucky he's been. He'll soon learn of course, it's a continuing process. What some people might call a learning curve.

And so with the new season approaching I watched

the news every day to see if anyone else had gone. Sebastien Schemmel had been fined for publicly criticising the club. Maybe his comments were out of order and badly timed – he had to admit he was only a shadow of the player he'd been in 2001-02 when he walked off with the Hammer of the Year award. But fining him seemed a bit harsh. He had already stated he was missing his family, who had moved back to France.

It seemed everything was starting to fall apart – not only for West Ham but for football as a whole. Roman Abramovic and his millions had rather spoiled everything for those of us with a degree of romance in our souls. What Jack Walker had done at Blackburn Rovers, when he effectively bought the 1995 league title, had seemed bad enough – but at least he had supported the club man and boy.

Herr Roeder continued to speculate in the transfer market and just before the season got under way took Neil Mellor on a year's loan from Liverpool. I'd never heard of Mellor and never seen him play but I knew that just because he was a Liverpool player, he wasn't necessarily brilliant. Remember Song and Camara?

The start of the new season was only a matter of hours away and rumours still abounded in the press that Defoe would be on his way by Saturday. They wrote with a confidence that suggested they really did know what was happening. Fortunately, as it turned out, they knew jack.

The season began at Deepdale with a 12.30pm kick-off courtesy of Uncle Rupert. I got on a Blackpool North train at Bradford Interchange, wondering why I didn't pick this mode of transport more often. For the first time in 10 years I was going to watch West Ham play a league match outside the top flight. In a way, I relished it. Now we were a big fish in a little pond – maybe we'd walk this division.

As I continued my walk towards the stadium I got jittery. What if we didn't walk the division? What if we got beaten every other week and ended up staying there for the duration? What if we did a QPR or a Sheffield Wednesday? My mood was not improved after a brief meeting with Gary Firmager and overhearing the conversations he was having with the punters. Boycotts and demonstrations were being hinted at. Not an ideal start.

The season kicked off and a high ball was pumped towards our area. Tomas Repka fell over. I held my head in my hands. Same old West Ham – here we go again. Two minutes later we were a goal down and the mood of unrest started to deepen. Had Defoe not equalised within seven minutes the protests could have arrived ahead of schedule. Had the Preston mascot not been riding round the perimeter track on an electric golf cart, I might have had nothing to laugh about at all in the first 45 minutes of what was already looking like a long, hard season.

David Connolly made his debut as a substitute in the second half and within minutes had notched the winner. Tired, happy and thirsty, I bought a couple of cold beers for the train ride home and indulged myself in a rare cover-to-cover reading of *OLAS*. It wasn't until I got home and turned on the radio, I found out about Connolly's astonishing outburst at Herr Roeder.

Connolly had expressed his disgust at the fact Neil Mellor had been given a starting place ahead of him when Mellor had only just arrived at the club, having met up with his new team-mates on the motorway the day before the opening game. I like to take these stories with a pinch of salt but they played the interview on the radio and that's exactly what he said.

I couldn't be sure whether to admire Connolly for his frankness, or be angry about this disturbance so early on in an important campaign. Whatever his motives he got his way and a starting place against Rushden and Diamonds in the Carling Cup the following Wednesday. He scored twice and Defoe got the other in a 3-1 win that hinted at better things to come. It was a novel experience to be playing in the first round of the League Cup. It was only a few years since we had received a bye into the third round due to European commitments. How times change.

Transfer deals continued. Kevin Horlock was signed from Manchester City. Horlock was a product of the West Ham youth team who had moved on after finding his opportunities limited in the early 90s. He had since proved himself with Swindon Town, Manchester City and Northern Ireland and was a welcome addition to the squad. He made his debut in a 0-0 draw with Sheffield United at Upton Park. I was disappointed. After the flying start we'd had, we needed to beat the likes of Sheffield United, who were likely to be close promotion rivals. But a clean sheet and an unbeaten start were still not to be sniffed at.

Rotherham United away was another matter. Losing to a team like Rotherham was inevitable at some point in the season. In the last promotion campaign we had lost at places like Oxford and Southend and still prevailed but this wasn't acceptable so early on. The story of the players refusing to use the dressing rooms at Millmoor, because they were not up to standard was, I am sure, exaggerated. Even so, it must have put an extra spring in the step of the Rotherham players.

Despite the 1-0 defeat and the continuing rumblings and rumours, the news that Herr Roeder had been sacked the next day almost toppled me from my step ladder as I scraped paint off the kitchen windows. I had to hold my hands up and say I was not disappointed by the news. I had defended Glenn as much as I could, I liked the bloke, but at the end of the day I just didn't feel he could hack it. The timing could have been better and it's a widely held view that the club let him continue long enough to do the dirty work of watching his prize assets being sold off, make a full recovery from his illness, then give him the old Spanish archer.

Football is a cut-throat business these days and we should never be surprised when El Bow arrives. It's sad, though. I always liked to think that West Ham United was above that sort of thing.

Trevor Brooking took over again in his caretaker role now becoming so familiar he was given a brown overall, a flat cap and a broom to go with it.

Schemmel, after his fine for criticising the club and Herr Roeder, predictably found himself and his alleged mental instability on the south coast at Portsmouth. Harry Redknapp was still providing a rest home for his favourite waifs and strays. Good luck to him.

Not only was there no immediate successor to Herr Roeder, the list of names being banded about numbered around 40. Again, my choice would have been Stuart Pearce and although his name was mentioned, he never appeared to be a serious contender. Trevor had made it clear he didn't want the job and to be fair to him, I felt once the honeymoon period had run out, he might struggle with it anyway. I speculated as much as the next man but in the end, we'd all just have to wait and see.

Meanwhile Trevor Brooking took charge for the game against Bradford City at Upton Park and maintained his unbeaten record with a 1-0 win before extending it further with a 2-1 victory at Ipswich the following Saturday. Maybe Trev could be persuaded to take on the role full-time? Apparently not. The powers that be had already fixed their sights and locked on to the man they wanted for the  job – Alan Pardew.

# 37. Can't Hold Us Down

**West Ham United 1 Reading 0  13.9.03**

I wasn't sure how to feel about Alan Pardew. He was just one name among many that had been mentioned, and while he had at least enjoyed success at Reading with limited resources, he still wasn't the big name that I felt we deserved. But I knew that a big name didn't always guarantee success, and as no appointment had been made, I was happy to stick with Trevor Brooking, his flat cap and brown overalls for the time being.

With the game against Nottingham Forest postponed due to the penultimate round of Euro 2004 qualifiers, it was ironic that our next game should be against Reading, at Upton Park. It seemed clear to me that Pardew was going to be the man who would take over, as he resigned from his post and spent the afternoon of Saturday, September 13, 2003 tending the roses in his garden.

I spent the afternoon heading down the A1 with Shauna for a well-earned break at my sister's caravan near Hastings. It was an opportunity to enjoy some early autumn sun, chill out and spend some time with my family. I took the opportunity to rummage through some old photographs and find the one of me with Pardew taken in Barcelona in 1998. It would take pride of place on my desk at work – at least until the first defeat.

Pardew's resignation as Reading manager had been rejected by their chairman, John Madejski, a man so arrogant he named a football stadium after himself and thought that he could retain the services of one of the most promising young managers in the Nationwide Football League by paying him a salary reported to be a mere £60,000 a year.

It seems odd to me but, in any other field, if a respected employee decides to move on, and is being offered more money, it would make sense to at least try to match the salary being offered elsewhere.

A Christian Dailly header was enough to secure a 1-0 win against Reading. It was their first defeat of the season, and even though Pardew's resignation had left them in something of a spin, it still represented a good result for West Ham, as the Royals provided our first real test of the season.

An away match against Crewe Alexandra the following Tuesday was the sort of game which, had it been a cup-tie, would probably have ended in defeat. Instead, a sparkling 25 minutes of football from West Ham raced them into a 3-0 lead by half time, thanks to two goals from David Connolly and another from Matthew Etherington. Now we were getting into our stride, level on points at the top with surprise leaders Wigan Athletic, and with an easy three points to come at Gillingham the following Saturday.

Furthermore, the Alan Pardew situation had been resolved. In an out-of-court settlement, Reading agreed to release him from his contract in return for a £380,000 fee and on the condition that he served out one month's notice.

I wasn't happy about the way the whole thing had been handled. We would be the first to complain if someone had come in and nicked our successful, bright, up-and-coming manager. We were the first to complain when Chelsea came in and took away our bright young playing talent. But then, if they hadn't, someone else would have. And if we hadn't prised Pardew away from Reading, he might be managing Tottenham now. It doesn't make it right, though, and I won't ever feel completely comfortable with it.

The Pardew affair, and the events of the following Saturday, underlined to me the way football as a game was heading, yet proved once again that no matter who has the most money and the biggest reputation, you can never guess what is coming next. Gillingham had lost 5-0 at Cardiff the weekend before and were struggling with injuries and suspensions. But the Gills treated the game like a cup final and, frankly, they had more desire than the Hammers, who went down to 10 men after Defoe was sent off for abusing a lino. Gillingham ran out 2-0 winners in a match that, it would be fair to say, West Ham lost for themselves.

The defeat at Priestfield Stadium meant an end to Trevor Brooking's unbeaten record as manager, and it seemed October 18th – Pardew's start date – could not come quickly enough.

The midweek trip to Cardiff offered another potentially early exit from a cup competition, particularly as we somehow found ourselves 2-0 down after half an hour in the Carling Cup despite City having seemingly only had one attempt on goal. Robert Earnshaw, the man with the most amazing teeth since Ronaldinho, scored twice and it looked like the reason why Brooking didn't want the job full-time was becoming clear.

The tie turned on a penalty award in Hammers' favour just before half-time and then there was no looking back. Defoe's hat-trick underlined his importance to us and made his petulance at Gillingham all the more unforgivable. It was one of those performances that restored the faith a little bit, and delivered the mouth-watering prospect of a fourth round tie at White Hart Lane. Following the sacking of Glenn Hoddle, there was the possibility of both teams having new managers in place by then and an early chance to let Fredi know what we think of his defection to the dark side.

Millwall at home was a huge disappointment after the midweek heroics in Wales and getting off to a good start with another goal from Connolly.

Crystal Palace provided the opportunity for Neil Mellor to grab a brace – his first goals for the club – and show that it wasn't just Defoe and Connolly who could find the net. Just as well, with both due to serve suspensions over the next couple of games.

Shauna and I had been having some disagreements over whether I should go to Derby. She said I should go. I felt that as it was on TV, and there were still items to be found and paid for to finish off the kitchen, I should give it a miss. At 5pm on the evening of the match, I prepared myself for a trip to the pub to watch the game. I switched on the TV to get the team news on Teletext. My heart sank as I realised Bradford Bulls were playing Leeds Rhinos in a bloody stupid game of egg-chasing. It was on one of Uncle Rupert's channels, too, so the chances of Derby v West Ham being shown anywhere in a 50-mile radius were slim. Non-existent actually. I checked with every pub in the area but they just laughed at me. A last-minute winner from Hutch just didn't feel the same when viewed on Teletext. Somehow, the excitement didn't register.

The decision was made. Now that things were better for us financially, I shouldn't miss out again. I was back on the road. The season was shaping up nicely. With Alan Pardew about to take over the reins, it was an interesting time to be a West Ham fan again. It was a good time to be a fan of a team outside the Premiership – with players from that league experiencing their own well-publicised problems. The first division is a hugely competitive league. After a year of complete turmoil; the future was again starting to look bright. A run of two defeats could see anyone plummet from second to sixth. It was going to be a roller coaster ride.

It was becoming clear that having teamed up with former Republic of Ireland manager, Mick McCarthy, Barry Green would, no doubt, be in the mix with his new club, Sunderland, come May. Their win at Sheffield United on the day we won at Derby was shown on the Sunday lunchtime, and John Helm's comments about their World Cup defender being "immaculate", made me chuckle inwardly.

Should we win promotion, we will be back at the stage we were at when we began our Premiership journey in 1993. Struggling, constant underdogs, but winning against the odds from time to time, and making us proud to be Hammers. Just how I like it. When we return to the Premiership we may find we have been overtaken by the likes of Fulham and Birmingham City in terms of size, status and finances. So what? We'll be back.

There will always be rich, there will always be poor, no matter how much money governments spend on benefits and improving conditions. Even in a purely socialist society, the opportunists thrive at the expense of the weak. A re-distribution of wealth within football wouldn't work – but a cap on the amount of money clubs are allowed to spend just might.

*This is sport, after all. Isn't it?*